LOCALISING POWER
IN POST-AUTHORITARIAN INDONESIA

A Series sponsored by the East-West Center

CONTEMPORARY ISSUES IN ASIA AND THE PACIFIC

John T. Sidel and Geoffrey M. White, Series Co-Editors

A collaborative effort by Stanford University Press and the East-West Center, this series focuses on issues of contemporary significance in the Asia Pacific region, most notably political, social, cultural, and economic change. The series seeks books that focus on topics of regional importance, on problems that cross disciplinary boundaries, and that have the capacity to reach academic and other interested audiences.

The East-West Center is an education and research organization established by the U.S. Congress in 1960 to strengthen relations and understanding among the peoples and nations of Asia, the Pacific, and the United States. The Center contributes to a peaceful, prosperous, and just Asia Pacific community by serving as a vigorous hub for cooperative research, education, and dialogue on critical issues of common concern to the Asia Pacific region and the United States. Funding for the Center comes from the U.S. government, with additional support provided by private agencies, individuals, foundations, corporations, and the governments of the region.

VEDI R. HADIZ

Localising Power
in Post-Authoritarian Indonesia
A Southeast Asia Perspective

Stanford University Press · *Stanford, California*

Stanford University Press
Stanford, California

Printed in the United States of America on acid-free, archival-quality paper

Library of Congress Cataloging-in-Publication Data

Hadiz, Vedi R.
  Localising power in post-authoritarian Indonesia : a Southeast Asia
perspective / Vedi R. Hadiz.
     p. cm.
  Includes bibliographical references and index.
  ISBN 978-0-8047-6852-8 (cloth : alk. paper) — ISBN 978-0-8047-6853-5
(pbk. : alk. paper)
  1. Local government—Indonesia. 2. Decentralization in government—
Indonesia. 3. Power (Social sciences)—Indonesia. 4. Elite (Social
sciences)—Indonesia. 5. Indonesia—Politics and government—1998–
I. Title.
  JS7192.H26 2010
  320.809598—dc22

                                                          2009007180

Typeset by Thompson Type in 9.75/13.5 Janson

With thanks to my friend and teacher, Dick Robison

Contents

Acknowledgments

I would like to thank the Department of Sociology and the Faculty of Arts and Social Sciences in the National University of Singapore, which has supported the bulk of my research over the last several years, much of the product of which has now been invested in this book. I would also like to express my appreciation for the Southeast Asia Research Centre, City University of Hong Kong (especially its former director, Kevin Hewison) and the Asia Research Institute at NUS (especially its former director, Anthony Reid), which provided additional financial support over the different legs of the long series of research projects to which this book owes its existence. My sincere thanks as well go to the Asia Research Centre at Murdoch University (especially its director, Garry Rodan, and also Kanishka Jayasuriya), where I spent my sabbatical of 2005 writing the first draft of most of the chapters of the book, and to the various colleagues who made it the perfect place to carry out this task. It would have been harder, I suspect, to complete this book if I had not started it there.

I also wish to express my appreciation to Richard Robison, with whom I have enjoyed and benefited from many years of collaboration. Many of the ideas explored in this book bear the mark of the various opportunities I have had to undertake joint-work, and engage in discussion and friendly debate with him.

I feel an immense sense of gratitude as well to all who provided me with invaluable help during my various periods of fieldwork in North Sumatra, East Java, and earlier, Yogyakarta. Over the years, the names became too many to mention individually, but it would be remiss of me not to refer especially to Elfenda Ananda and Safaruddin Siregar in North Sumatra, as well as Nurul Barizah and Yudi Burhan in East Java. Without their help, and that of their colleagues, respectively in FITRA/BITRA in Medan, and YSPDI, in Surabaya, and their amazingly broad social networks, there is no way that I could have completed this work. Ridaya Laode was also a most helpful contact person in Yogyakarta.

Thank you too to John Sidel, Linda Kay Quintana, Elisa Johnston, Stacy Wagner and Jessica Walsh for their encouragement and support in the publication of this book through Stanford University Press and the East-West Center Series on Contemporary Issues in Asia and the Pacific. It has been a pleasure to work with you all.

Finally—as usual—thank you Lina and Karla for putting up with me, my work and my absences, through all of these years.

Singapore October 2008

LOCALISING POWER

IN POST-AUTHORITARIAN INDONESIA

Introduction

Localisation and Globalisation

Two simultaneously occurring processes—economic globalisation on the one hand, and the localisation of power on the other—feature prominently today in debates about development issues (Harriss, Stokke and Tornquist 2004: 2). The first, not surprisingly, focuses predominantly on pressures for an ever-closer integration of national economies with global markets; the other is about rising demands within the geo-bodies of nation-states for increased local autonomy in the socio-political, economic and cultural fields in the face of the same economic globalising impulses. These debates are also reflective of real tensions and contradictions that have emerged in the actual experiences of simultaneously localising and globalising societies— of the kind that this book is concerned with especially in relation to post-authoritarian Indonesia.

It is suggested here that all the profound social, political and cultural transformations ultimately intertwined with the processes of economic globalisation have only come to reinforce one seemingly paradoxical point: issues of local power matter greatly in a globalised world (see Harriss, Stokke and Tornquist 2004). Not in the least, they matter in forging and mediating the conditions under which economic globalisation is experienced and made sense of by citizenries at sub-national levels of governance. Conversely, they also help in shaping local and national responses to seemingly relentless structural pressures that have to do with integration into the world economy, which may vary from embracement to resistance. As Kerkvliet and Mojares put it (1991: 11), 'Local communities are not only "affected" by broad national and world developments, they are continually being reconstituted by them.' But it is not a simple, one way process: 'extralocal systems' are unavoidably defined, too, 'through the overall configuration of local realities'. It is contended here that such 'local realities' cannot be understood in the majority of cases without taking into account the fundamental nature of concrete and tangible contests over power and resources. These can involve local, national and even international-based social forces and interests.

Thus contests over local power—which may take place through a range of vehicles and whose variety of expressions may be deeply influenced by what is locally available materially, culturally and ideologically—have taken on a new significance as the social transformations associated with capitalist development and integration into the world economy proceed. The dynamics of local power are understood, however, in radically dissimilar ways by different scholars, depending on their theoretical standpoints, political agendas and social values. The intellectually predominant neo-liberal view on what is often referred to rather expediently as the 'local/global nexus' is, not surprisingly, most powerfully articulated by international development organisations like the World Bank, along with most governments of the advanced, industrialised North, and the international media. It is well-encapsulated, too, in a range of scholarly works, such as the 'Democracy and Local Governance Research Program' undertaken in the late 1990s by the University of Pennsylvania; this study was carried out on the basis of a 'grand hypothesis' that 'globalization would give impetus to local democratic institutions, values, and practices'. It was also undertaken in the belief that globalisation invariably 'expands alternatives' and increases 'freedom of choice to entrapped locals', and 'stimulates local democratization' (Teune 2004).

It is useful to note, however, that growing interest in 'the local' has grown partly as doubts have surfaced about the social, political and economic ramifications of the march of economic globalisation. Thus the simultaneous and interconnected processes of globalisation and localisation can be associated with the rise of good governance, or local entrepreneurial spirit and innovation on the one hand; but also to such things as local corruption or abuse of power, xenophobia and ethnic or religious violence, on the other. Grindle (2007: 9) therefore cautiously observes that the expectations associated with 'going local' have had to be modified downward, though the 'promise of good governance and democracy' initially attached to it has not been abandoned.

Local Politics as Arenas of Contestation

The book is premised on the contradiction-laden relationship between pressures for economic globalisation and the continuing vitality of the local and how this is expressed in the vagaries of concrete contests over power. In important respects it follows on the observations of authors like Boone, who suggests that economic deregulation and open market policies have eroded central state authority, but without 'unleashing market-determined policies of social interdependence and resource allocation as neo-liberal reformers had hoped' (n.d.: 4). Instead, what have been activated in the Sub-Saharan African case she examined are complex, and often brutal, struggles to redefine territorial jurisdictions, relations between the centre and the periphery, and the nature of the state at the local level.

In these and other contexts, a crucial task is often to understand how predatory systems of power remain resilient in the face of international pressures for market-facilitating 'good governance'. The answer to the puzzle, it is argued here, will frequently lie in the fact that entrenched local predatory interests have been able to usurp the agenda of good governance reforms, including that of decentralisation, to sustain their social and political dominance. From this point of view, the advance of local democratic politics does not *necessarily* constitute any direct threat to the position of assorted local oligarchs, strongmen and notables; neither are they always supportive of 'rationally' organised free markets.

Local power is thus but another arena of contestation among a range of interests concerned with the forging of economic and political regimes that would govern the way wealth and power are distributed, just as nation-states and the world at large are sites of such contestations.[1] What is important in any empirical analysis is identifying the kind of social forces and interests that actually affect the dynamics of power at the local level. Obviously one cannot assume the homogeneity of interests among state, market or civil society actors in any context. One *needs to concretely examine what kind of interests*, ascendant, or subordinated, are involved or marginalised in actual contests over power. This entails an examination of prevailing 'political topographies', to borrow a phrase used by Boone (2003),[2] or historically specific constellations of power and interest.

It is notable that much of the literature on local power in Southeast Asia has focussed on the phenomena of 'local strongmen', corrupt local machineries of power, or the resilience of pockets of authoritarianism (e.g. Sidel 1999). The Indonesian case is particularly intriguing because the heavily centralised authoritarianism of the New Order actually left little room for the emergence of relatively autonomous local strongmen frequently associated in the region with the experiences of Thailand or the Philippines (Sidel 2004).[3] Nevertheless, it is argued here too that institutional reforms pertaining to the localisation of power, inspired by neo-liberal notions of 'good governance', have ironically assisted in 'clearing the way' for the kind of social and political milieu for their emergence and consolidation, rather than their pre-emption or eradication.

From a broader regional perspective, a major question that needs to be examined is why the localisation of power in Indonesia—like in Thailand and the Philippines—has failed to usher in more fundamental transformations in the prevailing relations of power that tend to be dominated still by long-entrenched predatory interests. In all of these cases, the localisation of power—through much lauded decentralisation policy—has notably taken place under distinctly post-authoritarian conditions.[4]

Neo-Liberalism and the Reconfiguration of the State

It has to be stated clearly at this juncture that the book diverges greatly from much of the neo-liberal/neo-institutionalist inspired work on decentralisation (see the discussion in Chapter 1) as the institutional expression of the localisation of power. It has to be noted that neo-liberals and neo-institutionalists, whether as consultants or academics, tend to see a close relationship between receptivity to global free markets and democratic governance, and more lately, decentralisation. Simonsen argues, for example, that 'Failure of economic performance within an increasingly globalised economy can be considered the most general underlying cause behind the demise of authoritarian regimes around 1989' (Simonsen 1999: 399). The distinguished works of Crook and Manor (1998) and Manor (1999)—as well as innumerable reports and policy papers produced by an array of international development organisations and policy think tanks—then attempt to make the link between market rationality, democratic governance and decentralisation.

The development of local village elections in China, therefore, has been viewed in relation to the new economic giant's massive experiment with market and local governance reforms (see Craner 2004; IRI n.d.), even if a highly autocratic Communist Party still rules unchallenged and deeply suspicious of the democratic aspirations of domestic groups of 'dissidents'. If there is irony involved here, it does not pre-occupy those who emphasise the 'market preserving' character of Chinese decentralisation. Such scholars place importance on how a 'federal'-like institutional framework of governance has emerged to support the growth of market forces, however, without explaining the persisting lack of democracy accompanying the shift to markets (e.g. Montinolla, Qian and Weingast 1995; Qian and Weingast 1996; Singh 2007). The ambivalent nature of the Chinese experience has led critics to stress how the localisation of power in globalising China has produced corrupt local governments (e.g. Gong 2006), with little accountability to the governed in the context of a rigid one-party system (Lin, Tao and Liu 2006: 322).

There has been less ambiguity in some treatments of other cases that have involved a similar shift to the market. The World Bank, for example, notes that the fall of Communism in Eastern Europe and Central Asia introduced its peoples to new opportunities generated by the combination of market capitalism and electoral democracy. It has also lauded the experience of administrative and fiscal decentralisation—as the accompaniment to electoral democracy—in these societies.[5]

Significantly, decentralised governance has been established as part of a broader and more fundamental project of rolling back the pervasive role of inefficient central states for the sake of the growth of healthy market economies. This project constitutes an exercise in defining the parameters of a desired state role in facilitating the operations of the market. The economist Bardhan, for example, notes that 'free-market economists tend to emphasize the benefits of reducing the power of the overextended or predatory state.' According to Bardhan, the occurrence of 'market failure' has led proponents of free markets to turn 'for their resolution to the government at the local level, where the transaction costs are relatively low and the information problems that can contribute to central government failures are less acute' (2002: 186). The assumption being made is that local states are inclined to be more receptive and flexible when it comes to the task of facilitating market operations (Montinolla, Qian and Weingast 1995; Qian and Weingast 1996).

Economic globalisation, therefore, does not signal the demise of sovereign states and of politics, even for market-oriented neo-liberals. Instead, it means a transformation of the nature and functions of state power. This is because under the pressure of global markets, 'many states are undergoing transformations toward *de-statisation* (that is, reduced state authority in favour of market liberalisation) and toward *de-nationalisation* (that is, the scalar reconfiguration of state power in favour of regionalisation and localisation)'. The consequence is that 'political authority is becoming increasingly diffused among state, market and civil society actors at local, national, regional and global scales' (Harris, Stokke and Tornquist 2004: 2). The degree to which such pressures have actually resulted in these transformations, of course, must be examined empirically from case to case.

It is well known that organisations such as the International Monetary Fund (IMF) and the World Bank have acted as the main advocates of a particular view of decentralisation and 'good governance' that has become influential in the developing world. Their view highlights how integration in the global economy imposes market forces that pressure local governments to behave responsively as well as efficiently in the delivery of a range of services. The effect of their influence is to 'create and sustain political and discursive frames for thinking and acting, frames that are strongly influenced by a technocratic and apolitical approach that is itself rooted in the most powerful global institution of all—the market (Harriss, Stokke and Tornquist 2004: 2–3). As we shall see, this creates problems in terms of deciphering the sorts of social outcomes produced by the decentralisation experiences in post-authoritarian Southeast Asian societies like Indonesia.

Odd Anti–Neo-Liberal Alliances?

However, the allegedly unstoppable rise of global markets has been understood as endangering the autonomy of local communities by those who challenge the neo-liberal view (see Escobar 1995; Hines 2000). Especially disadvantaged according to such dissenters are the urban and rural poor, as well as marginalised groups such as ethnic religious minorities, and 'indigenous peoples'.

Abers, for example, notes the view that globalisation can kill off the possibility of genuine democracy. Thus, mobilising the resources of local communities *against* the forces of encroaching market capitalism (see Abers 2000) is the only way of saving democracy *from* globalisation. In a nutshell, while neo-liberals see globalisation as generating new vitality and entrepreneurship in local communities, their populist opponents effectively see globalisation as a great threat both to local cultural diversity (see Abdullah 2005) and local capacities that tend to get subordinated to the logic of the global market (Hines 2000). They also see the incursions of global capitalism, more often than not, as detrimental to the welfare of the poor in local communities; for example, they will lament the environmental degradation caused by the intrusion of capitalist enterprise or the propensity of global markets to destroy local community self-reliance (see Govan 1997; Maffi and Woodley 2005).

For localist populists, who are often represented in activist communities, neo-liberal economic globalisation is inherently anti-democratic in nature. As one observer (in the neo-liberal camp) writes in summarising their viewpoint: 'Among the many evils' perceived in globalisation 'is the suspension or blockage of local democratic processes in deference to more encompassing and generally more powerful systems, whether of a region, a state, transnational regions or the world as a system'. Thus, globalisation's successful inroads into local communities frequently 'by-pass local institutions, including democratic ones', and tend to 'nurture anti-democratic and corrupt local institutions and practices' (Teune 2004).

It is important to point out that localist populism of any kind is not a 'free floating idea'; its bearers can range from critical non-governmental organisations (NGOs) to the advocates of state development programmes. The 'guiding principle', however, is almost always the stated desirability of rooting the development process in 'people's own practices'. Its claims to being participatory are thus embedded in the already existing cultural reference points of local communities (Connors 2001: 3). Moreover, localist populism is not necessarily anti-capitalist in nature, though its social agents are typically suspicious of globalisation's consequences on local productive capacities. Instead it is more frequently about the innate morality of protecting local agriculture and business from the encroachment of the forces of international capital (Connors 2001: 4).

From this last observation, another important point can be made: localist populism can take forms that merge readily with the official, statist-nationalisms of much of the developing world's most well-known leaders. Thus, prominent figures in Asia, such as former prime ministers Mahathir Mohammad of Malaysia or Thaksin Shinawatra of Thailand, can make strident appeals for the protection of local cultures—and simultaneously, domestic capitalist forces—while selectively engaging with the most salient actors of the global capitalist order. It is therefore possible to imagine newly ascendant local politicos in post-authoritarian Indonesia adopting a similar position—in relation to extra-local actors—especially if it serves their material interests.

Given the above observation, it is notable that localist populists have been supported intellectually by a hotchpotch of former Leftists, as well as academic post-structuralists and post-modernists, who are equally suspicious of the neo-liberal globalisation project (see Harriss, Stokke and Tornquist 2004: 1). These have largely dismissed grand historical narratives and, consequently, political contestation on grand scales. Having been let down by History, their hopes and aspirations are pinned on the revitalisation of democratic, humane impulses within members of local communities and citizenries (e.g. Laclau and Mouffe 1985). For them, meaningful politics are direct, local and subaltern (Chatterjee 1993).

The latter also tend to be critical of the culturally homogenising threat posed by economic neo-globalisation. Thus local communitarianisms believed to be underpinned by local 'knowledge' systems (as understood by Geertz 1983)—as well as values, norms, beliefs and lifestyles (Harvey 2000: 84)—are thought to be under threat by 'development' (Diawara 2000). In effect, these threatened cultures and ways of life signal some sort of benevolent 'other' possibility—representing mankind's last hope of escape from the ravages of the impersonal and homogenising forces of capitalism on a global scale. In the concrete struggles over the localisation of power in Southeast Asia, such views are frequently found among representatives of the NGO community (Hewison 2000).

The irony, of course, is that the notion partly rests on an atavistic call to restore old religious or cultural values that can serve as the basis for various kinds of narrow ethno-religious solidarities and xenophobic nationalisms. Like notions associated with populism in general, such atavism easily falls into the hands of politically conservative, even reactionary, social forces that the aforementioned critics of the neo-liberal globalisation project would be averse to support. While atavism represents uneasiness toward the consequences of the march of global capitalism on the diversity and richness of the human experience, its deployment by conservatives may result in outcomes that are much less meaningful for emancipatory struggles imagined by those dissenting against the neo-liberal project.

Socially and politically conservative forces in the United States, for example, that are suspicious of interventionist big states *as well as* the 'anarchic' tendencies unleashed by the free market, will find commonalities with intellectual and political positions that uphold the virtues of 'traditional' or 'Christian' values (see Harvey 2000: 70). In Indonesia and Southeast Asia— the parts of the world that this book is most concerned with—localism and atavism have certainly been valuable weapons for some of the most distinctly un-progressive of social forces—even if they do not necessarily find expression in overtly post-modernist discourse. In Thailand, for example, Pasuk's (2004a) otherwise sympathetic treatment reveal how inward-looking notions of 'Buddhist economics', emphasising local community, are conceptually linked to an idealised notion of village life that appears to be equally attractive to NGO activists, monks, the Ministry of the Interior, as well as the King. In Indonesia, particularly conservative and rigid interpretations of Islam have been utilised by a range of forces since the advent of democratisation in 1998 to provide ideological legitimacy to their fight for power (e.g. Irianto 2006: 20).

An intriguing development, therefore, as Harriss, Stokke, and Tornquist (2004: 1) rightly observe, relates to the importance now placed on local power by those espousing a wide variety of social and political agendas. Neo-liberals, and assorted populists and Leftist critics of globalisation, who often fiercely disagree on issues such as the social effects of globalisation and marketisation, have lately coalesced around the virtues of local grassroots politics. There is consensus that local initiatives are especially crucial for social change in a 'positive' direction, however 'positive' is to be defined.

Likewise, Bardhan notes the oddity of free marketeers joining with 'a diverse array of social thinkers: post-modernists, multicultural advocates, grassroots environmental activists and supporters of the cause of indigenous peoples and technologies' in espousing the cause of strengthening local-level governance. According to Bardhan, though the latter 'are usually both anti-market and anti-centralized state', they 'energetically support assignment of control to local selfgoverning communities' (Bardhan 2002: 186), much like mainstream economists who view central states as a cumbersome obstacle to local initiative and development.

It is, therefore, not surprising that in Indonesia, as well as Southeast Asia more broadly (Ungpakorn 2003a: 299; also see George 1998), many largely populist NGO activists have been drawn into the World Bank-sponsored discourse on 'good governance', which has come to emphasise local community and civil society participation in development (World Bank 2000). This has occurred despite their usual hostility toward many other facets of the neo-liberal economic globalisation agenda, including those of privatisation and marketisation (see Culla 2006). For their part, organisations like the World Bank realise that support from NGOs could be useful in terms of garnering broader public acceptance of market reforms. The World Bank (2003a: 3) now highlights, for instance, that civil society organisations, including NGOs, 'are important actors in building a necessary social consensus for economic reforms and long-term development, in promoting effective governance by fostering transparency and accountability of public institutions'.

Indonesia and the Southeast Asian Experience

The position taken in this book—that of 'localisation as an arena of contestation'—involves a fundamental critique of the sort of convergence described above, which is developed in dealing with the main case study of post-authoritarian Indonesia, in comparative Southeast Asian perspective. It undertakes this critique by concretely examining the constellations of social interest that have presided over the localisation of power, especially in the Indonesian regions of North Sumatra and East Java. As Rodan, Hewison and Robison (2006: 7) point out, existing regimes anywhere 'cannot be dismantled at will because they embody a specific arrangement of economic, social, and political power.' Furthermore, 'Institutions that might appear dysfunctional for growth and investment often persist because elites are prepared to sacrifice efficiency where their social and political ascendancy is threatened'. Importantly, however, institutional reforms, including those pertaining to decentralisation and democratisation, may be advanced in such a way that already dominant forces might 'further their control or weaken their opponents in broad struggles over social, political, and economic ascendancy'.

As in other societies, the localisation of power has been expressed institutionally in Indonesia through the renewed salience of contests over decentralisation policy. After the fall of the late dictator Soeharto in 1998, Indonesia implemented a decentralisation programme that has been quite dramatic in many ways. Inheriting its far-flung borders from the Netherlands East Indies, this archipelagic country has struck many observers as being remarkable because it has remained intact despite an incredible diversity of cultures, religions, ethnicities, economies and geographies (see, for example, Bourchier and Hadiz 2003: 255). However, the combination of the Asian Economic Crisis of 1997–98, political instability, regional demands for autonomy or even independence, and the perceived rise of 'failed states' globally brought concerns about the long-term viability of the Indonesian nation-state as we now know it (Gelbard 2001). Such concerns have clearly been exacerbated by the rise of religious and other forms of 'communal' violence in post-authoritarian Indonesia (see van Klinken 2007; also see Sidel 2006). Not surprisingly, 'local autonomy' has been linked in Indonesia to issues pertaining to the revival of local traditions and customs (see Davidson and Henley 2007), which is reflective of the potency of mobilisations based on local cultural identities in spite of notions about the homogenising effects of globalisation.

It is no wonder, therefore, that the Indonesian case has been simultaneously placed at the heart of international policy and academic debates on both decentralisation and democratisation. The Indonesian case is also particularly instructive because it so readily displays the primacy of constellations of power and interest vis-à-vis institutional crafting in determining how institutions actually work at the local level in post-authoritarian situations—a theoretical point that is argued throughout this book. The Indonesian experience is especially valuable given the sharp contrast between the heavily centralised and authoritarian New Order and the highly decentralised and diffuse democracy that has replaced it.

Analysing the Indonesian case is therefore particularly useful because in spite of the caution of Grindle mentioned above, Bardhan (2002: 185) remains essentially right when he announces that 'All around the world in matters of governance decentralization is the rage'. Furthermore, according to Bardhan and Mookherjee (2006: 1):

> The last two decades of the twentieth century witnessed a significant rise in the scope of local democracy throughout the developing world, with increasing devolution of political, economic, and administrative authority to local governments. Along with privation and deregulation, this shift represents a substantial reduction in the authority of national governments over economic policy. The phenomenon is geographically spread, occurring simultaneously in Latin America, Africa, Asia, and Eastern Europe. The earliest changes were initiated in the 1970s, picked up momentum in the 1980s, and accelerated after 1990.

But what is really the appeal of decentralisation, especially for the intellectually dominant proponents of the neo-liberal and technocratic view of statecraft?

To put it succinctly at this juncture, the centralised state 'has lost a great deal of legitimacy', and decentralization is believed to promise a range of benefits as 'a way of reducing the role of the state in general, by fragmenting central authority and introducing more intergovernmental competition and checks and balances'. As a considerable bonus, 'In a world of rampant ethnic conflicts and separatist movements, decentralization is also regarded as a way of diffusing social and political tensions and ensuring local cultural and political autonomy' (Bardhan 2002: 185).

But the relationship between decentralisation, democracy and transparent and accountable governance is understood here as being essentially problematic and contentious. In the case of Indonesia, it will be shown here that the rise of local politics has been instrumental in—and become part of—the emergence and consolidation of newly decentralised and predatory networks of patronage that have become politically ascendant after the fall of Soeharto. These have continued to have a vested interest in resisting many institutional reforms or have usurped them in a number of creative ways. From this standpoint, this book also represents an attempt to explain the processes through which power has been reorganised in post-authoritarian Indonesia through the lens of local politics.

It should be added that there have now been a few edited collections produced that deal with the politics of the local in Indonesia (e.g. Aspinall and Fealy 2003; Kingsbury and Aveling 2003; Erb, Sulistiyanto and Faucher 2005; Schulte-Nordholt and van Klinken 2007. But this is a relatively new development because the particularly centralised nature of power during Soeharto's New Order meant that only rare studies of local power were previously ever undertaken. The few exceptions included those by Antlov (1995), Schiller (1996) and Malley (1999). Given this relative dearth, the study of post-authoritarian Indonesia will benefit from the insights provided by the experience of the Philippines or Thailand, where the study of local power is far better developed, partly because the Cold War-era authoritarian state was arguably never as successfully centralised as in Indonesia.[6]

It is for this reason that the discussion on the localisation of power in Indonesia is continually interspersed in this book with discussion of other cases of post-authoritarian decentralisation. The Indonesian case is far from unique in terms of its 'unintended consequences'—to borrow a well-known term from Weberian sociology. Across the world, decentralisation has produced 'unanticipated problems' (Grindle 2007: 2), perhaps especially for the technocrats, domestic or international, whose main task is to craft policy frameworks. In Southeast Asia, the cases of post-authoritarian Thailand and the Philippines provide some particularly useful points that help decipher the Indonesian situation due to certain commonalities in the prior experience of authoritarianisms born in the Cold War era.

Of course, these two cases are not meant to have a 'status' within the book that is equal to that of Indonesia. There is no full-fledged analysis of Indonesia's neighbouring Southeast Asian democracies being offered here. However, key developments in the Philippines and Thailand, as well as in such places as Russia and China, will be cited to help shed light on such fundamental issues as the politics of institution-building, power and contestation, and on the determinants of societal trajectories.

Structure of the Book

Chapter 1 provides a critical analysis of dominant (economics-inspired) neo-institutionalist and neo-liberal perspectives on decentralisation, development and democracy. These perspectives essentially view the relationship as a mutually reinforcing process that is sustained by the free market. They typically highlight the importance of designing the 'correct' institutional frameworks to govern state, society and economy; and they have lately given much weight to Putnamian notions of social capital. These perspectives fail to seriously address conflict; they treat it mainly as a managerialist problem of insulating good policy-making from certain kinds of societal pressure. The chapter offers a contrasting position that highlights the importance of constellations of power and of social conflict in determining the way that institutions, including that of the state, actually work.

Chapter 2 extends the contrasting position by relating it to the role and composition of state and local elites in determining societal trajectories, especially in connection with experiences of democratisation in Southeast Asia. In particular, the chapter reassesses modernisation approaches in their myriad more 'classical' and contemporary forms to the question of technocratic design of social change. But this is no perfunctory revisit of old theories. The suggestion being made is that much of the social thinking that has emerged in relation to decentralisation constitutes a rebirth of modernisation theory assumptions about development, politics and technocracy. It then juxtaposes this sort of thinking to that which latches on to the role of predatory 'local strongmen' or 'oligarchies' in post-authoritarian Southeast Asia. In the process, the chapter provides the background for a concern that is pursued in later chapters: local elite responses/adaptations of/resistance to the allegedly homogenising effects of globalisation pressures.

Chapter 3 takes the book deeper into the complexities of the specific post-authoritarian Indonesian situation. It does so by examining the background of broader social and political changes since the demise of Soeharto's New Order in 1998 and then inserts into this context the actual contests over institutional reform. The chapter pays particular attention to debates about reforms pertaining to decentralisation and local governance in Indonesia in relation to those that have taken place in Thailand and the Philippines. In the process, the chapter expands the argument about the complex and often contradictory relationship between institutional reform design and concrete struggles over power at sub-national arenas of contestation.

Chapter 4 presents an analysis of the sociological background of Indonesia's newly ascendant local elites—particularly through case studies in North Sumatra and East Java. Chief among these are the former local apparatchik, and local entrepreneurs incubated within the New Order system of political patronage, as well as assorted goons and thugs who have managed to cast themselves as democratic actors. The chapter demonstrates how these have reinvented themselves as reformist local democrats, and pays particular attention to their appropriation of democratic institutions like political parties and parliaments. Comparisons with the social origins and bases of local elites in post-authoritarian Thailand and the Philippines are also presented to augment the view put forward about the primacy of constellations of power and interest over institutional frameworks in driving change.

The processes and mechanisms through which the social and political ascendance of local elites are secured and maintained in post-authoritarian Indonesia are more deeply examined in Chapter 5. In this chapter, the experiences of other post-authoritarian societies in Southeast Asia are shown to be particularly instructive. The focus of the chapter is on the vagaries of alliances and coalition-building in Indonesian local electoral politics, and the way in which localised networks of predatory power are now being developed through money politics, and to some extent, local instruments of coercion.

Chapter 6 presents an analysis of the modes of political inclusion and exclusion in post-authoritarian Indonesia, contrasting these at important junctures with other post-authoritarian Southeast Asian experiences. The chapter pays attention to the mechanics of electoral democracy at the local level as well as to the position of social groups that had been marginalised during the New Order. Chief among the groups to be examined in the context of the actual operations of local power is organised labour. In the process, the chapter raises crucial issues related to political participation and contestation, and the position of civil society in post-authoritarian situations. It also raises questions about the emergence of localised oligarchies.

The Conclusion offers observations that re-link the experiences of post-authoritarianism with the localisation of power. It also reviews the main arguments of the book as a whole in relation to the question of the entrenchment of distinctly localised forms of oligarchic power. The chapter offers speculations too on some of the possible implications of the outcomes of the localisation of power for particular kinds of integration with the global capitalist economy.

Chapter One

Decentralisation, Development and Democracy
Theoretical Issues and Debates

The main objective of this chapter is to examine the way in which the localisation of power has been understood in the contemporary literature on the developing world, especially as it pertains to Indonesia and other post-authoritarian Southeast Asian cases. The focus is particularly on the contradiction-laden relationship among decentralisation, economic development and democracy. As mentioned previously, decentralisation policy has been the institutional form in which the localisation of power has taken place (Harriss, Stokke and Tornquist 2004: 3).

This chapter questions why a particular kind of understanding, mainly associated with neo-liberal and neo-institutionalist schools of thought—and primarily originating from within the discipline of economics—has come to predominate in both the academic literature and that produced by international development agencies, while also appealing to many civil society organisations in the region.[1]

The intention is not to suggest a process by which developing societies merely swallow whole the framework of thinking predominantly advanced by technocrats perched in the offices of international development organisations. In fact, the agenda of neo-liberal governance reform, including the aspect of decentralisation can be appropriated by a range of local interests with little regard for upholding 'good governance' principles. These interests may even be strenuously opposed to the incursion of demands for accountability and transparency while fighting for greater local autonomy over a range of social, economic and political fields. At the same time, such interests seek to negotiate the terms of local engagement with the forces of economic globalisation, as the expansion of markets potentially produces new rent-seeking opportunities. Thus the neo-liberal reform agenda can morph into something completely different when the aspect of concrete political struggle is inserted into it.

Central Themes

ADVANCING DECENTRALISATION

In agreement with Bardhan and Mookherjee (2006), the World Bank has observed that decentralisation is 'a global and regional phenomenon', and that 'most developing and transitional countries have experimented with it to varying degrees' (World Bank n.d. a). Writing before the end of the twentieth century, Crook and Manor (1998: 83) specify in a highly influential work that 'more than sixty governments, mainly in developing countries' have experimented with decentralisation in some form since the mid-1980s. Observing Latin America in the late 1990s after a decade of decentralisation policy, Willis, Garman and Haggard (1999:7) noted that decentralisation has been 'championed' as the 'route to greater accountability and transparency in governance', as well as to other objectives like 'increased participation by ethnic minorities and social groups excluded under semidemocratic and authoritarian rule'. Writing on China, Montinola, Qian and Weingast (1995) argue that decentralisation protects pro-market reforms undertaken by local governments from central government intervention, and induces healthy economic competition within countries that leads to economic efficiency. Concomitantly, the link between decentralisation and corruption eradication is also often proposed.

Authors writing for the World Bank have put forward the case for decentralisation most confidently in relation to Asia. White and Smoke (2005: 1) thus declare:

A fundamental transformation in the structure of government has been taking place across East Asia. Before 1990 most East Asian countries were highly centralized; today subnational governments have emerged as the fulcrum for much of the region's development . . . Though East Asia's decentralization has come later than in some other parts of the world, it is now here to stay.

Since 2001, Indonesia too has been pursuing policies of decentralisation that have profoundly transformed the institutional framework of governance in a country that was ruled for more than three decades in a highly authoritarian and centralised fashion, to the extent that Indonesia's decentralisation approach has been described as a 'Big Bang' (World Bank 2003b; Bunte 2004). Thus, according to a document produced by the United States Agency for International Development (USAID) (2000:17), 'Indonesia is moving rapidly from years of tight central control to a far more decentralized and autonomous system of local government', which will help 'create the basis for national and local democratic governance' (USAID 2000: 17).

Moreover, in 'opting for a decentralised model of government', Indonesia appeared to be sensibly 'following a global trend' (Turner and Podger 2003: 2), which was in any case 'well suited to the particular geography of Indonesia' (Turner and Podger 2003: 1; also see Bunte 2004: 379). The observation about Indonesia's geography is unsurprising given the sprawling, archipelagic form of the country, which is inhabited by hundreds of ethnic groups with distinct languages and customs.[2]

Geographical and ethno-linguistic factors notwithstanding, Indonesia's abrupt decentralisation turn would not have been possible without the fall from power of Soeharto in May 1998 and the consequent demise of the New Order. This occurred amidst a deep economic crisis that led to a harrowing political one—eventually leaving the entire institutional framework of the New Order largely unviable. The fall of Soeharto thus in many ways truly marked the beginning of a new chapter in the social and political history of Indonesia. This vast country—with over 220 million people of diverse ethnicity and belief systems, spread irregularly across an archipelago comprising some 17,000 islands—was to embark on a massive experiment in forging new, more democratic, transparent and participatory political and economic regimes. A cornerstone of the experiment was the much heralded programme of decentralisation that devolved considerable powers, resources and responsibilities to the local level.

The end of the Soeharto era therefore commenced an exciting, albeit short-lived, period of high expectation in Indonesia; this was in sharp contrast to the preceding long era of highly stifling, centralised and authoritarian rule. Some believed that decentralisation in particular would pave the way for a more genuine participatory form of democracy, especially if enough of the right kind of 'human capital' was produced to institute 'policies for the interests of the public' (Pratikno 2005: 33). Others saw great opportunities for the development of an empowering form of politics at the grassroots level (e.g. Antlov 2003a)—in spite of many structural and cultural impediments left over from the New Order—as communities in towns and villages re-learn the art of politics after decades of living in a starkly depoliticised environment. For the Indonesian bureaucrat-academic Ryaas Rasyid (2002), moreover, decentralisation was indisputably the natural extension of democratisation.

But a theme also running through the discussion on post-Soeharto Indonesia, especially during the early years, was of the possibility of national disintegration (Tadjoeddin, Suharyo and Mishra 2003;[3] also see Berger and Aspinall 2001). This accounts partially for the rise of interest both within academia and international development organisations in Indonesian decentralisation. According to the World Bank-led Consultative Group on Indonesia (CGI), decentralisation 'continues to be one of Indonesia's most significant reform initiatives' after the end of the New Order, and its successful implementation is 'crucial for Indonesia as a nation' (CGI 2003).

It should be recalled that following the fall of Soeharto in 1998, demands for greater local autonomy emerged from many parts of the Indonesian archipelago against a background of evidently rising violent ethnic or religious conflict, especially in such places as Maluku and parts of Kalimantan (e.g. Bertrand 2003; Kingsbury and Aveling 2003; van Klinken 2007). The fear commonly expressed was of Acehnese or Papuan secession, no doubt sparked in part by the successful attainment of independence by East Timor in 1999 after years of insurgency. In both natural resource-rich Aceh and Papua, the Indonesian military had also been long embroiled in armed conflict with local pro-independence forces. Other natural resource-rich provinces such as Riau soon also clamoured for greater local autonomy. It is worth noting that in the Philippines decentralisation was partly a response to the chronic instability in Mindanao and the communist insurgency in Cordillera;[4] in Thailand, more substantive decentralisation has been put forward as a partial solution to the renewed violence in the predominantly Muslim South from 2004 (National Reconciliation Commission 2006).[5] In other words, a stated commitment to decentralisation policy has repeatedly been an avenue pursued to hold together nation-states in the region troubled by threats of secession and rebellion. Indeed some of the literature produced by international development organisations suggests how decentralisation can enhance political stability as well as strengthen national unity in troubled polities.[6]

But the concerns about the disintegration of Indonesia following the abrupt departure of its Cold War-era strongman have far outweighed worries about threats to the integrity of post-authoritarian Thailand or the Philippines. This is an irony given the more successful centralisation of state power that the New Order achieved in Indonesia. Neither Thailand under Cold War military dictators Sarit or Thanom and Praphat, nor the Philippines during the martial-law period under Marcos, quite displayed the kind of centralised authoritarianism as existed in Soeharto's Indonesia, where officials 'at all levels of the state hierarchy were highly responsive to demands and directives from "above"' Sidel 2004: 61),[7] and where policy-making and implementation was the undisputed purview of Jakarta, only to be followed compliantly by the regions.

It would not be an exaggeration to place concerns about Indonesia's breakup in the context of the international security environment that emerged following the promulgation of the American 'War on Terror', for which the political disintegration of this largest nation-state in Southeast Asia constitutes a major source of distress. If Indonesia truly became a dreaded 'failed state' (Mallaby 2002), then there would have been some major consequences for American and Western security and economic interests in the Southeast Asian region, which has been presented as the 'second front' in the 'War on Terror'. As a former U.S. Ambassador to Jakarta once observed with some trepidation: 'Strategically, the security of most of Southeast Asia rests on a stable Indonesia and would be seriously threatened if a number of mini-states emerged from a political collapse here' (Gelbard 2001). A USAID (2005) document thus proclaims:

As the world's largest Muslim majority country, Indonesia is too important to fail. The outcome of Indonesia's democratic transition has profound implications for U.S. strategic interests in fighting terrorism; preserving regional stability in Asia; strengthening democratic principles, the rule of law and respect for human rights; and expanding access for U.S. exports and investment in the fourth largest country in the world. Indonesia's importance also stems from its substantial natural resources, rich biodiversity, and strategic location across key shipping lanes linking Europe, the Middle East, and Asia.

Indonesian policy-makers no less presented decentralisation as the ostensible answer to the dreaded prospect of the disintegration of the country as we know it (Rasyid 2005: 17). Decentralisation also appeared to be the expedient political compromise between the idea of a highly central, unitary republic as existed under Soeharto's rule and the contending idea of a much looser federal republic of Indonesia, with the latter idea winning supporters among sections of the intelligentsia (see Mangunwijaya 2003; Sukma 2003). One major post–New Order political party, the National Mandate Party (PAN)—at the time led by the Muslim politician Amien Rais—had even placed the establishment of federalism in its official platform for the 1999 elections.[8]

It was under these circumstances that a 'team of experts' led by bureaucrat-academic Ryaas Rasyid was charged by the Habibie government, which immediately took over following Soeharto's resignation on 21 May 1998, with developing a blueprint for decentralisation. Habibie's enthusiasm for decentralisation was partly attributable to his intent to cling to power; he needed to distance himself from the New Order's centralised authoritarianism, while at the same time find ways of garnering political support from the outer regions (Hofman and Kaiser 2006: 83) for his precarious rule. The final product of the Habbie-appointed team's work comprised Laws no. 22/1999 on Regional Governance and no. 25/1999 on the Financial Balance Between Central and Regional Government.[9] These laws have been characterised by international development observers as no less than 'radical' (Betts 2003; Rohdewohld 2004) in their aims.

NEO-INSTITUTIONALISM AS A VARIANT OF NEO-LIBERALISM

What might be called the 'neo-institutionalist' variant in the neo-liberal development literature, in which decentralisation emerged as a crucial theme, has been most prominently, though not exclusively, represented in the work of international development organisations. A great deal of the literature on decentralisation thus originates from within the prolific intellectual production lines of the World Bank, USAID, the Asia Foundation, the Asian Development Bank (ADB), the German Organisation for Technical Cooperation (GTZ), as well as such private grant-making institutions as the Ford Foundation. These have a significant presence in much of the developing world and, because of their financial as well as intellectual resources and clout,[10] have profoundly affected development planning and internal policy debates in a range of countries. For example, decentralisation featured in a number of the 'Letters of Intent' signed between the IMF and the Indonesian government after the Asian Economic Crisis of 1997/98 as a condition of a long-term programme of assistance and loans, although the IMF was always concerned that revenue sharing with the regions did not create an unsustainable central budget (Buentjen 2000: 14). Turner and Podger (2003: 15), among others, note how various advisers and consultants from GTZ and USAID provided significant input to the design of Indonesia's decentralisation framework.

Some authoritative accounts suggest that input from international development organisations played a major role in forging the decentralising agenda in the Philippines during the period of reforms that immediately followed the fall of Marcos in 1986.[11] This is the case even though prominent domestic spokesmen for decentralisation, such as the politician Aquilino Pimentel, Jr., were to also emerge, as did Ryaas Rasyid in Indonesia. However, international organisations played a less significant role in the case of Thailand, where a group of domestic technocrats were the prime movers in getting decentralisation clauses prominently placed in the now defunct 1997 Constitution, and in drafting the 1999 Decentralisation Act.[12] The latter was facilitated by the support of the Democrat Party of then Prime Minister Chuan Lekpai,[13] who led a government that was already very much in sync with the economic reform agenda promoted in the region by the IMF and the World Bank after the Asian Crisis. Nevertheless, here too, synchronicity with the international good governance reform agenda was married to domestic political exigencies: the then ascendant Democrat Party had geared elections for local executive bodies as a means through which it could establish a stronger local base of voter support and bolster its local machineries (Nelson 2003: 8).

However, whether or not the localisation of state power through decentralisation policy was primarily driven by external or domestic technocrats in Southeast Asia is not really a key issue. Both kinds of technocrat share common assumptions about the largely mutually reinforcing relationship between decentralisation, good governance and the advancement of market economies. On this basis alone, neo-liberal and neo-institutional development thinking has left an indelible mark on the localisation of power in post-authoritarian Southeast Asia.

It is therefore appropriate now to consider more fully the ramifications of neo-institutionalist thought, as a variant of economic neo-liberalism, on decentralisation policy. It is first necessary to specify the kind of neo-institutionalism that is the subject of discussion here.

The term *neo-institutionalism* has been associated with a variety of actually quite disparate intellectual traditions of scholarship (Zysman 1994; Hall and Taylor 1996; Steinmo 2001; Sangmpam 2007), in spite of there being some common forebears and overlapping interests among them. It should be especially clear that a distinction is being made between the primarily economic neo-institutionalism (which, however, has made major incursions into sociology and political science) and the 'historical institutionalism' that was revived in sociology and political science by the work of Evans, Skocpol and others in the 1980s. The latter was developed further by authors such as Pierson (2000) and Thelen (1999), and adopted to analyse rapid East Asian growth in the state-centred work of Weiss (1998).[14] What is scrutinised here is mainly the economics-inspired neo-institutionalism, often described perhaps too narrowly as rational choice institutionalism (Steinmo 2001; Sangmpam 2007).

This type of neo-institutionalism should be placed within a broader neo-liberal orthodoxy that has been ascendant within governments, international development agencies and policy think tanks globally for nearly three decades. Importantly, its deep influence on shifts in thinking among neo-liberals generally in the 1980s and 1990s marked a distinct point at which many came to reassess their earlier market fundamentalism in ways that take into account the role institutions play in getting markets to actually work.

Yet that most important form of neo-institutionalism is simultaneously much more than this; it is no less than a school of thought that seeks to explain the history, existence and functions of a wide range of institutions (government, the law, markets, the family and so on) and social relationships. Specifically, it focuses on how institutional frameworks, norms, rules and regulations affect human behaviour and societal development. It does so by largely adhering to neo-liberal economic principles about the 'rationality' of the marketplace, even as it constitutes a partial internal critique of neo-liberal thought. Thus sociologists partially influenced by the economic neo-institutionalism, such as DiMaggio and Powell (1991), hold that human behaviour in modern society can take on 'irrational' forms, because they are embedded in pre-existing organisational or institutional structures. To be sure such sociologists have a greater tendency to speak in terms of a 'socially constructed rationality' (Scott 2005) that to an extent departs from the more strictly utility-maximising rationality that imbues neo-institutionalism in its manifestations in economics. In broad terms, however, the neo-institutionalist project addresses development in terms of the presence or absence of market facilitating institutions and complimentary cultural and behavioural norms; not surprisingly, this leads to a proclivity for social engineering and design among its proponents.

The neo-institutionalism tied to neo-liberal economics has undoubtedly driven the policy objectives of international development organisations, think tanks and foundations, as well as the policy agendas of the governments of leading industrial nations of the 'North'. But it has become increasingly influential in the wider social science community as well, from which development consultants are regularly recruited. This has been possible because the methodologies of mainstream economics have lately been increasingly absorbed by disciplines like sociology and political science (see Fine, 2001; Harriss, 2002)—as demonstrated in the influence of variations of rational choice or 'game theory' across the academic disciplines, as well as a particular notion of 'social capital', especially as advanced by theorists such as Robert Putnam and James Coleman.[15]

Interestingly, in the 'South' as well, we see otherwise critical NGO activists indirectly provide support for the neo-liberal globalisation agenda as it has come to be 'softened' by neo-institutionalist appeals for 'good governance' and 'social capital', and for public participation of 'civil society'. The Philippines scholar and activist Rocamora (2000), for example, suggests that it is in the interests of international mobile capital now to have authoritarian governments in the Third World ousted and replaced with democracies that espouse new governance practices that are more amenable to international investment. A key factor was the end of the Cold War; allegedly, this made authoritarian regimes such as existed in the Philippines during its height, redundant and often a mere barrier to the free movement of capital (for a contrasting view, see Rodan and Hewison 2006). Such an idea is of course appealing to NGO activists and scholars of a broadly 'progressive' political inclination in the Philippines and elsewhere in Southeast Asia.

The way that decentralisation as the manifestation of the localisation of power actually takes place requires careful empirical investigation, however. This requires a rejection of the notion that governments can just 'choose' the most appropriate form and pace of decentralisation, as is implied by the World Bank.[16] In fact, finding the 'right balance' of decentralisation in various areas of governance, or settling on the right 'pace', is almost never largely a matter of rational policy-making or of recognising and implementing the best policies. It more fundamentally involves constellations of social power and interests, and the outcomes of social conflict. In drawing attention to this aspect of the problem, it is not being suggested here that neo-institutionalists are unaware that policy-making is entangled in a highly political process of contestation. Of course they are not. Still, neo-institutionalists inspired by neo-liberal economics have a marked tendency to invoke politics largely as a process whereby rational policy-makers try to neutralise vested interests that lie as obstacles to the real business of technocratic weighing of policy options. As a consequence, democracy is embraced especially if technocrats/ technopols can preside over policies relatively unimpeded by societal inter-ests, which might include organised labour or other sources of social demo-cratic or more radical agendas. Such a position has important theoretical as well as practical ramifications.

In contrast, it is put forward here that policy-making is fundamentally shaped by contests between competing interests, the outcomes of which are highly indicative of modes of distribution of power in state and society. Such a position entails an understanding of neo-institutionalism, not just as an intellectual endeavour, but as part of a highly influential and political (even if hardly ever made explicit) neo-liberal project of reconstituting state power and state/society relations in market-facilitating ways. Significantly, there is nothing that guarantees that the social agents representing the world view and interests of technocratic rationality will prevail in arenas of social con-flict. Perhaps this is why neo-institutionalists have become embroiled in an ambiguous relationship with democracy. Their emphasis on the political in-sulation of technocratic policy-making from market-distorting societal pres-sures (for example, from labour unions or environmental movements) is also particularly conspicuous given the supposition that decentralisation paves the way for broader public participation in development.

Thus, China can be lauded for having undergone political reform, even if this is defined in rather minimalist fashion: strengthening local govern-ment, ideologically embracing the market, and opening the economy (Mon-tinola, Qian and Weingast 1995: 52). Moreover, when explaining the *politics* of China's economic success, some writing from within the neo-institutionalist tradition can draw attention to decentralised institutional configurations that are supportive of the market to the extent of highlighting commonalities among the contemporary Chinese state, and the American and English states of respectively the nineteenth and eighteenth centuries (Qian and Weingast 1996), without seriously broaching the presence or absence of democratisation impulses.

In other words, the theoretical position proposed by neo-institutionalists is one that expresses a kind of liberalism that is in many ways highly exclusionary in its political aspects (Jayasuriya 2000). Again the obvious problem is that the outcomes of representative democracy cannot always be harnessed to the requirements of technocracy. Hence, Grindle's otherwise complex analysis of the success and failures of thirty Mexican municipal governments ultimately rests on the presence or absence of reformist 'state entrepreneurs'— effectively heroic figures who will push through innovations in spite of public opposition and the lack of a social base (2007: 11).

As demonstrated in subsequent chapters, the Indonesian case strongly suggests that what really matters in terms of social analysis is the system of power relations within which decentralisation takes place. In Indonesia, neo-liberal governance reform in the shape of decentralisation was already 'hi-jacked' in its early years by a range of local predatory interests.[17] In fact, decentralisation provided a lifeline for them when the authoritarianism in which they were incubated had become no longer tenable. It is no coincidence that in the Philippines, too, fervent supporters of decentralisation acknowledge that it had the 'unintended consequence' of providing a windfall for predatory local bosses and dynastic families, whose power was strengthened rather than eroded, as might have been the case if good governance practices were to really take hold.[18] In Thailand as well, decentralisation converged with the interests of local predatory forces, which in the context of broader democratisation processes arguably enhanced their influence on national-level political contests.[19]

But could the kind of benign 'democratic decentralisation' envisaged by Crook and Manor (1998) take hold in the foreseeable future as Indonesia's new institutions of democratic governance take root? Could benign democratic decentralisation, as opposed to one dominated by predatory elites, evolve through a more or less natural process once a particular set of institutional changes have been set in motion, as they have been now? Again, the same questions could be put forward in the instances of Thailand and the Philippines, although it should be noted that they would sound especially strained in the latter case, where the Local Government Code was promulgated as early as 1991. From the point of view adopted here, there can be no guarantees; the real questions are whether reformist coalitions of power will sweep away already entrenched predatory interests, and from where would these coalitions emerge in the first place.

Today, most major Indonesian political parties would include a range of former apparatchik, military men, entrepreneurs and assorted political operators and enforcers of Soeharto's New Order—at both national and local levels (Robison and Hadiz 2004). While political parties and parliaments have now become real vehicles of political contestation, a key issue is the kind of interests that are embedded within them and, therefore, the kind of roles they actually play. As touched upon in a later section of this book, Indonesian political parties do not fit the 'ideal type' associated—rightly or wrongly—with the experiences of Western liberal democracies, and neither do their counterparts in post-authoritarian Southeast Asia generally.

It should be pointed out that there are instances in which local officials in Indonesia have emerged to perform relatively well under difficult circumstances.[20] Still, the comparative rarity with which such instances emerge indicate that the circumstances under which power is gained and maintained make it extremely difficult for a genuinely reformist impulse to take hold and not dissipate under the pressure of predatory politics. Yet, understanding cases that deviate from the norm of predatory ascendancy, if and when they do occur, is no doubt important. Dasgupta and Beard (2007: 237), thus maintain on the basis of field data from five urban and peri-urban communities in Java that decentralisation has variously produced outright 'elite capture', considerable democratic self-governance or combinations of both. While the finding is very useful, explaining outcomes that may deviate from what strongly appears to be the norm across the archipelago also requires more systematic attention to issues of contestation and social interest than is provided. Did reformist coalitions establish themselves in the cases of more democratic self-governance, and if so how did they emerge, what are their components, and how did they hold sway against local predatory interests that were embedded in the broader New Order structure of power?[21]

In Kebumen in Central Java (*Straits Times* 8 September 2003), for example, a *bupati* elected in 2000 was reported to have cracked down on local corruption with some success , so much so that its experience with decentralisation and reform was held as being exemplary. Significantly, however, even here a culture of good governance was not achieved well enough to prevent subsequent accusations of electoral fraud and abuse of power when the *bupati* won the re-election in 2005 (*Suara Merdeka* 13 June 2005).

Two of the contributors to an otherwise quite grim book edited by Schulte-Nordholt and van Klinken (2007) notably describe cases in which decentralisation appears to have resulted in relatively peaceful and prosperous local democracies. These are respectively the cases of Jepara (Schiller 2007), in Java, and North Sulawesi (Henley, Schouten, and Ulaen 2007).[22] The editors to the volume explain these as anomalies partly having to do with relative local prosperity and peacefulness during the Soeharto era and the role of entrenched traditional religious elites in maintaining order (Schulte-Nordholt and van Klinken 2007: 27), though the articles are really suggestive of the need for a more detailed and explicit scrutiny of local political topographies. For example, Schiller's own previous detailed work (1996) on what he called the New Order's 'power-house state' in Jepara, calls for a re-examination of what happened, after 1998, to the constituents of the system of patronage that underpinned it.

But it is the case of Jembrana, in Bali, that is perhaps most frequently held up as a decentralisation success story. Here, a *bupati* (district head) elected in 2000 is commonly seen to have effectively pushed for local administrative reforms as well as led a drive for economic innovation and entrepreneurship (Erawan 2007). What is often forgotten about the Jembrana case, moreover, is that even this *bupati* is widely believed to have won power by bribing members of the local parliamentary body that voted him into office and later pushing for personal control over the local branch of the party that had been a source of opposition to his rise. Such was the extent that Schulte-Nordholt (2007: 406–407) does not categorise the *bupati*, Gede Winasa, as an enlightened technocrat, but as a new local strongman.

The evidence for 'success' using good governance criteria employed by technocrats or of people's or civil society 'empowerment' employed by localist populists commonly residing in NGOs is patchy to say the least throughout most of Indonesia. The case studies discussed in later parts of this book are intended to explain why this is so in spite of the general consensus across the political spectrum after 1998 for the need for Indonesia to decentralise.

Decentralisation, State and Society

Another aspect of the theoretical discussion that requires examination is how 'decentralisation' has become—along with 'civil society, 'social capital' and 'good governance'—an integral part of the contemporary neo-institutionalist lexicon that focusses attention on the 'social' and 'human' aspects of capitalist development. As mentioned previously, neo-liberal and neo-institutionalist thought suggests that a vibrant civil society contributes to good governance and democratisation by ensuring greater public participation in development. As the World Bank put it, 'we now approach economic reforms and the development process in a much more decentralized fashion. Individuals and various social groups are now seen not only as beneficiaries, but also as active forces that support the process of development (World Bank n.d. b).

From this point of view, the logical consequence of decentralisation is that local communities would be in a better position to demand more adequate provision of services (Grindle 2007: 12). Local officials are more accountable and 'closer' to these communities and can better identify their needs. As Harriss, Stokke and Tornquist (2004: 3) put it, the 'common assumption is that mutually enabling relations between decentralised state institutions, local businesses and civil associations will generate economic growth, poverty alleviation and good governance'. Such an argument provides a seemingly appropriate riposte to populist criticism about the socially marginalising effects of neo-liberal economic globalisation.

This faith in civil society and political participation, however, has some definite limits. A different World Bank-sponsored document declares that: 'the success of decentralisation frequently depends heavily on training for both national and local officials in decentralized administration' (Decentralization Thematic Team n.d.). This distinct 'training for success' explanation underscores that local governance reform must be enforced by technocratic and managerialist interests constructed within the state bureaucracy. Thus 'successes' cannot really depend on vital elements within broader civil society after all.

In keeping with this perspective, a USAID document on decentralisation in Indonesia states that 'local governments have little experience with participatory self-rule and will need assistance to create adequate mechanisms for participation, transparency and accountability'. These local governments are also recognised to have only 'limited technical capacities, particularly to perform functions that have been provided by central agencies'; thus, 'they will need assistance to demonstrate to citizens that autonomy does lead to improvements in services and the environment'. The document adds that 'particular attention will be paid to ensure women's participation and concerns are included at all levels' (USAID 2000: 18).

What is especially astonishing is that there is no mention of the lack of influence of local environmental lobbies, or the only limited clout of the women's movement in Indonesia. Nor is there acknowledgement of how in the Indonesian context, large domestic and foreign corporations can simply ignore environmental regulators, or that young female workers in low-wage manufacturing industries continue to face harassment and violent intimidation as they attempt to exercise their legally guaranteed right to organise. That such politically marginalised female workers will substantively 'participate' in decentralised development is assumed, without explaining how this might come about in the context of very unequal relations of power.

Given all the above, there are sound reasons to question the underlying assumptions about the link among decentralisation, good governance and civil society participation as understood in the neo-institutionalist literature, especially, but not exclusively, that produced by international development organisations. The following section therefore offers a closer examination of the ways in which the-neo-institutionalist literature proposes the existence of such a link.

CIVIL SOCIETY, SOCIAL CAPITAL AND PUBLIC PARTICIPATION

Particularly through the work of Putnam (1993; 2000), social capital has become an ever more important part of neo-institutionalist thinking about civil society's role in the decentralisation process. As is well known, the social capital discourse emphasises the common norms and values that create 'trust' among development actors as well as between those who govern and are governed.[23] Decentralisation is believed to be particularly helpful in setting the institutional environment for the nurturance of the social capital necessary for a vibrant civil society that can work together constructively with governments. Thus, the World Bank, too, has come to develop major social capital-inspired policy initiatives (Fine 2002: 220).

A too rarely acknowledged but contentious problem is the very concept of civil society that is utilised. Following the Tocquevillian tradition adhered to by Putnam, the Bank tacitly assumes a civil society defined by a homogeneous, common set of fundamental interests and values, generated by autonomous associational life, while academics like Diamond have stressed the democratic and rule of law-oriented culture that should arise out of civic activity (Diamond 1994). A counterweight to state power, pro-market and democratic values should emerge from a vital civil society to promote 'tolerance, moderation and a willingness to compromise' (Diamond 1994: 8), according to such views. They sit uncomfortably, however, with the usually existing reality of competing interests within civil society itself and discrepancies of access to wealth and power which is often rooted in class structures. They also do not accord with the finding that important sections of civil society may be profoundly anti-democratic or anti-market (Rodan 1996: 4–5; see also White 1994) including,[24] ironically, the bourgeoisie and the middle class, which on the basis of assumptions most established in the classic work by Lipset (1959), are conventionally put forward as modernising and democratically inclined.

As Fine (2001) reminds us, 'social capital' actually began its life as part of a critique of the cultural aspects of class inequalities in contemporary capitalism (Bourdieu 1986) but was soon appropriated by the followers of theorists such as the economist Becker (1996), the sociologist Coleman (1988) and the political scientist Putnam (1993, 2000). The main purpose of 'social capital' at present appears to be to conceptually downgrade the importance of social conflict and the dynamics of unequal power relations in determining the development trajectories of societies. Social capital in its most well-known manifestations, therefore, has become an essential part of the wider technocratic project of conceptually depoliticising development itself (Fine 2001; Harriss, 2002).

In this respect, the functionality of social capital is to privilege the normative bonds assumed to be present in well-adjusted societies, and to cast social conflict as aberrations much in the same way as 1950s and 1960s sociological theories of the modernisation mould used to privilege social equilibrium. What has thus transpired is the successful reformulation of 'civil society' by neo-liberal and neo-institutionalist thought by way of a link to the intellectually spurious but attractive notion of social capital. Fukuyama (1999), for example, states that: 'An abundant stock of social capital is presumably what produces a dense civil society, which in turn has been almost universally seen as a necessary condition for modern liberal democracy'). As a consequence, civil society—actually an arena of struggle between competing interests—becomes conceptually sterilised and sanitised.

It is true that the Bank defines civil society as the space among family, market and state consisting of 'not-for-profit organizations and special interest groups, either formal or informal, working to improve the lives of their constituents' (World Bank 2000: 10). In this way, an array of organisations—research and policy design organisations, labour unions, the media, NGOs, grassroots associations, community-based organisations, religious groups and many others—can be placed within this definition as 'typical examples of the actors that comprise the dynamic web known as civil society' (World Bank 2000: 10). Still, there remains too little recognition that the so-called 'dynamic web' may embody a range of interests that are mutually antagonistic—of the powerful and the exploited—that may promote or resist good governance reforms.

The point is that by painting a picture of civil society free of fundamental contradictions, it can be overlooked that democracy, public participation, accountability and social and economic rights are all historically tied to the outcome of the struggles of social forces and interests; that they are not simply the product of intentional policy design. Liberal democratic regimes in the West, for example, are undoubtedly the product of wrenching social change over centuries, coloured by often violent and bloody confrontations, not the least between labour and capital. The neo-institutionalist view, however, would 'hold out the prospect of a democracy with substance and depth but without political competition or conflict between different social groups and classes'. For the World Bank a conflict-free democracy 'created through the crafting of local organisations and facilitated by NGOs' is a condition for good governance and economic development (Harriss, Stokke and Tornquist 2004: 8).

The rise of 'social capital' is indicative of the enhanced status of public participation in the mainstream developmental discourse. A glowing assessment of decentralisation policy in the Philippines thus claims that the 1991 Local Government Code there has been responsible for greater public participation in development, as well as rising levels of public accountability and greater local control over local resources. But the story is obviously not a simple linear one, for besides the presence of a more mature civil society, the author acknowledges the continuing salience of predatory local political bosses, who regularly deploy 'guns, goons and gold', in the post-Marcos era. Still he holds out hope that a more 'modern' and 'technocratic' elite will eventually arise out of their families (Rood 1998)—pointing to the case of the son of a notorious old local boss who is 'an American-educated sophisticate quite at home with technocratic modes of governance'.

Away from Southeast Asia, a broad survey of decentralisation and democratisation in southern Africa by Wunch is quite instructive and thus worthy of mention. It cites studies that show how 'democracy must be rooted in functioning local, participatory self-governance institutions'. It points to 'untapped local capacity to make collective choices and take collective action'. At the same time, however, Wunch notes that 'experiments' in local governance and democracy in virtually every place in Africa he mentions has met with failure. The way out of the quandary is to suggest that these failures are rooted in 'specific policy choices and strategies pursued by African governments', including deliberate withholding of resources from 'local entities' (Wunch 1998). But why were the policy choices and strategies made, and what made them more possible than others? What was concretely at stake? What was the specific constellation of power and interests that made it difficult for others to challenge these policy choices?

These same questions could of course be readily transferred to the Southeast Asian experience. Rocamora (2000), for example, believes that decentralisation in the Philippines, specifically the Local Government Code of 1991, opened up new political space for progressive movements. 'People's organisations' and NGOs are now in a better position to genuinely strive to empower society's politically and economically marginalised, according to his assessment. One important innovation has been the building of a political party vehicle to directly contest power via elections by these movements.

Insofar as the efforts described by Rocamora are successful, they point to the fact that it is necessary for coherent, reformist or progressive social and political coalitions to exist—and successfully contest processes that might otherwise only result in new space for established local elites. But there are real structural impediments that must be overcome. Thus, Hutchcroft, also writing on the Philippines after Marcos, emphasises the existence of old political clans that dominate the institutions of representative government, and elections that are marred by money politics and intimidation. He points to the 'the enormous expense of running for election' that serves as an 'effective barrier to the entrance of reformist forces into the political arena', and that 'many so-called new faces often retain strong connections to old centers of power' (Hutchcroft 1998b). This observation is highly relevant to the case of post-authoritarian Indonesia, as we shall see.

In other words, the crafting of democratic institutions of public participation, while important, is not sufficient. This is seen clearly in the other post-authoritarian Southeast Asian case, Thailand. Here, the 1997 Constitution (abrogated after the September 2006 military coup against Thaksin) stipulated a decentralised structure of governance that contradicted the logic of the famed 'bureaucratic polity' (Riggs 1966)—though it should be noted that it had already been undermined progressively with the emergence of local politicos over the decades (Sombat 2000). Democratisation, especially after the 1992 public uprising against the military, was accompanied by a drive to more formally decentralise power from Bangkok, and to create new local administrative entities endowed with greater power and responsibilities (Patpui 1999). As the Asian Development Bank put it, the aim of decentralisation in Thailand was to 'reconfigure the political, legislative, judicial and administrative machinery of government.'[25]

As in post-Soeharto Indonesia, the expectation was that successful decentralisation would make governance in Thailand 'more decentralized and participatory' and induce government institutions at all levels to become 'more transparent, accountable and responsive' (ADB 1999: 7). But of course there were to be structural impediments. These included a 'number of influential forces have a vested interest in the status quo', as well as the presence of 'fierce bureaucratic resistance to the decentralisation initiatives envisioned in the constitution, and widespread perceptions of corruption' (ADB 1999: 7). Another obvious obstacle was the widespread practice of vote buying, especially in rural areas where politics remains an exclusive sphere dominated by 'strongmen', notable families and informal networks of patronage (see Arghiros 2001; Nelson 2005). Thus even the modes of political participation involved in the local workings of democracy could be tied to the persistence of corruption, another issue with which the neo-institutionalist literature on decentralisation and good governance is concerned, but finds difficult to resolve.

DECENTRALISATION AND CORRUPTION

Besides civil society empowerment, it was already mentioned that decentralisation is also linked conceptually with corruption eradication in the neo-institutionalist literature (e.g. Fisman and Gatti 2002). Fjeldstad (2003) notes the widely-held assumption that decentralisation would bring the government 'closer to the people'; hence, it would help discipline the state, resulting in the improvement of 'service delivery' as well as the decline of corruption.[26]

He also notes, however, that there is little empirical evidence to support this assumption across cases.

Today Indonesia has the well-deserved reputation for being one of the most corrupt countries in the world. In fact, Transparency International listed Indonesia as the joint third most corrupt country in the world in its 2001 survey and joint-fourth in 2002, although improvements were 'achieved' in 2003 when Indonesia took position 122 out of the 133 countries surveyed, and position 130 out of 163 countries in 2006. The Philippines stood respectively at positions 92 and 121 in 2003 and 2006, while Thailand stood at 70 and 63.[27]

Long-term observers of Indonesia or corruption issues in general will not be surprised by these results. In 2000, for example, the Hong Kong-based Political and Economic Risk Consultancy (PERC) showed that expatriates working in Asia viewed Indonesia as the most corrupt country in the continent (*Kompas* 23 March 2000). Indeed, Indonesian government data show that the state lost some Rp 22 trillion (US$2.35 billion) in nearly 1,200 corruption cases from January 2002 to April 2004 (*Jakarta Post* 18 June 2004).[28] It is impossible to ascertain the number of cases that go unreported in the sprawling archipelago, and therefore, this must be considered a very conservative estimate.

It should be recalled, however, that rampant corruption in Indonesia is hardly a post-Soeharto phenomenon. In fact, Indonesia did not rate much better under the New Order, which was often praised by international development agencies for its economic performance. Transparency International, for example, ranked Indonesia at position 80 out of 85 countries surveyed in 1998 (Wee 2002: 5),[29] the year Soeharto was finally toppled.

Understandably, a major fear is that rampant corruption will deter much-needed investment, especially of the foreign kind, given that Indonesia still struggles to re-emerge from the ruins of the Asian Economic Crisis of 1997/98 (Winters 2000). While corruption and cronyism were notoriously unbridled in the Soeharto era, the key difference is that corruption now is especially unpredictable. If foreign investors easily accommodated the more predictable form of corruption, they are less keen about today's more decentralised form. Of course this is not surprising; no less than Max Weber (1978: 240, 1095) had famously recognised the importance of the predictability of corruption for business at the much earlier development of capitalism in Europe.

Instead of necessarily creating conditions favourable for investment, the newly decentralised and unpredictable form of corruption may promote new business uncertainty. This is why no less than Indonesian Vice-President Jusuf Kalla, himself a prominent businessman, warned local administrations against adopting policies of increasing local revenue through levies on business. He was responding to a study that found that 30 per cent of these would lead to 'high-cost economies', as well as a survey in which '24 per cent of 5184 respondents in 214 regencies and cities complained about business distortions' caused by local government edicts. These edicts, as we shall see, have been particularly controversial because of the perception that corruption has particularly grown at the local level of governance, leading one seasoned Indonesian observer to declare that 'People got nothing out of autonomy, while local officials got rich.'[30] Significantly, the survey also showed that businesses had to bear the burden of illegal payment demanded by 'security forces, the courts, social organizations and mobsters' amounting to '6.81 percent of total production costs' (*Jakarta Post* 21 March 2005); many will rightly regard this as a rather conservative estimate. So rather than inducing the kind of healthy competition between localities envisaged by authors writing on China like Qian and Weingast (1996), decentralisation has produced local governments, armed with greater autonomy in various spheres, such as taxation (Lin, Tao and Liu 2006: 324), that provide sustenance for predatory interests.

The World Bank has of course long suggested policy and institutional frameworks that are crucial to the successful eradication of corruption.[31] A World Bank-sponsored compilation on fighting corruption in Asia (Bhargava and Bolongaita 2004) concludes by recommending a fairly uniform set of policy measures geared toward strengthening institutions tasked with curbing and monitoring corruption, while also inviting civil society participation. Clearly, in the case of Asia, the emphasis on constructing anti-corruption institutional frameworks is a direct response to the Asian Economic Crisis of 1997/98, which has been portrayed as being triggered fundamentally by corruption and market-distorting policy choices. Given that Indonesia's experience of the crisis was uniformly regarded as the worst, it is little surprise that curbing corruption has been at the front of the reform agenda pertaining to Indonesia.

While anti-corruption institutions have now been established in Indonesia, the outcomes of Indonesia's *reformasi* contests described earlier constrain their effectiveness. Not surprisingly, entrenched predatory interests have had some success in resisting measures to monitor and constrain corruption, which Dick (2002: 71–86) calls the 'new frontier in social engineering'. Some of the worst offenders among New Order tycoons, bureaucrats and politicos thus remain unscathed by anti-corruption probes, in spite of some notable convictions. In such a context, decentralisation may only 'multiply existing opportunities for corruption' as well as offer 'unrestrained possibilities of wealth accumulation' (Harris 2003: 62) on the part of bureaucrats and criminals alike. In fact the line of differentiation between the two could become exceedingly blurred.

The recent experience of the Philippines is particularly instructive given the high hopes that inevitably accompanied 'People Power' in 1986, not just in terms of democratisation but also eradicating corruption and cronyism. Hayllar shows that institutional changes did not loosen the hold on power of traditional economic and political elites, despite the stated intentions. Decentralisation resulted instead in 'the institutionalisation and considerable enlargement of pork-barrel funds necessary to maintain congressional and elite support for the government's reforms' (Hayllar 2003: 257). The system of patronage fuelled by corruption was, therefore, actually perpetuated by decentralisation, as privatisation and deregulation policies provided new rent-seeking opportunities for predatory elites.

Given rising local corruption accompanying decentralisation in Indonesia, much attention is now being paid to corrupt practices by local officials. Such local corruption often relates to contests for control over the local state machinery and resources, as well as developing potential bases for localised predatory networks of patronage. In the process, it has also involved a misallocation of local government budgets for private gain by local politicos. It was estimated in late 2001, for example, that 40 per cent of central government subsidies to the regions under a fiscal assistance scheme had been misappropriated—and this less than one year after the official implementation of local autonomy (*Kompas* 27 November 2001).[32]

Re-Politicising Decentralisation

The discussion above suggests that largely depoliticised accounts of actually messy and contradictory decentralisation processes are being produced in the intellectually predominant accounts written from within the neo-institutionalist perspective inspired by neo-liberal economics. However, the problems of institutional design, civil society participation and corruption eradication, to name a few, are those that cannot be treated adequately on the basis of politically sanitised narratives.

The point to be made here is that neo-institutionalists inevitably are often trumped by the very power relationships that they would like to wish away with theory. This is because the agenda of democratic decentralisation, whose broad outlines may have been drawn by technocratic experts, has frequently been usurped by decidedly non-technocratic interests that may only selectively engage with neo-liberal inspired governance reforms. These could be even threatened by good governance reforms that demand transparency, as will be shown in more detail in the case of post-authoritarian Indonesia—even if they are advantaged by other facets of decentralisation.

Such an observation paves the way for a more realistic, and overtly political, understanding of why decentralisation in Indonesia has failed thus far to achieve its stated aims, and in the process sideline those that champion the worldview of 'technocratic rationality'. It also allows for the incorporation of important insights from other experiences, such as that of Thailand and the Philippines, to help explain the trajectory that Indonesia is presently on and the social and political outcomes of the localisation of power.

Another implication of the above analysis is that because decentralisation is primarily about contestation of power, rather than technical policy-making, its course is hardly ever linear; there can remain strong tensions between centralising and decentralising impulses over long periods. Thus, one ambition of the demised Thaksin government[33] in Thailand was to recentralise state power, involving renewed efforts to exert control over, or absorb, the local politico-economic alliances that had particularly thrived in the 1980s and 1990s.[34] In other words, even after decentralisation has been set in motion, it might still be partially rolled back, as appears to be the case to some extent in Indonesia today—to the detriment of ambitious local politicos who thought their fortunes were to be continually rising.

Chapter Two

The Post-Authoritarian Context

Technocratic Ambitions and
the Challenge of Predatory Power

Indonesia, Thailand and the Philippines make up the three major post-authoritarian Southeast Asian societies in which the localisation of power has emerged as a key part of debates about democratisation and governance. In all three cases, decentralisation policy has been instituted as an ostensibly key pillar of reform, although the outcomes have been contentious and ambivalent. On the one hand, these cases have been featured in the varied and voluminous literature on 'democratic transitions' and technocratic 'good governance' reform; on the other hand, they have been included too in the literature on the resilience of predatory local elites.

Several issues are grappled with in this chapter. First, what could the Indonesian experience with decentralisation and, more broadly, the Southeast Asian, contribute to our understanding of the driving forces behind the localisation of power in post-authoritarian societies? What could they tell us about the factors that may prohibit the emergence of the kind of 'democratic decentralisation', characterised 'accountability' and 'transparency', as understood in the neo-institutionalist literature? What is the role of technocratic 'modernising elites' on the one hand, and what is often referred to as predatory local bossism, on the other, in the concrete struggles pertaining to the localisation of power, according to the experience of Indonesia and other post-authoritarian Southeast Asian societies?

In spite of important differences as products of distinct histories, post-authoritarian Southeast Asian societies share features that demonstrate serious problems in envisaging the replacement of authoritarian regimes with liberal forms of democratic governance, certainly in any 'rationally' and technocratically engineered manner. Instead, they tend to show how old interests or such un-civil forces as predatory local notables and political gangsters may find a strong niche in or even usurp the democratisation and decentralisation processes when circumstances allow. They therefore indicate the limits of engineered processes of institution and capacity building that take place within certain terrains of power. Such observations are crucial to a deeper understanding of the 'successes' and 'failures' of decentralisation in post-authoritarian contexts. In particular, the case of Indonesia, which has undergone substantial transformations in the sphere of governance institutions since 1998, provides ample evidence to support an analysis that privileges power, interests and contestation over technocratic institutional crafting.

Post-Authoritarian Trajectories

As is well known, an international literature on 'democratic transitions', including the 'crafting' of 'democratic institutions', grew quite spectacularly after the 1980s (see Munck 2001) and continues to develop even today. Some of the most influential works on the subject can be attributed to such scholars as O'Donnell and Schmitter (1986), Linz and Stepan (1996), Huntington (1991) and Di Palma (1990). Though the starting point was democratisation in Southern Europe in the 1970s and Latin America in the 1980s, the literature soon came to deal with the experiences of post-communist Eastern Europe/Central Asia (see McFaul 2002) and later, the globalising capitalist economies of East and Southeast Asia (see Johannen and Gomez 2001). A central characteristic of the literature is the concern with how benign elite pacts could emerge in very fluid situations following the fall of authoritarian or totalitarian regimes, and how they might give rise to lasting institutions of democratic governance. Especially for the East European post-communist cases, a major concern has been the relationship between 'transitions to democracy' and the nurturing of capitalist market economies (see Haggard and Kaufman 1995; Przeworski 1991).

Though remaining influential,[1] the assumptions and approaches of 'transitionists' or of 'transitology' are now being placed under more scrutiny than before. Notwithstanding the privileged position still held by ideas like 'democracy promotion' within governments like that of the United States and by extension, many international development organisations, the 1980s euphoria concerning waves of democratisation—accompanying globalisation and market-friendly economic reforms—had somewhat abated by the beginning of the twenty-first century. Thus, Thomas Carothers of the Carnegie Endowment for International Peace in Washington, DC, writes about the 'End of the Transition Paradigm' (2002). He notes with conviction that 'reality is no longer conforming to the model' and that 'it is time to recognise that the transition paradigm has outlived its usefulness' (2002:6). One of his main laments is the disingenuousness with which transition authors had categorised a host of countries as being on the way to democracy in the 1980s and 1990s; he suggests only a small minority of them today can be unambiguously labelled 'democratic'. With regard to Indonesia, one vociferous critic, Schulte-Nordholt (2004: 29), has labelled the use of the transitions paradigm as 'outdated sociology'.

Writing on Chile, Posner critiques the fixation among 'transitologists' with elite pacts. He notes that whether or not it is acknowledged, the participants in such pacts represent sets of concrete social and economic interests, and that any 'institutional crafting' of the new 'rules of the game' that ensues will inevitably reflect this. He points out too that there is no real reason to assume that 'pacted democracies' will incrementally become more broad-based or accountable, or result in more equitably shared power. In fact, elite pacts may result in institutional arrangements that hinder such a development because they are against the interests of the dominant participants (Posner 1999: 63). Such observations are very relevant in particular to the case of post-authoritarian Indonesia and issues related to the localisation of power, as we shall see more clearly below.

In this book, the messy and often volatile changes in Indonesian politics and society are *not* seen as a characteristic of any transitional stage to an idealised democratic form. It is proposed, following Robison and Hadiz (2004; also see Hadiz 2003), that the patterns and essential dynamics of the exercise of social, economic and political power have more or less been established, and will remain relatively unaltered in the foreseeable future. This is a direct product of the fact that old oligarchic and predatory interests were not overcome by *reformasi* but managed to reinvent themselves as democrats and reformers and then preside over newly constructed institutions of governance. The presence of predatory elites and a variety of local bossisms, the rise of money politics and notable tendencies toward political thuggery are therefore not the symptoms of the 'growing pains' of a society whose political development was stunted by decades of authoritarianism. They are essential characteristics of the logic of an (illiberal) type of democracy, variations of which can be found in the Philippines, Thailand and in many other post-authoritarian situations, and which have now become well entrenched. The consequence is that Indonesia is following a well-traversed historical trajectory that differs significantly from that associated with the entrenchment of liberal or social democracy.

Nevertheless, Indonesia has been at the core of recent discussions about 'democratic transitions'—not just as represented in the academic literature (see various chapters in Budiman, Hatley and Kingsley, 1999; Liddle 2001; Aspinall 2005a) but also in the more technocratic kind spawned by experts based in international development agencies or consulting institutions (see USAID 2000; also see Bjornlund 2000).[2] In fact the discussion on democratic transitions in Indonesia depicts the ease with which the assumptions of 'transitology' and neo-institutionalist good governance can be combined.

In response to the fact that local elections from 1999 tended to produce local governments that were unresponsive to local needs and thrived on money politics, Turner and Podger (2003), for example, suggested the need to revamp the electoral system by making heads of local executive bodies directly elected by the local electorate, rather than the local parliament, as was the practice until new legislation requiring direct elections started being implemented in 2005. They also suggested that a system that had more district-based features might make elected members of local parliaments more accountable to those who elect them. However, governors and mayors have long been directly elected in the Philippines (as they have been in Indonesia since 2005), as is well known, and both Thailand and the Philippines have electoral systems that have strong district-based features; yet, money politics obviously abound in both cases. Therefore, what seems to be more important than electoral and institutional reforms per se is the context within which they take place.

But the product of generous infusions of neo-institutionalism into transitology has significant implications, especially in relation to the strategies of international development organisations. A USAID document thus describes part of its activity in Indonesia for the year 2004 in the following manner:[3]

USAID will provide technical assistance and training to the national legislature and political parties to enable them to become effective agents of
democratic reform. Technical experts will work directly with legislative commissions deliberating key pieces of legislation, including bills on freedom of
information and justice sector reform. Training will be provided to office-
holders, youth groups, and women's groups of political parties. The training
will strengthen internal democratic features of the parties, including how to
make the parties more responsive, policy-driven and able to communicate directly with their constituencies.

What is overlooked in the USAID document is that the kind of groups
that have coalesced in Indonesian political parties may not have a genuine
vested interest in governance reforms that would make them more accountable to the citizenry and place restrictions on predatory, rent-seeking opportunities. Moreover, being 'policy-driven' is not necessarily compatible with
the persistent interest in rent-seeking. The key point to keep in mind is that
the demise of authoritarianism in Indonesia—as was the case in the other
Southeast Asian societies—did not produce any kind of clear liberal victory.
As McFaul (2002: 225) states in a useful internal critique of the transitions
literature in relation to the former communist bloc, 'if powerful democrats
draft the rules, it does not matter what electoral system is adopted or whether
a parliamentary or presidential system is adopted'.[4]

Helping to ensure such persistence of predatory politics in democratic Indonesia is the continued marginalisation of cohesively liberal, social democratic, or more radical social forces from the processes of political contestation. This is partly indicated in the fact that in just six years after Soeharto's
fall, the former state party of the New Order, Golkar, had already regained its
status as the country's premier political organisation. Winning the presidential poll in 2004 was a former senior New Order general, although one whose
reputation is not nearly as sullied as that of the majority of his peers. The
vice-president that emerged from the same poll is part of a group of businessmen that gained much from New Order patronage of *pribumi* (indigenous)-
owned enterprises in the 1980s (see Pangaribuan 1995) and is head of Golkar.
Indonesia's new Regional Representation Council (DPD), resulting from a
major Constitutional amendment and modelled to a degree on the American
Senate (though much less powerful), came to be led by Ginandjar Kartasas-
mita.[5] Implicated in corruption scandals, he was no less than one of Soehar-

to's most important economic aides outside of the so-called 'Berkeley Mafia'. Down to the local level, in fact, one finds that a range of former New Order petty apparatchik and state-connected entrepreneurs or gangsters have achieved pre-eminent status in local politics (see Chapter 4).

Further complicating the analysis of Indonesian democratisation is the fact that the military has not been completely eliminated from politics nationally or locally. Though it has had to give up seats previously automatically allocated in national as well as local parliamentary bodies, military commanders are still able to engage locally in political and business alliances on the basis of the so-called territorial command structure, which provides for a military counterpart to each level of civilian governance (see Mietzner 2003). Nico Schulte-Nordholt (n.d.) proposes that decentralisation has facilitated corrupt practices on the part of local military commands, especially in resource-rich areas like Kalimantan and Papua, while Jun Honna (2005) argues that in line with the need of each local/regional military command to remain financially viable, military commanders have had the tendency to enter into accommodations and alliances with locally or regionally ascendant political parties. It should be remembered that many of these military commands have long been involved in illicit economic activities (for example, in illegal logging, human trafficking, drugs and prostitution); therefore, they have an interest to continue working with local gangsters, businesspeople and officials to ensure that money continues to flow into the local military coffers (Honna 2005: 3–5).

Again, Indonesia's situation is not unique. The collapse of the Soviet Union, for example, was followed by the emergence of a Russian Federation within which party competition and parliamentary politics have been prominent. For quite some time, studies of Russia's 'transition' tended to closely look at the degree to which institutions of democracy, like legislative bodies, had developed and matured (e.g. Hahn 1996). As in Indonesia, however, the new salience of such institutions did not rule out the repositioning of old ruling party apparatchik in new positions of power, or the rise of political gangsters as powerful officials or as rulers of thriving politically-connected business empires.

Thus, it is incorrect to present the main lines of conflict in Russia as being between conservative, backward-looking survivors of the Soviet *nomenclatura* and a business 'oligarchy' representing 'free market' interests. The business oligarchs, who are far from being champions of the free market, infamously made their huge fortunes by politically usurping the process of privatisation in the 1990s (Oversloot 2006). Moreover, many present-day Russian tycoons were also the field operators of the old Soviet regime, acting as functionaries of such organisations as the Communist Youth League.[6] The very genesis of the post-Soviet tycoons therefore was at the intersection between politico-bureaucratic power and business, and riddled with all kinds of criminal influences. Organised crime, already in existence during Soviet times, grew and proliferated with the rise of Russian capitalism and the corruption that characterises business and state relations (e.g. Lynch 2005).[7] Such developments in democratic Russia can be viewed as having been directly affected by the social configuration of power that existed during the late Soviet era.

The legacy of authoritarianism is one aspect of the problem that certainly requires a significant degree of emphasis in the case of Indonesia. Immediately following the fall of Soeharto, the social forces that were not directly nurtured by the New Order and, therefore, would possibly have an interest in challenging the system of predatory capitalism that it forged (for example, sections of the liberal intelligentsia and professional groups in society, or the politically marginalised working class or peasantry) were not able to organise and develop into a coherent social force. This in turn allowed for the continued ascendance of many of the elements of the ancien regime—who were always more organised, coherent and endowed with material resources in the first place—in the context of an illiberal form of democracy that was mainly to be run by the logic of money politics. In a nutshell, these elements were better positioned than others in taking advantage of the opening up of Indonesian politics after 1998.

In this regard, another of McFaul's observations about Eastern Europe and Central Asia after the fall of the Soviet Union seems to be quite relevant. According to McFaul, democracy only emerged out of the ruins of the Soviet Union when there had been a clear political defeat of the forces of the ancien regime by strongly reformist interests, while new dictatorships have resulted from the alternate situation (McFaul 2002). Although no new dictatorship has emerged in Indonesia, a core argument made by Robison and Hadiz (2004) is that the constituents of the ancien regime in Indonesia were much less than unambiguously defeated, and certainly not replaced by any coherent liberal or reformist coalition.

In the Philippines, another icon of the Cold War, the anti-communist dictator Ferdinand Marcos, was dramatically toppled more than a decade before Soeharto. Here, the broad-based political opposition in 1986 benefited from having relatively sustained organisational activity over the years, owing to the authoritarian regime's comparative lack of success in domesticating sources of political dissent. The latter is partly shown in the fact that the Marcos regime continued to confront substantial armed insurrections on the part of both communist rural-based forces and of Moro separatism while in power and lacked authority over swathes of territory where such insurgencies were prominent.

Boudreau observes, however, that the celebrated People Power Movement of 1986 displayed the important role of social and economic elites which included politicians and entrepreneurs who presided over social movement organisations. For this reason, 'elite activists', as Boudreau terms them, never feared that social protest 'would have *socially* revolutionary consequences' (see Boudreau 2004: 187; also see Thompson 1995) in the sense of radically redistributing power and wealth in society. Not surprisingly, the local political dynasties that were subordinated to Marcos when state power became more centralised under martial law subsequently found new opportunities to reclaim the privileged social and political positions they had enjoyed, under the subsequent money-politics run democracy typically presented as being characterised by the salience of 'goons, guns and gold'. In other words, the sway that elite families hold over local politics in the Philippines was strengthened by democratisation and the 1990s turn to decentralisation. Moreover, Hedman (2006) notes that more recent, post-authoritarian, civil society-based mobilisations against dominant oligarchic groups have frequently elicited counter-mobilisations spurred by conservative elements, operating with equal vigour in the name of a civil society—which by now has amply displayed its heterogeneity and internal contradictions.

Democratisation in Thailand has also been beset with problems that are eerily similar in several respects, especially in relation to the features of sub-national politics. Like in Indonesia, but with a degree of violence more closely approximating that of the Philippines, local politics long became the preserve of local strongmen and notable families and their informal networks of patronage, or *phuak* (Nelson 2005). This is in spite of any criticism that one might advance against the stereotyping of Thai local political figures (see Nishizaki 2006) in the style of the godfather-like *chao pho*. In the Thai context, decentralisation policy further entrenched the social and political position of predatory local notables rather than empower local citizenries.

In Indonesia, the system of power that came to replace the heavily centralised and authoritarian 'New Order' had already developed the following
features within just a few years (see Hadiz 2004b: 619):

1)   The decentralisation of power from the presidency to political parties
      and to parliament.
2)   The rise of political parties mainly as expressions of shifting alliances
      of predatory interests, primarily those incubated by the New Order.
3)   The decentralisation of power from Jakarta to the regions and the as-
      sociated new importance of local offices such as that of *bupati* (regent)
      or town mayor, and of party branches and parliaments at the local level.
4)   The emergence of decentralised, overlapping and diffused patronage
      networks built on the basis of competition for access and control over
      national and local institutions and resources.
5)   The rise of political fixers, entrepreneurs and enforcers previously en-
      trenched at the lower layers of the New Order's system of patronage.
6)   The related emergence of hooligans and thugs organised in party mi-
      litia and paramilitary forces, many of which have taken over some of
      the functions of the security forces proper.

Given the above, one could rightly ask from where the social base of support for the neo-liberal/neo-institutionalist agenda of reforms would emerge
as it concerns decentralisation in post-authoritarian societies like Indonesia
(or the Philippines and Thailand). From where would be found the social
agents that could win the liberal victory that is required for these reforms
to become politically ascendant? One answer that might be given appears in
the form of an old favourite of modernisation theorists of a prior age: state
bureaucratic and technocratic elites.

Elites, Decentralisation and the State

One view that has been highlighted is that the experience of Indonesia after
1998 demonstrates how the legacies of authoritarian rule can remain essential even as the institutional structures of authoritarian regimes dissipate.
While decentralisation has accompanied the institutional unravelling of authoritarianism in Indonesia, good governance in the technocratic sense has

not transpired because of the persisting legacies of the New Order. Thus is Indonesia's current quandary insofar as decentralisation is concerned: the centralised authoritarian system is no longer viable, yet democracy combined with decentralisation has failed to break down the predatory relations of power that underpinned the old system.

If one legacy of the New Order is that of instrumental control over state power, its institutions and resources, by powerful predatory forces, another is the severe disorganisation of civil society and independent societal movements— a development that followed the elimination of the Left in the 1960s. These legacies persist even as the institutional framework of governance in Indonesia has been radically reconfigured, and even as technocrats aided by able consultants and experts in international development agencies attempt to 'craft' or 'design' the appropriate sorts of institutions that are expected give rise to a culture and practice of good governance, and even political participation.

Neo-liberal and neo-institutionalist thinking might suggest that the way out of this predicament depends on the nurturance of forward-looking elites, whether within the state or sections of civil society—thus, the 'training for success argument' already alluded to. The aim would be to nurture strategic elites that would act as the vanguard of any push toward the desired form of decentralised governance by equipping them with the right skills and imbuing them with the right world views. There is clearly something eerily reminiscent here with early modernisation-style sociological understandings of social change. Because of this, it is useful to revisit some of the ways in which the roles of modernising elites have been understood as far as Indonesia and Southeast Asia are concerned, particularly as some of these have reappeared in new guises and implicitly come to inform much of the conventional thinking on decentralisation policy today.

It is well known that classical modernisation theory conceived the state as an intrinsically interest-neutral and, therefore, potentially benign agent of development and modernisation. From this perspective, the absence of a solid entrepreneurial class in virtually all the newly independent countries of Asia and Africa in the 1950s and 1960s left the state with the role of being the main agent of the modernisation project. It was in this context that technocratic elites were invariably invoked to safeguard economic and political modernisation, frequently in a social and cultural environment that was understood to be 'pre-modern'. It was through the moulding of such technocratic elites that the emergence of a kind of 'civic culture' (à la Almond and Verba 1963) preconditioning democratic life was supposed to emerge. Moreover, it was no coincidence that at the height of the Cold War, these same elites were also imagined to be the main safeguards against the threat of communism. In the context of the Vietnam War's escalation, institutions like the Ford Foundation and the Rockefeller Foundation, with close links to American policy-making circles, came to be very active in providing academic scholarships to selected members of the intelligentsia and bureaucracy in Indonesia and other parts of Asia (Hadiz and Dhakidae 2005: 11–13).

In Indonesia, the Ford Foundation was particularly instrumental in the emergence of the Faculty of Economics of the University of Indonesia as a major intellectual centre, from which the Soeharto regime would be provided with a steady stream of economic technocrats and experts (Ransom 1970). Many of these went on to key economic positions in his various cabinets over the years. The Cold War (and Vietnam War) context was very important in dictating this development—a similar process of training technocrats that would become bastions against the incursion of communist ideology occurred in Thailand and in the Philippines (Suehiro 2005; Tadem-Incarnacion 2005). Needless to say, particularly insofar as Indonesia and Asia in general are concerned, much of the emphasis on technocratic elites pre-dated the period of rapid capitalist development from the 1980s in the region that ultimately produced vibrant middle classes and bourgeoisie. The latter social actors would much later be seen as the most vital of modernising agents, the rise of which gave the state reason to retreat, especially from the economy.[8]

It is useful for our purposes to note the significance of Samuel Huntington's work, especially in his late 1960s and early 1970s incarnation (see Huntington 1968). It is not an exaggeration to suggest that this work signalled the beginning of a new variant in modernisation thinking that came to define society's modernity in terms of its institutional capacity to successfully maintain political order and stability. As a consequence, modern political systems of power and their institutions were to be increasingly understood as those that were capable of averting a society's descent into revolutionary chaos, which would be a sign of a lack of modernity. For the political scientist Emmerson and others who studied Indonesia broadly in this vein, a return to the party-based parliamentary system that had preceded both the New Order and the late Soekarno period's so-called 'Guided Democracy' offered political instability (Emmerson 1978: 104, 105; 1976: 250) rather than a way to political modernisation. In contrast, the New Order's 'bureaucratic pluralism' (Emmerson 1983) allowed institutions of state charged with economic policy a significant measure of autonomous space. In other words, state technocrats were insulated from societal pressure for the sake of the common good.

It is suggested here that the disposition within the neo-liberal and neo-institutionalist literature today—including on decentralisation—to emphasise benign technocracies able to rise above narrow interests, partially harks back to this particular phase of modernisation theory. Such is the case in spite of the actual history of overtly political links between technocrats and dictators in Southeast Asia and elsewhere during the Cold War. Thus, after a period of decline, modernisation theory has more lately been undergoing resurgence, taking the form of an economics-inspired neo-institutionalism as well as the predilection of social theory for rational choice and/or Putnamian notions of social capital—all of which feature significantly in the decentralisation literature.[9]

Not surprisingly, the Huntingtonian version of modernisation theory had become attractive to the intellectuals, technocrats and ideologues of authoritarian capitalist regimes, such as those in Soeharto's New Order (see Moertopo, 1973; Boileau 1983: 68), as it helped to legitimise their harsh treatment of detractors within society. In other words, the Huntingtonian revisionism helped to provide intellectual legitimacy for state policies that systematically maintained the disorganisation of civil society in order to guarantee the sort of political stability that was said to be conducive to economic growth (see Bourchier and Hadiz 2003). It should be recalled too that Marcos' vision of a New Society in the Philippines was partly formed with the help of Western-trained economic technocrats whose influence grew in the context of harsh authoritarian rule (Abinales and Amoroso 2005: 207–212), and yet were either complicit in or could not stop the looting of the economy by regimist cronies (e.g. Hutchcroft 1998a, chapters 6 and 7).

As is well-known, the New Order in Indonesia emerged in the mid-1960s out of the victory of an alliance of anti-communist forces led by the military, and which consisted of elements of the urban and rural propertied and middle classes. These groups were threatened by the increasingly strident radical populism of the Indonesian Communist Party (PKI), then the third largest in the world, which had forged a political alliance with President Soekarno—the nationalist firebrand whose autarchic (and ultimately disastrous) economic strategy and anti-Western foreign policy ostracised Indonesia from the major powers of the capitalist world. Soekarno's downfall was accompanied by the annihilation of the PKI through the mass slaughter of hundreds of thousands of real and alleged communists as well as detainment without trial of innumerable others. The violence that characterised the elimination of the PKI from Indonesia's political and historical landscape in turn paved the way for the development of a political regime that was not only designed to curtail the re-emergence of the Left, but also to pre-empt any substantial independent organising activity within any group in civil society. Labour, for example was to be organised only through one state-initiated and controlled labour union, as were other groups in civil society (Hadiz 1997).

This was the environment of systematic depoliticisation in which modernisation perspectives became influential in the scholarship on Indonesia. Borrowing from Riggs's (1966) classic analysis of Thailand, scholars like Jackson (1978) produced works that transferred to the Indonesian case many of the assumptions of modernisation theory, and incorporated such concepts as the 'bureaucratic polity' dominated by a narrowly-based elite freed from societal pressure. Other scholars, like Liddle, thought that the authoritarian New Order could be the incubator of a rational capitalist system and believed that Soeharto was being ably assisted toward fulfilling this task by a team of economic technocrats trained in the neoclassical tradition of economics (1991: 403, 404, 1992: 796–798).

In spite of some variations, Indonesian development problems were thus more or less posed in terms of producing the values conducive to modernisation or ensuring that agents possessing those values were politically or economically ascendant. Western-trained economic technocrats (MacDougall 1975)—starting with the University of Indonesia's so-called 'Berkeley Mafia' (Ransom 1970)—were usually portrayed in many accounts as the 'heroes' of modernisation who had to struggle to enforce rational policy decisions in the face of a pervasive pre-modern social and political culture.[10]

In Indonesia, another period of technocratic optimism was spurred after the fall of Soeharto, when the importance of educated 'modern' elites capable of making rational choices and rising above petty politics was once again regularly invoked. President Susilo Bambang Yudhoyono, for example, declared upon his election in 2004 that he would appoint a cabinet made up of experts and technocrats, and limit the participation of political party figures driven by narrow interests. This was a promise he was notably unable to keep due to the realities of the constellation of power (*Kompas* 11 August 2004). Indeed the appeal of a supposedly interest-free technocracy has never completely abated in the region, although in Thailand, Thaksin had more or less marginalised the departments and agencies traditionally equated with technocratic influence (Suehiro 2005). In the Philippines, the case of President Arroyo is particularly interesting, as she is simultaneously a traditional oligarch and self-professed technocrat with advanced training in economics. Though keen to emphasise the latter part of her identity by assembling a so-called 'technocratic dream team' (Tadem-Incarnacion 2005) in her cabinet, the continuing corruption and cronyism that has tarnished her government speaks volumes about the limits of technocracy when placed in a broader social constellation of power that remains inhospitable.

Pro-technocracy positions obviously do not only arise from within sections of the state apparatus. A staunchly pro-technocracy approach has been more recently championed outside of the state in Indonesia by Mallarangeng (2002), an admirer of the economic historian Friedrich von Hayek. A U.S.-trained political scientist and now public commentator, Mallarangeng espouses a rather exceptionally blunt form of market fundamentalism in the Indonesian context. In fact, he has argued for the innate wisdom of technocratic pro-market policies and ideas as opposed to the objections typically put forward by groups representing populist and distributional coalitions. The Jakarta-based Freedom Institute, which he leads, has become a leading advocate of neo-liberal policy and technocratic decision-making. Mallarangeng certainly has his intellectual counterparts in the region—among them is Thammasat University's Medhi Krongkaew (2000), whose work ultimately portrays economic policy-making as the province of 'power-elites' that are essentially defined as technocrats perched in the state bureaucracy. Besides recalling Riggs's bureaucratic polity, his work largely and conveniently leaves out sustained discussion of the range of societal interests, including the Thai capitalist class, that profoundly influence the direction of policy-making; not the least after one of its leading representatives assumed the office of prime minister in 2001.[11]

There are different ways, of course, of understanding the role of the state, and its bureaucratic or technocratic elites. Robison (1986), for example, proposed that state power in Indonesia, as elsewhere, needed to be understood in the context of the wider system of class relationships (Robison 1986: 117–118). He analysed developments in Indonesia around the mid-point of New Order rule by postulating the emergence of an increasingly powerful domestic capitalist class and the implications this might have for the country's future. He later suggested that a version of 'Bonapartism' had taken hold in Indonesia insofar as a bourgeoisie forfeited power in favour of an authoritarian state, in order to maintain political stability. In Indonesia, the state thus proved especially vital to the consolidation of both capitalism and the capitalist class (Robison 1993: 41), and provided the catalyst as well for the emergence and consolidation of a capitalist oligarchy. Significantly, this capitalist oligarchy was to appropriate state power and to use it instrumentally to further its own interests (Robison and Hadiz 2004).

Still, what was the position of the technocrats within this oligarch-dominated system of power? Many Indonesian populists made the error of equating New Order economic policies with the interests of the technocrats (see Chalmers and Hadiz 1997, especially chapters 1, 2 and 6). On the other hand, those more favourably inclined toward the technocrats saw them as pushing through 'good' policies *in spite* of the rapacity of Soeharto-era politics. Such a view perhaps lingers on. It has been suggested, for example, that decentralisation policy was successfully advanced after 1998 through the efforts of technocratic 'agenda setters' who were endowed with superior information and knowledge vis-à-vis politicians who needed something to prove their reformist intentions (Smith n.d.). However, the neo-classically trained economists in Soeharto's various cabinets only provided a façade of technocratic rationality for a regime that exercised arbitrary power and was irreparably corrupt, and it is hard to sustain that they have become any more powerful subsequently. Lindsey (2001) thus likened the New Order not to rule by technocracy but rule in the style of criminal gangs, in which highway robbery as well as coercion and violence were formalised in the practices of the state.

It is indeed arguable that these much-lauded economic technocrats, in spite of international support, only enjoyed periods in which they were especially influential. This was during the early years of the New Order, when Soeharto was particularly eager to court international aid and investment, and when the Indonesian oil 'boom' of the 1970s ended around the mid-1980s. It was during these times that technocrats were able to promote economic agendas, such as that of partial economic deregulation and privatisation in the 1980s, as was strongly advocated by the World Bank.[12] The economic technocrats' influence, however, was noticeably very low even during the New Order's final economic crisis in 1997–98, when Soeharto brushed aside IMF conditionalities that would have harmed the economic interests of the oligarchy, including the business fortunes of his family members and cronies (see the discussion in Robison and Hadiz 2004).

Even as Indonesia continues to struggle to re-emerge from the effects of this crisis in the post-Soeharto period—for several years amid continuing pressure from the IMF to institute neo-liberal economic reforms—there are few signs of more powerful economic technocrats as would-be 'modernising elites', who are able to spearhead the process of designing and constructing new institutions of markets and economic governance. This is in spite of the role of various groups of technocrats in helping outline the blueprint of post-crisis reforms, including with regard to decentralisation, with the assistance of international development experts and consultants. Thus the basic problem of the absence of a coherent domestic coalition of interest to underpin the neo-liberal agenda remains, excepting rather woefully isolated pockets of neo-liberals in a few government ministries and agencies, and some vocal academics who typically air their views through the media.

In short, it is true that Soeharto's fall marks the end of a long chapter and the beginning of a new one in Indonesian history, but it is not the sort of chapter that neo-liberal reformers or neo-institutionalists would have written. To their chagrin, the social, political and economic legacy of the New Order will likely prove quite enduring and continue to influence Indonesia's trajectory in the near future. Thus, powerful coalitions of modernising elites espousing genuine good governance reform agendas, and effectively contesting local power, remain rather difficult to find.

So, if not the social agents of neo-liberal technocracy, then what kinds are instead presiding over the process and outcomes of decentralisation in Indonesia? It is here that we me must turn to the already significant literature on predatory local bossism in Southeast Asia.

The Resilience of Predatory Power: Bossism and Its Cousins

As already pointed out, the post-New Order Indonesian experience has inspired comparative analyses with post-authoritarian Thailand and the Philippines (see Heryanto and Hadiz 2005). One area of comparison involves the role of local bosses or notables and predatory networks of patronage in the context of the rise of the institutions of democratic politics (see Savirani 2004). Sidel notes that as 'power has shifted "downwards" and "upwards" from within a centralised bureaucracy firmly rooted in Jakarta to elected members of assemblies in regencies, municipalities and provinces around the archipelago', scholars of Indonesia 'were quick to pick up on the rapid rise to prominence of local powerbrokers' (Sidel 2004: 67). This is the case although Indonesia's previously exceptionally centralised system of authoritarian rule made it difficult for anything resembling local bosses—prominent individuals with control over local coercive and economic resources and political machineries (Hedman and Sidel 2000: 88)—to have emerged.

By contrast, local strongmen or 'godfathers' are far better established in Thailand's recent history. Dubbed the *chao pho*, their social origins were at the junction between formal politics and criminal activity. According to Kasian Tejapira (2006: 13–14), these men 'usually had a provincial entrepreneur-cum-local mafia-boss background' for whom the 'establishment of a parliamentary democracy were unexpected gifts, which provided them with a golden opportunity to convert their hitherto shady local wealth and influence into legal power at the centre of national politics.' Kasian also considers such individuals as comprising a layer of 'electocrat' within Thai democracy: people who would typically have built personal fortunes in the 1960s and 1970s 'exploiting American aid intended for war efforts against neighbouring states and the military government's market-oriented development projects.' They are engaged in businesses 'such as land speculation, logging, public works, trucking, cash crops, entertainment, gambling, underground lotteries, prostitution, bootlegging, gunrunning, drug-trafficking, smuggling, etc.' Government contacts and violence were key features of their rise, as 'Intractable conflicts with business rivals and uncooperative officials were often solved with the help of hired gunmen.'

Still, according to Kasian Tejapira (2006: 14):

> the electocrats themselves were transformed from lowly mafia businessmen who had to kowtow to local officials into respectable members of parliament or Cabinet ministers, with jurisdiction over the promotion (or demotion) of their former 'patrons'. Once elected, they treated politics as a kind of business, effectively selling public policy, office, concession or title deed to the highest bidder. Shameless avarice was fuelled by the need to gather enough 'ammunition' for election campaigns to enable them to stay in power.

In the Philippines, however, local political bosses come from traditionally dominant families and clans, the *cacique*, who were able to reclaim their ascendant position in society and politics after their authority was curtailed for so long by the state-centralising ambitions of Ferdinand Marcos. These families and clans could typically trace their lineage and dominant position back over many decades.[13] As a lawyer-politician who did not emerge from the ranks of the cacique-proper, Marcos's rule, particularly during the period of martial law after 1972, was aimed at empowering the central state and its apparatus 'an active weapon against landed privilege'. Attacking the economic base of these clans, Marcos established quasi-government monopolies in such important export industries as sugar and coconut, and established control over other, smaller, export crops. Control of these monopolies was placed under businessmen whose position was dependent on Marcos's personal patronage (Rocamora 1995: xiv–xv). In the process, the latter cobbled together a new coalition of 'new entrepreneurs, newly professional politicians and technocrats' (Boudreau 2004: 79) who similarly resented the 'traditional' politicians or *trapos*. Anderson (1988) came to dub the system in the Philippines, post-People Power, as *'cacique* democracy', dominated as it is by the traditionally dominant social forces that had been threatened by Marcos's state-centralising project.

Nevertheless, it is certainly necessary to be mindful of significant differences within Southeast Asia with regard to local bossism.[14] Clearly, insofar as it has emerged in Indonesia, local bossism has been coloured by less outright violence than in either Thailand or the Philippines, where assassinations of politicians and activists are regarded as being a much more 'regular' part of political life. Furthermore, Tornquist (2000: 388) comments that bossism 'in the Philippines is characterised by the long history of US colonialism, partially elected government and more private control of resources'. In Indonesia, however, 'primitive accumulation through political and administrative means' has been comparatively more important. Therefore, most local Indonesian bosses are likely to be comparatively 'petty' in terms of having less private wealth, and in their dependence on public resources, according to Tornquist.

In this connection, Sidel (2004) provided a rather systematic basis for distinguishing the specific manifestations of the local bossism/local strongman phenomenon in post-authoritarian Southeast Asia. He does this by explaining their origins in diverse historical settings. He points out, for example, that local bosses only appeared as major players in Thailand in the 1980s in the context of the rapid industrialisation that coincided with the gradual withdrawal from politics of the military, which in turn opened the way to power for a range of civilian forces. The Thai so-called *chao pho* also essentially came to flourish within a European-like parliamentary system of democracy, but in which figures of authority in local and provincial components of parties have become very important partly due to the strategic nature of the rural, non-Bangkok vote. Moreover, the bureaucratic polity of Riggs (1966) did not completely dissipate; as Sidel notes (2004: 60), career civilian bureaucrats still retained much authority over local executive bodies, while military generals continued to wield influence through senatorial appointments and various forms of economic and political interventions. A major function of the chao pho in Thailand's democracy is to guarantee votes by 'delivering parliamentary constituencies, or regional clusters of constituencies, to Bangkok-based patrons, local clients, or themselves'. They do this on 'elections day, through a combination of coercion, vote-buying, and electoral fraud' (Sidel 2004: 59).

In the Philippines, it is the legacy of U.S. colonialism that was the most decisive factor in determining the evolution of bossism and the peculiar system of rule that characterised it. This system of rule gave rise to politically powerful, even dynastic, local families[15] within a highly decentralised state, with a U.S.-style presidential system and a 'multi-tiered pattern of municipal, congressional, and provincial bosses (Sidel 2004: 60). Local bossism in the Philippines, in this sense, has a longer, more entrenched and formal history than the Thai 'strongman'. In the Philippines, local bossism has sometimes given dynastically entrenched families firm control over elected office, which in turn 'provides access to a broad array of state resources and prerogatives'. Here, political violence, intimidation and money politics all 'work in tandem with the mobilisation of local machines for self-perpetuation in office' (Sidel 2004: 56–57). It is well known that political violence in the Philippines can become exceedingly stark: in Sulu, for example, competing local clans are documented to have openly fought battles by fielding hundreds of armed men against each other in the provincial capital's streets (Gutierrez 1995).

Sidel is certainly correct about the aspects of 'timing' and 'context' that distinguish local bossism in Thailand from that of the Philippines. Nevertheless, it is still possible to trace the social origins of the chao pho to a more distant past. In fact, they arguably go back to a time when, despite King Chulalongkorn's administrative reforms initiated in the late nineteenth century and geared to develop a modern bureaucratic form of governance, the state failed to apply control and surveillance effectively in the hinterlands. This provided the chao pho, or at least their antecedents, with the opportunity to develop profitable illicit trades (drugs, gambling or smuggling) that enabled them to emerge as feared but respected leaders. Such leaders typically became 'strongmen' to whom locals could turn for protection against state and capitalist encroachment (Nishizaki 2002). As a result, they came to wield enormous influence in their communities and carved out loosely defined territorial bailiwicks largely beyond the control of the central state bureaucracy (see various chapters in McVey 2000; also see Nishizaki 2002). As capitalism developed in Thailand, especially during the 1960s and 1970s, such individuals increasingly developed a more varied range of economic interests.

In contrast, it has already been said that Indonesia's heavily centralised and bureaucratic New Order, which presided over a rapid period of industrialisation from the 1970s to the 1990s, provided comparatively little opportunity for the emergence of local 'strongmen' or 'bosses'. Insofar as they existed, they were subordinate to a broader system of political patronage based on Soeharto himself and also more distinctly based within the state and its local apparatus. According to Sidel, the fall of the New Order made it possible for bureaucratically-rooted 'local 'mafias' and 'networks', once an organic part of Soeharto's system of rule, to emerge 'around the country in tandem with the shift to competitive elections and the devolution of considerable state powers to elected regency-level,[16] municipal and provincial assemblies'. Thus, local bossism in post-Soeharto Indonesia is less dominated by 'individual strongmen' or 'dynasties' than in Thailand and the Philippines than it is by more fluid clusters and cliques of businessmen, politicians and officials (see Sidel 2004: 68–69).

Nevertheless, there are variations even within the individual societies. Thus, many local politicians in Thailand could no doubt rightly object to the chao pho label given the many connotations involved, and Hedman and Sidel (2000, chapter 5) note how bossism within the Philippines can take different forms. Contrasting two economically advanced provinces—Cavite, just south of Manila, and Cebu—they observe that the former is characterised by the predominance of single-generation families of gangster-style politicians or warlords. The latter, by contrast, is notable for the predominance of more stereotypically paternalistic and dynastically-entrenched families at different levels of governance who manage to pass on power to succeeding generations.

As we shall see, predominant within the 'clusters' or 'cliques' that Sidel identifies as having emerged in Indonesia are politico-bureaucrats, entrepreneurs, military officers and gangsters—many cultivated within a range of youth and paramilitary organisations—that see democratisation and decentralisation as opportunities to now break free from the shackles of Jakarta-based interests to pursue their own predatory objectives. They also include actors, old and relatively new, whose social base lies within the corporatist and social organisations from which the New Order regularly recruited new apparatchik and local functionaries for decades. Again, the social actors most prominent in the local scramble for power and in forging regimes of governance at the local level are those who represent forces that had been nurtured in the provinces, *kabupaten* and towns within the formerly vast New Order system of patronage (Hadiz 2004a, 2004b).

It is therefore correct that the politics of 'local bossism' in post-Soeharto Indonesia are more fluid than in the Philippines or Thailand, in the sense of the more easily shifting nature of local coalitions of interests as well as the actual sites of local centres of power. Thus, Sidel refers to 'local mafias' in Indonesia rather than bosses per se to highlight the distinction. This Indonesian divergence is a legacy of having had to emerge 'out of' a more 'successfully' centralised authoritarian regime.

The tantalising question that arises as the localisation of power proceeds, however, is whether local bossism in Indonesia will develop features that are more 'solid' and give rise to more coherent, entrenched interests and alliances dominated by local notables of various sorts, leading toward local oligarchies. This is not merely a 'matter of time' question, but an important acknowledgement of how democratic politics can be consolidated in such a way that the mechanics and coalitions of interest that underpin them can be very different from those that characterise liberal forms.

Therefore, in spite of historically-defined differences, all three post-authoritarian Southeast Asian cases are characterised by regimes distinguished by the appropriation of state power, its prerogatives and resources; and by local predatory interests, whether through executive bodies, parliaments or both. The Philippines case may stand out in the way that power is expressed in the form of local political dynasties that wield such extensive control over local political and economic machineries. In all three cases, however, the maintenance of political ascendance involves different combinations and degrees of money politics, electoral fraud, political intimidation, selective mass mobilisations and parastatal or non-state security groups.

Moreover, one of Sidel's main reasons for asserting the continuing lack of opportunity for either Thai- or Filipino-style strongmen in Indonesia is an electoral system that remained prohibitive of the emergence of influential individuals or powerful 'dynasties'. He notes that in the Indonesian system, the heads of local and provincial governments are elected by their respective parliaments; this is in 'sharp contrast with the direct elections—and unrestricted powers—of mayors, governors and congressmen in the Philippines, and parliamentarians (MPs) in Thailand.' Hence, there are supposed to be 'institutional obstacles' in Indonesia to the rise of Thai- and Filipino-style local bossism (Sidel 2004: 70).

However, as discussed more fully especially in Chapters 3 and 6, there have been many changes applied to Indonesia's electoral system, including the institution of direct elections for the positions of *bupati*, mayor, governor and president/vice president. Although such changes have been welcomed by Indonesian democracy activists and neo-liberal/neo-institutionalist advocates alike, ironically, they also help newly ascendant and ambitious local politicos to secure their privileged positions in post-Soeharto Indonesia, relatively free from the shackles of a Jakarta-directed dynamics of party politics. Thus, as we shall see, direct local elections are providing new possibilities for those who aspire to be 'local bosses' in the Thai or Filipino sense. For those with higher ambitions, this might yet fuel a more vociferous appetite to build more coherent local networks of patronage based on less diffused economic and political alliances.

It should be re-asserted that the ascendance of local bosses and the like is not at all about the absence of a civil society cemented by enough social capital—civil society does exist in post-authoritarian Indonesia, in spite of the ravages of the Soeharto era, and it remains rich and dynamic in the Philippines and Thailand. Evidence of a measure of civil society dynamism in Indonesia is seen in labour organisations, for example, which have proliferated since the demise of the New Order, even though they remain largely ineffective as workers go about re-learning the business of organising in the context of large-scale unemployment and the pressures of international capital mobility, as well as intimidation from hired goons and thugs. Business and professional organisations exist in abundance as well, and the media is free despite having experienced some setbacks from time to time (see Heryanto and Hadiz 2005). NGOs, too, remain quite vibrant; even during the New Order there was a rich diversity of NGO-type activity in Indonesia (see Hadiwinata 2003; see also Eldridge 1995); the government had regarded some of these as potentially troublesome. Furthermore, though their origins cannot be separated from links to the state, it is fruitful to view many of

Indonesia's current aspiring local bosses as occupying a space within civil society, or at least where civil society intersects with the state. In recognising this, it is not necessary to adopt Migdal's (1988) overly dichotomous arguments about local strongmen being the products of societies that are 'strong' and states that are 'weak'. It is significant that their political socialisation and incubation were in societal organisations, though of the kind previously patronised by the state.

The real issue with regard to civil society, therefore, is that most of its salient elements in post-authoritarian Indonesia, including at the local level, are those that were organised and nurtured under a rabidly predatory system of power and therefore were really placed at what might be conceived as an intersection between state and civil society. Most significant among these were the kinds of groupings of political operators, entrepreneurs, and goons and thugs that were so instrumental in the operations and sustenance of New Order rule at the local level. The interests of civil society are often tacitly understood in the neo-liberal tradition to favour free markets, rule of law, and democracy; thus, basically those associated with idealised notions of a vibrant and independent middle class or bourgeoisie. The reality is that there is a diversity of often competing interests within civil society itself. The political rise of such elements as goons and thugs constitutes nothing less than a 'glowing' testimony to that diversity, as well as the failure of other kinds of interests to successfully challenge them.

Comprehending the nature of this diversity is necessary in getting to the heart of contemporary struggles over power and the way these are organised at the local level. It is not some vague and lofty ideological battle about preferred systems of economic and political governance that is at stake. The contest is also not about the supposed rationality of the market in contradiction to the irrationality of politics, including identity politics; the way that markets actually operate is politically defined in the most basic sense. The struggle is more about the moulding of rules through which the fruits of rent-seeking are to be distributed among competing coalitions of local and national predatory interests. As we shall see, one of the major vehicles for these battles in Indonesia is now about control of the institutions of democracy par excellence, such as political parties and parliaments. But what kinds of political parties are they, and what sort of interests underpins them? These questions are addressed in the discussion to follow.

Chapter Three

The Localisation of Power
and Institutional Change

When placed firmly within a concrete societal and historical setting, the dynamics of electoral and party politics can provide important clues about the nature of the localisation of power. They may provide insights into the way in which the institutions of decentralisation and democracy at the local level actually operate and the kinds of interests that they advance and marginalise. Local electoral and party politics in post-authoritarian Indonesia are therefore worthy of the same kind of scrutiny given by Kerkvliet and Mojares (1991) to local politics in the Philippines in the immediate post-Marcos period. Whether in the Philippines, Indonesia or elsewhere, the dynamics of local electoral and party politics provide indicators of the way in which 'the articulations between the "local" and the "national" in politics' (Kerkvliet and Mojares 1991: 3) takes place in practice. They have ramifications as well for our understanding of the contradictory relationship between local power and pressures for pro-market good governance reforms.

In Indonesia, Golkar was for decades the vehicle that lent Soeharto's authoritarian rule a significant facade of electoral legitimacy. Notably, this was a vehicle that had begun life in the early 1960s as a mass organisation created by the military and its civilian allies to counter the influence of the PKI and its array of mass organisations (Boileau 1983; Reeve 1985). Throughout New Order rule, Golkar never failed to overwhelmingly win a national election, and it was only rarely defeated in elections at the local level (see Suryadinata

2002). As is well known, the People's Action Party (PAP) in Singapore and United Malays National Organisation (UMNO) in Malaysia also provide good examples of dominant one-party rule in Southeast Asia that remain relevant to this day—though in the latter case it has lately been destabilised. In fact, not all attempts at establishing dominant state parties have been as unambiguously successful in the region as it has become ever more integrated with the global capitalist economy in the last few decades.

Ferdinand Marcos in the Philippines, for example, had attempted to form the so-called New Society Movement in the 1970s which, like Golkar in Indonesia, was intended to extend his reach and authority into the farthest corners of a vast archipelagic country. Although Marcos was highly successful in rigging elections so that the New Society Movement would convincingly triumph—much in the vein of Golkar—the façade of electoral legitimacy was decidedly more flimsy in the Philippines case. Thus, the last election held under Marcos actually helped to stimulate the emergence of the People Power Movement that would topple him in 1986 (Thompson 1995; Boudreau 2004). Clearly, part of the problem that Marcos's authoritarian centralising project faced was the legacy of strong local ruling families.

State and political party centralising endeavours have, in fact, been taking place in Southeast Asia more recently. Thailand's controversial businessman-politician Thaksin Shinawatra, for example, was known to have expressed his admiration for the Malaysian and Singaporean models of one-party rule. According to Pasuk, Thaksin once declared his preference for 'a parliament like Singapore where an opposition exists to give the state democratic credentials, but where the opposition is too small to have any effect.' As prime minister, he openly strived 'to achieve an effective one-party state' partly by ensuring that his Thai Rak Thai party absorbs 'smaller parties on what is a modified version of the UMNO model' in Malaysia (Pasuk 2004b: 2–3; also see Ockey 2003: 663). The state centralising project was cut short in September 2006 with the Thai Rak Thai's ouster by military and royalist elements (Nelson 2007) hostile to the Thaksin-led bourgeois appropriation of the state.[1]

It is Indonesian party and electoral politics, however, that have come to resemble those in post-authoritarian Thailand and the Philippines rather than the other way around. This is because state power has become much more diffuse since the end of the New Order, thereby providing opportunities for the development of a new dynamic that involves the rise of more localised coalitions of power and interest. At present, the institutions of governance and of electoral politics, national and local, contrast ever so starkly with those that seemed to be so permanently enshrined during Soeharto's long tenure, and which hindered the development of Philippines- or Thai-style bossism. Such a situation provides a unique opportunity to analyse breaks and continuities in power relations beneath the surface of institutional change.

This chapter provides an overview of the dynamics of institutional change in post-authoritarian Indonesia, including the format within which electoral and party politics now take place, with a focus on issues of localisation of power. The overview is premised on the idea that, as with all institutional frameworks of governance, those that define electoral and party politics can be regarded, first and foremost, as expressions of the way in which power is distributed in a specific context of time and space—of what sorts of interests tend to be dominant and which ones tend to be subordinated.

The Dynamics of Institutional Change

REORGANISING POWER INSTITUTIONALLY

The most observable and dramatic change in Indonesia since the fall of Soeharto has undoubtedly been the prominence of electoral politics, now so energised and animated after decades of stringent and rigid controls. This change has involved the rise of political parties and parliaments, national and local, which play an important role in the post-authoritarian framework. Thus, few observers will dispute that while elections and political parties merely provided a façade for an essentially predatory, authoritarian regime during Soeharto's rule, they are now genuine vehicles of political contestation. The importance of political parties, and national and regional parliaments, is currently reflected in the often intense competition among elites to wield control over them and the increasingly vast resources expended in the process.

It should be noted that the main pieces of legislation that came to regulate the workings of Indonesia's electoral and democratic institutions following the demise of the New Order were Laws no. 2/1999 (on political parties), no. 3/1999 (on elections) and no. 4/1999 (on the constitution and status of various representative bodies). Most of the content of these laws was notably produced under the auspices of the same 'team of experts' led by scholar-bureaucrat Ryaas Rasyid, who was appointed by Habibie and played the most instrumental role in drafting the legislation that was to govern 'regional autonomy'. The original drafts produced by the team, however, were revised considerably as political parties ensconced in the last Soeharto-era parliament were already taking advantage of the demise of authoritarian rule and made important interventions (for details, see Robison and Hadiz 2004, chapter 9). The set of new political legislation was finally passed in January 1999, although it was a contentious process that involved objections from some civil society groups on some clauses they considered still too restrictive.

Thus, free parliamentary elections took place in June 1999, contested by 48 political parties out of the 150 or so that initially registered. These were Indonesia's first democratic national elections since 1955. Except for the first New Order-era elections, held in 1971, which involved a number of parties left over from the late Soekarno period,[2] electoral contests had always pitted Golkar against only two other vehicles in a highly uneven race: the 'Islamic' United Development Party (PPP) and the 'nationalist' Indonesian Democratic Party were both actually strange, state-enforced amalgamations of otherwise highly disparate and even mutually antagonistic political parties. The historic 1999 elections thus contrasted sharply with elections implemented during the New Order (Suryadinata 2002; Antlov and Cederroth 2004), which were controlled and fixed to ensure the resounding victory of Golkar.

As is well-known, the 1999 legislative elections in Indonesia also ultimately opened the way for the largely unexpected emergence of Abdurrahman Wahid as president in October that year and brought an end to the seventeen-month tenure of B. J. Habibie, Soeharto's immediate successor and former protégé, as well as an embarrassing symbol of lingering New Order influence. For the first time in its history, Golkar was placed in an unfamiliar position of electoral loser, although its resources and still intact machinery ensured a respectable second place showing. In first place was the Indonesian Democratic Party for Struggle (PDI-P) led by the enigmatic but then wildly popular Megawati Soekarnoputri, daughter of Indonesian first president and independence hero, Soekarno. But she failed to win the presidency at that time due to intricate, behind-the-scenes manoeuvrings in the MPR, which was still the supranational body that elected Indonesia's presidents and vice presidents, on behalf of Wahid. Nevertheless, PDI-P's victory did stimulate a process of migration to the party from Golkar and associated organisations, including in the towns and provinces.

The erratic Wahid, leader of Indonesia's largest Muslim organisation, the Nahdlatul Ulama, and with a reputation of a liberal-minded reformer, also did not last long as president. He was impeached by the MPR in July 2001 (see Barton 2002, especially chapter 12, for the long saga) ostensibly because of his implication in corruption scandals, notably involving the alleged misappropriation of Indonesian State Logistics Body (Bulog) funds (Baswir 2000) as well as a donation from the Sultan of Brunei. Wahid was replaced in July 2001 by his vice president, Megawati Soekanoputri.

There was more to Wahid's abrupt fall than 'mere' corruption scandals. In reality, he had become increasingly besieged the more he had challenged the authority of parliament, which was still full of New Order luminaries, as well as still-powerful institutions like the military and the police force. For example, he interfered unsuccessfully in military leadership squabbles, replaced political party figures from cabinet positions in favour of his confidantes, reshuffled the composition of the Supreme Court in a process that involved a scuffle with the political parties, and tried to dismiss the head of the national police in the face of parliamentary objections (for details of the Wahid presidency, see Barton 2002, chapters 11 and 12). Members of the NU-linked National Awakening Party (PKB) or those personally close to him often received positions as heads of institutions with significant rent-seeking opportunities at the expense of members of other parties.[3]

It seemed that Wahid the erstwhile reformer was increasingly being sucked into the system of money politics and patronage networks as he attempted to secure his own position in the face of institutions that remained obstinately predatory. The Wahid experience provided interesting glimpses, essentially, of the way that political power was being reorganised within Indonesia's new democratic institutions by a range of elites concerned with securing their positions and access to state power and resources in a highly uncertain period. Such a reorganisation would not just take place in Jakarta but occurred even in local political arenas. It may be said that Wahid was an initial victor but later became one of the chief casualties of this often highly intense process of reorganisation.

Although the unpredictability of events in Indonesian politics after the fall of Soeharto can be discomforting to those used to New Order-era 'orderliness', by the majority of accounts, Indonesia is now well and truly on the path of electoral democracy. This is in spite of fears that persist about the possibility of a future military comeback should Indonesia's civilian politicians botch things so badly that the country descends into a 'failed state' or risks disintegration. Although the military still retains its territorial command structure (as well as charitable foundations and companies), Indonesia has almost certainly gone too far away from the kind of heavily centralised authoritarianism of the New Order to slide back to it very easily.

More proof of democracy at work in Indonesia was displayed in 2004. On the occasion of the national and local legislative elections held in April that year, twenty-four political parties met the formal criteria that enabled them to participate. This time, Indonesia took one major step further—the legislative elections were followed by Indonesia's first ever direct presidential election in July 2004. Such a development saw incumbent Megawati Soekarnoputri run against such rivals as former Soeharto-era military strongman General Wiranto and other New Order-era notables. At the run-off stage of the process, which took place in September, Megawati lost to Susilo Bambang Yudhoyono, yet another retired key New Order General. Yudhoyono was a former chief of military social and political affairs and a member of the cabinets of various post-Soeharto governments. More importantly, these direct presidential polls were made possible by one among several amendments and reforms to Indonesia's 1945 Constitution, which during the Soeharto era was regarded as 'sacred' and unalterable as a matter of supposed national interest. All these changes paved the way for the next logical step, the holding of direct voting polls for provincial and local government heads in 2005 (see Chapter 6).

In spite of the move toward a popularly elected president, a series of reforms had actually been previously introduced, significantly, to formally reduce the powers of the president in relation to the national parliament. Given the long rule of both Soekarno and Soeharto, this was best reflected in the new limit of just two five-year terms for any president. Moreover, an amendment to Article 20 of the 1945 Constitution paved the way for an MPR decree, which stated that bills passed by the legislature would have to be made law within one month regardless of presidential approval. These changes expressed the fact that under the circumstances that came to prevail after the fall of Soeharto, no single individual could harness the kind of authority and power that the dictator had enjoyed in almost unchallenged fashion for decades. More specifically, the conjuncture of factors that made possible Soeharto's rise to such a dominant position in the 1960s was not there for any new aspiring national strongman to exploit. Among these the international Cold War context could be mentioned, as well as such domestic factors as the emergence of an army-led coalition of elite urban and rural interests that was seriously threatened by the presence of well-organised radical social forces.

What all these changes signalled was the flow of power away from the presidency and toward the legislature (and almost concurrently, from Jakarta to the periphery, as we shall see more clearly later). There was, however, more than that—also transpiring as presidents came and went, and election after election came to be held, was the development of a system of money-politics through which old and some new predatory interests found the means of reconstituting themselves within new networks and vehicles (Robison and Hadiz 2004, see chapter 9).

Thus, the advent of a new period that more prominently emphasised electoralism, parties and parliaments must be fundamentally understood from the vantage point of the survivors of a fallen regime struggling to ensure their survival within what seemed like new, uncharted territory after May 1998. The ascendance of parties and parliaments cannot be extricated from the strategies employed by a variety of interests to secure their position in a changed social and political environment. The survival of salient New Order elements as leading forces in Indonesia's democracy has led some observers to lament that the fall of Soeharto 'has seen massive institutional changes but little true reforms' (Antlov 2003b: 144). What such a sentiment actually expresses is the sense that even important institutional changes have failed to redistribute power in post-authoritarian Indonesia.

POLITICAL PARTIES AND NEW CONTESTATIONS

Given this context, it not surprising that most of Indonesia's political parties have not emerged as 'natural' political entities that carry out 'aggregating' and 'articulating' functions, as conventional political theory would have it. Instead, these parties are the institutional expressions of temporary tactical alliances that draw from the same pool of predatory interests (Robison and Hadiz 2004: 228). In this sense, they are similar to most major parties in the Philippines and Thailand, which are also largely pragmatic alliances in nature and devoid of distinctive programmes or political vision (Shatkin 2003; Rocamora 2005; also see Ockey 2003). Indeed, it is essential to understand the logic of party politics in post-authoritarian Southeast Asian societies as being quite fundamentally different to those associated with liberal forms of democracy.

Aquilino Pimentel, a prominent Senator and political party leader in the Philippines, as well as a major advocate of decentralisation, has suggested that (2006: 8–9):

> In my country, today, crossing over from one party to another can easily be done because the political parties are not differentiated by ideologies. They are differentiated only by the depths of the pockets of their political leaders and the charisma that their financial fortunes create. And sad to say, what passes for their political platforms are mainly motherhood statements that have no bearing on the real needs of the people.

Following the fall of Soeharto, not only did a plethora of new parties—major and minor—appear, but several were significantly strengthened by close links to old New Order elements that found them convenient vehicles to protect and further their interests. Thus, the mass migration of former Golkar and military bigwigs to a number of so-called *reformasi* parties like the PDI-P took place, which at the provincial and local levels was accompanied by a similar migration of the New Order's former lower level operators and apparatchik (Hadiz 2004b). In Thailand, too, instructively, the abrupt fall of Thaksin was followed by the mass exodus of Thai Rak Thai stalwarts and members to rival parties (*The Nation*, 3 October 2006)—providing credence to Nelson's view that Thai politics are much less based on parties proper than they are on informal networks of patronage (2003: 9, 2005).

In Indonesia, the bureaucracy was always a major pillar of Golkar's supremacy, mobilised as it was on behalf of the state vehicle in every electoral contest held in the New Order. Malley suggests, instructively, that career civil servants have now taken over many of the top elected positions in local governments since the fall of Soeharto, riding on the coat tails of political parties, old and new. Of the eighty-nine cases of new mayoral and *bupati* appointments that he examined across several Indonesian provinces from November 1999 to December 2001, two-thirds were reportedly career civil servants, while only a quarter were 'other civilian' (another 6 per cent were from the military) (Malley 2003: 115). This is not only an indicator of continuity with the old New Order but is also indicative of the success that Soeharto-era local elites have had in reconstituting their power in the new democratic environment dominated by parties and parliaments.

Given this background, it is not surprising that schisms within and between political parties are not, therefore, primarily ideological or policy-related; their function has primarily been to act as vehicles for old and some new predatory elites to contest access to the spoils of state power. It is instructive as well that in spite of being provided with the opportunity to do so after 'Pancasila' was dropped as the ideology to which all organisations in Indonesia must adhere,[4] few parties have come to develop distinctive social, political and economic platforms,[5] aside from some that emphasised their adherence to Islam, such as the Justice and Prosperity Party (PKS). Even such Islamic parties, however, have tended to 'moderate' their focus on Islamic identity over time. Thus, as we shall see, local politics are so fluid that inter-party alliances at the local and provincial levels can take forms that have nothing to do with alignments at the national level and allow individuals and groups to regularly switch their allegiances with little or no concern for ideology, policy or programme.

This view, however, is contested by a number of analysts. In a paper published by the International Institute for Democracy and Electoral Assistance (IDEA) based in Sweden, Schneier (2005) acknowledges that Soeharto's abrupt departure from political power 'left the entire structure of New Order people and positions essentially intact', but he views this as no real obstacle to incremental change toward democracy and good governance. Schneier specifically suggests, that 'there is a dynamic by which a legislature's growing ability to make marginal changes in policy emboldens its members and outside groups to seek incrementally larger inputs' (2005: 21). More broadly, he argues that 'the success of the constitution-building process' that has taken place as part of the process of establishing a new framework of governance in Indonesia 'is contingent on a continuing dialogue between elite and reform elements in Indonesia and their counterparts in the global environment'. He also points to the experience of the United States, where the Constitution was written by wealthy property owners to protect their interests, but 'the institutions they created deliberately opened the system to progressive democratization and social justice'. Schneier ventures, moreover, that this is exactly 'what is happening in Indonesia' (2005: 24), where the process is being helped along in a global context that is generally more conducive to democratisation.

Apart from simplifying the historical experience of the United States, and the social conflicts and struggles that gave the descendants of Southern slaves many of the rights of citizenship almost two centuries after the Constitution was drafted, Schneier's analysis demonstrates some of the pitfalls of analyses that privilege institutional change as the central dynamic of social change. One of these is his implied 'matter of time' argument. His is a view that assumes that because new institutions are in place, new possibilities for important shifts in the structure of power and opportunities to consolidate liberal democracies will also be created in due course. Indonesia's democracy, according to such a view, will ultimately become more liberal in character as the constitutional liberalism that Schneier emphasises is nurtured gradually.

However, institutions do not have a life of their own that is independent of context. So, rather than mirror the United States, Indonesian developments after 1998 reflect more closely post-authoritarian developments in the former American colony of the Philippines. Here, political parties, for example, are described by one source from the early 1990s (Marlay 1991) as lacking 'coherent political programs', and generally tend to champion 'conservative social positions'. Political parties in both countries also have to go to great lengths to enforce any semblance of 'party discipline', which is so low that 'politicians switch 'capriciously back and forth' between vehicles, as Pimentel (2006) had observed for the Philippines. Rocamora (1998) regards political parties in the Philippines as belonging to elites who do not even attempt to organise support from broad segments of society but are underpinned by shifting coalitions centred on wealthy families. Such families may be wealthy enough to unite municipal political organisations and finance electoral battles at the provincial level or for congressional district seats. Shatkin's (2003) analysis of local leadership in Thailand displays how informal power blocs, sometimes linking local bosses engaged in a range of illegal economic activities to Bangkok bigwigs, lie beneath the surface of electoral and party politics and determine such matters as candidate selection. Such a world as exists in Indonesia, Thailand and the Philippines is far from the liberal-pluralist model of aggregating and articulating functions, even if the model inadequately captures the empirical reality of the West itself.

Since political parties in post-authoritarian Southeast Asian societies tend to be captured by conservative and predatory elites, they have little interest in pursuing programmes or policies that threaten the prevailing social relationships of power. As a consequence, Indonesia, the Philippines and Thailand may have parties, just like in the United States, and parliaments just like in Western Europe, together with a range of other institutions associated with democratic politics. However, the question remains: why do they operate so differently? To understand this apparent puzzle, one must go beyond institutions.

Here we must go back to a recurring theme in this book as far as Indonesia is concerned: the possible survival and continued salience of predatory interests both at the levels of national and local politics in spite of a raft of institutional reforms in the neo-liberal vein. In Indonesia, as was mentioned earlier, Golkar had regained its ascendance over Indonesian political party life just six years after the fall of Soeharto. It would be a grave mistake, however, to distinguish the interests that pervade in Golkar too starkly from those that underpin its rival political parties. As Robison and Hadiz have pointed out (2004: 227), other parties are 'also well populated by a variety of elements—political entrepreneurs and fixers, business and bureaucratic interests, both central and local'—that constituted the building blocks of the New Order's system of patronage, 'albeit sometimes ensconced only in the second or third layers'. For these sorts of interests, parties and parliaments are now the main avenue to political power and control over state institutions. Thus, varying concentrations of old oligarchic forces are dispersed among virtually all the major political parties, which are joined by an array of relative newcomers variously emphasising statism or social justice appeals, typically with reference to nationalist or Islamic ideals. Here and there, one will also find scattered bands of neo-liberal reformers, some with a high public profile but limited weight in terms of internal political party wrangling. Thus it is not possible to speak of a clear reformist or anti-reformist political party in Indonesia today, whether or not reformism is to be strictly defined in the neo-liberal vein.

These developments are in turn partly attributable to the absence of effective organising vehicles representing social groups, such as labour and the peasantry, which were most politically marginalised under the New Order. The consequence is that the struggle over *reformasi* became the domain of vehicles that drew on the interests of those who were part of the New Order's extensive system of patronage, though not necessarily those who were ensconced at the very top layer. Democratisation and decentralisation, the rise of parliaments and political parties in Indonesia has meant, in a nutshell, the rise in fortunes of individuals and groups that had been nurtured and cultivated by the New Order as its local notables and apparatchik, minor political party operatives, fixers and entrepreneurs, and as its contractors, gangsters and thugs. It is these sorts of people and groups whose ambitions have been raised by the new opportunities opened by decentralisation and democracy, as shown in Chapters 4 and 5.

Perhaps most instructive of the nature of Indonesia's democracy has been the repositioning of the role of organised goons and thugs in politics. Formerly, these served as the informal henchmen of the New Order. Together with local military and police commands, they helped to 'maintain order' in local communities by keeping crime organised, while simultaneously profiting from illegal trades like gambling, prostitution and drug trafficking. It was an open secret that much of this organised crime was taking place with gangsters working in cahoots with their military and police patrons and protectors locally (see Ryter 2002; Wilson 2006). These criminals and thugs also helped to sustain a culture of fear that was important to the longevity of the New Order in spite of its periodic rituals of demonstrating popular legitimacy through elections. As explained further, although these sorts of links to local military or police commands continue to be maintained by some 'youth' organisations, the 'landscape' of organised thuggery is now far richer and more diverse than it used to be.

Thus, within the first few years of the fall of Soeharto's centralised regime, we witnessed the sudden proliferation of paramilitaries often related to individual political parties (see Wilson 2006). Henk Schulte-Nordholt (2002: 51) reports that there are about thirty militia organisations in Indonesia with an estimated membership of 700,000 people. Of course, it is difficult to corroborate such figures; however, they are a good indicator of the proliferation of uniformed, though essentially civilian, groups of goons and thugs in post-authoritarian Indonesia. Among the most notorious of these have been the PDI-P *Satgas* or Task Force, which seemed to have absorbed a large number of local thugs especially in and around such major cities as Medan in North Sumatra and Surabaya in East Java. Another feared outfit has been the Banser, a much older organisation linked to PKB, and its parent organisation, the 'traditionalist' Islamic Nahdlatul Ulama. The latter was heavily implicated in the anti-PKI actions of the 1960s. Filling some of the space left by a military forced to take more than a step or two back from its previously pervasive role in politics as well as the informal security services business, some paramilitary forces have been hired by capitalists to protect factories during labour disputes.[6] Moreover, some representatives of these organisations have achieved success in local electoral contests, though they have certainly not been able to achieve all of their lofty ambitions, as we shall observe in more detail later.

Decentralising Governance or Institutionalising Local Predatory Power?

CENTRALISATION VS. DECENTRALISATION

According to the World Bank (2003b: 1), Indonesia is now 'one of the more de-centralized nations in the world'. Its degree of decentralisation 'is higher than the OECD average, and all other East Asian nations, except China'. For the most part, decentralisation has been deemed a success. The Asia Foundation (2004), for example, reports that local governments have coped well with the task of carrying out new functions and responsibilities delegated by the central government. However, much of the foregoing discussion suggests that such assertions should at least be questioned, especially with regard to objectives like the empowerment of local citizenries, public participation and the like.

Rather than aimed at substantively strengthening civil society participation at the local level, in more important ways decentralisation policy can be understood in relation to new quandaries arising from the politically and materially rising ambitions of local and regional elites immediately follow-ing the fall of Soeharto. Thus the so-called 'Big Bang' of decentralisation was a tangible response from Jakarta to the new, growing aspirations of local elites (World Bank 2003b; Bunte 2004) given the unravelling of the New Or-der's institutional framework of governance.[7] These local elites had quickly latched on to the language of localism and of asserting local identities, often in ways that were quite distinctly if selectively atavistic, and which recalls some of the populist positions alluded to earlier in this book (see Introduc-tion). Though many of these same local elites had been fastened to the New Order juggernaut, they were cognisant of the new opportunities being pre-sented in the context of the very real diminishing capacity of the central state to impose its will and agenda.[8]

It should also be noted that the national parliament that passed Indonesia's decentralisation legislation was a leftover from the end of the Soeharto era. Schulte-Nordholt (2004: 37) argues credibly that its most dominant element, the former state party, Golkar, perceived that its position was particularly vulnerable on the main island of Java in any future electoral contest. Thus, supporting the decentralisation thrust constituted an attempt to maintain key support bases in the outer islands, a strategy that also suited the aims of then-President Habibie—who needed to distance himself from the centralising and authoritarian tendencies of his predecessor.

It may be useful to recall at this time just how centralised the New Order was in its mechanics. As the anthropologist Antlov notes, economic growth, which 'integrated the diversity of regions in Indonesia', was 'managed through a regulated and centralized system of plans and programs emanating from Jakarta down through provinces to districts, sub-districts and villages.' In the heyday of the New Order, 'Government offices, from central agencies in Jakarta to village branches, were in control of this process and policy blueprints', rather than local governments (Antlov 2003b: 143).

The formulation of these blueprints was a process that was no less heavily centralised. Thus, 'Priorities and initiatives were determined from atop and seldom in line with local demands. The diversity of Indonesia's socioeconomic conditions and cultures—the array of customary rights and modes of decision-making associated with the peoples of different localities—was effectively ignored' (Antlov 2003b: 143). In other words, due to the absence of vehicles through which resistance could be effectively and cohesively organised, policies and regulations were not only established but also implemented from above. Policy-making, not surprisingly, hardly ever required the targeted sections of the population to be involved in any substantive way.

Such a strategy of rule was reflective of the way in which a centralised system of patronage, centred on Soeharto himself, had come to evolve and become entrenched over the course of the New Order. Antlov (2003b: 143) describes it in the following way:

> A massive patronage system was created in which the central government awarded local governments with budget allocation in exchange for loyalty. Budget allocations were not based on performance or need, but rather on how close local governments were with the central government, and how well local elites could lobby decisions-makers in Jakarta. The resulting rent-seeking system was effective in rapidly building the economy, but was not transparent or sustainable and created great regional dissatisfactions.

The overall product of these circumstances was a rigid and politically stifling regime, both for the locals and, arguably, for local officialdom. Again, Antlov's description of the situation that existed (2003b: 144) is apt:

Local government officials were accountable to central government authorities rather than local constituencies and thus had very little grassroots liability and support. Afraid of repression, citizens could not demand changes from their government. Public policies were determined by the state. The centralistic and authoritarian governance system also ruptured the social texture of local politics and community institutions. The crippling uniformity that the Suharto regime imposed on ordinary people undermined critical thinking and extracted a heavy price in the form of uniformity, standardization, co-optation of community leaders, abuse of power, and corruption.

Indeed, the New Order upon its inception had quickly enforced Jakarta's grip over the country, which had experienced a number of regional rebellions of varying levels of seriousness in the 1950s. The New Order achieved this by centralising the military apparatus and the state bureaucracy, a process that saw thousands of military officers appointed to strategic positions in local government, and the establishment of a military territorial system in which each layer of 'civilian' government was 'shadowed' by a parallel military command structure. Until the post-Soeharto decentralisation laws, the institutional foundations for twenty-five years of central domination of the apparatus of governance were laid down in Law no. 5/1974, which made heads of local and provincial governments accountable to superiors in Jakarta. A further measure of centralisation was administered with Law no. 5/1979, which standardised village administration throughout Indonesia on the basis of a Java-centric model and effectively reduced village heads to the status of subservient civil servants (MacAndrews 1986: 39; Kahin 1994: 209–210; Bourchier and Hadiz 2003: 255).

It is because of such a background that Laws no. 22/1999 and no. 25/1999 that spearheaded Indonesia's decentralisation seemed quite impressive. Some of the more salient stipulations of these laws included:[9]

a)   The scrapping of a regional hierarchy in which provinces supervise *kabupaten* (regencies) and cities. The consequence was the establishment of the *kabupaten* and the city, instead of the provinces, as the focal points of regional governance. As a result, provincial governors are henceforth relegated to the position of mere 'representatives' of the centre, with little authority over the city mayor or *bupati*.

b)   The related granting of permission to the *kabupaten* and the town/city, as the focal points of governance, to deal directly with various Jakarta agencies and ministries.

c)   The awarding of jurisdiction over a large number of administrative and financial functions to the *kabupaten* and the city, but *not* over such matters as foreign policy, the judicial system, monetary/fiscal policy, religion, defence and security; these continue to be the domain of the central state.

d)   The election of members of local parliaments (DPRD) among the local citizenry, from candidates offered by authorised political parties. The DPRD, in turn, were to elect the local *bupati* or mayor (and in the case of the provincial-level DPRD, the governor). This provided local parliamentarians with a great deal of latitude in terms of dealing with heads of local governments, whose election and tenure depended on them and the kinds of loose alliances and coalitions assembled in local parliaments.

e)   The establishment of the mayor/*bupati* as being accountable to the DPRD or local parliament. The mayor or *bupati* must present periodic accountability reports to the relevant local parliament, which has the power to reject them.

f)   The vesting of the DPRD with an array of broad powers. For example, members of the DPRD are to be involved, together with their respective *bupati* or mayors, in the formulation of the budget of the *kabupaten* and the municipality as well as in formulating other legislation. The DPRD also 'supervises' the implementation of bylaws/edicts.

g)   The simplification of local level administrative structures. During the New Order, numerous national government bodies were represented through offices at the level of the town/city or *kabupaten*, as were local representations of provincial government offices. Thus, a dual structure had existed that, under Law no. 22 /1999, was to be scrapped. The array of nationally- and provincially-affiliated offices was to be amalgamated and integrated under a single structure headed by the mayor of a city/town, or *bupati* in the case of a *kabupaten*.

h)   The transfer of an array of personnel functions to the local level of government, including those that deal with the appointment, transfer or dismissal of officials, as well as those that deal with their remuneration.

i)   The provision by the central government to the regions of a General Allocation Grant (DAU) that is to be 'at least' 25 per cent of domestic revenue. Ninety per cent of this fund goes to regencies and cities and 10 per cent to provinces. Distribution to individual sub-national territories is done according to a special formula' (Turner and Podger 2003: 26).

j)   The introduction of revenue sharing between central and regional governments in areas such as land and building taxes, forestry, fishery, mining and the important oil and gas sectors. According to the legislation on the fiscal balance between central and regional governments (Law no. 25/1999), 85 per cent of oil revenues (after tax) were to be taken by the central government. The remaining 15 per cent is to be taken by the region from which the oil is extracted.

k)   The stipulation of a Special Allocation Grant (DAK) through which special regional initiatives could be funded. Significantly, local governments are also given the opportunity to secure loans, including loans from overseas sources.

l)   The vesting of the Ministry of Home Affairs with the power to cancel any regional decree or regulation deemed to be in contradiction to higher legislation or the 'common good'.

In Indonesia, therefore, the initial design of decentralisation policy meant power being distinctly shifted from Jakarta to sub-provincial *kabupaten* and cities/towns, with the provinces in danger of being overlooked. As a point of comparison, decentralisation in the Philippines meant the establishment of a multi-tiered system of governance supervision involving the president, provincial governors as well as city and municipal mayors; whereby the central government has limited supervisory power over local government beyond the provincial level. In Thailand, by contrast, there exist separate administrative bodies responsible for the same territorial areas, one linked to the Ministry of the Interior and the other being units of elected local governments at different territorial levels. Here it is the empowerment of the latter that is intended in the institutional design of decentralisation. The point, however, is that in all these cases, the institutional design of decentralisation—regardless of whether intended to facilitate technocratic and market rationality or pave the way for the empowerment of local communities—would prove to be less important than the kinds of social interests and forces that would actually preside over actual institutions.

It should be noted in the Indonesian case that some of the stipulations on decentralisation listed above were later revised as a result of Law no. 32/2004, which replaced Law no. 22/1999. As has been pointed out earlier, the very limited official role of provincial governors became a bone of contention as elites at the local, provincial and central levels of governance jostled over control of state institutions and resources. Thus, the status and power of the provinces and the provincial governors—and provincial level elites, in general—were to be partially restored in subsequent revisions of the decentralisation legislation. If governors had complained that mayors and *bupati* no longer recognised their authority because of the vagueness of 1999 legislation,[10] they were partially placated by the amendment that once again placed them more firmly in the role of superiors. Again this was no mere wrangling over technical details. Coalitions of interests ensconced at the provincial level feared being left out of the spoils of local power.

Furthermore, the 2004 legislative changes also established that mayors and *bupati* would be, for the first time, popularly elected. It is possible to view the changes to the 1999 legislation as being induced by conflicts related to growing challenge to the authority of Jakarta (and provincial governors) presented by *bupati* and mayors alike; paradoxically, these expressed both an attempt to rein them in and the growing propensity of aspiring local political bosses to carve out some form of institutional independence. In particular, one highly contentious issue between Jakarta and the regions pertained to the inclination of local DPRDs and heads of local governments to produce edicts and bylaws to supplement revenue in local budgets, many of which were controversial not the least because of the growth of predatory, rent-seeking activities at the local level (*Media Indonesia* 15 June 2006). Nevertheless, an important change was already achieved by 1999 and was reflective of the newfound bargaining position of some local elites vis-à-vis Jakarta: by then the heads of local government were no longer to be appointed by power-holders in the capital as had been the practice during the New Order. Although the earlier change represented achievement in carving out a real degree of autonomy from the dictates of interests entrenched in Jakarta, the subsequent introduction of direct local elections represented the successful extrication of *bupati* and mayors from their great dependence on the local legislative bodies that had been charged with electing them in the interim system.[11]

THE FISCAL REGIME

It is important to note that much of the wrangling about the rules for governing regional autonomy or decentralisation has pertained to its material basis; it most often concerned the financial arrangement set up between Jakarta and the regions to redistribute revenue. This arrangement also made accommodation for natural resource-rich areas to especially enjoy economic advantages.[12] Significantly, the outcome of the financial stipulations contained in the 1999 legislation was that the revenues of *kabupaten* and city governments would derive from the DAU, the transfer of revenue shares and income accruing from local taxes and levies.

The World Bank (2005b: 1) soon came to enthuse that regions in Indonesia 'are responsible for one-third of all government spending, and half of the development budget', and that most 'spending on education, health and infrastructure is local'. Many like Turner and Podger, however, have noted a pertinent fact: according to Indonesian official data, the main source of revenue for 92 per cent of the sub-provincial governments of cities and *kabupaten* came from the DAU, 'with half the regions depending on it for 90 per cent or more of their revenues' (see Turner and Podger 2003: 40). According to a GTZ assessment, 'there are no significant own-source revenues of the regions since all major taxes are still kept by the central government', including property taxes which in other countries are typically a local source of revenue (GTZ n.d.).

Such sobering assessments suggest that most local-level governments do not in fact enjoy a significant level of financial autonomy from Jakarta in spite of the bombastic rhetoric. According to Lewis and Chakeri (2004), moreover, the central government of Indonesia spends a little less than half its development budget outside Jakarta and provides more than one-third of the development spending of the regions; moreover, the central government spending sometimes covers costs that, under the decentralisation legislation, have actually been transferred to sub-national governments.

In reality, therefore, the majority of sub-provincial governments remain financially dependent on centrally-allocated funds, particularly governments of provinces that are not particularly rich in natural resources. The Indonesian situation is not very different from those of Thailand and the Philippines. But the problem in each case is not simply a lack of political will to genuinely decentralise. Much of the hesitancy surrounding fiscal decentralisation in particular is no doubt tied closely to continuing tug-of-wars between national-based coalitions of interests and those ensconced sub-nationally.

With reference to Thailand, for example, one document described the situation there in the late 1990s in the following terms:[13]

> (L)ocal government in Thailand is subjected to strong control by the central government . . . most resources and revenues generated are drawn into the centre . . . What is left to the local government is hardly adequate to meet the needs of local communities, both urban and rural.

Like their counterparts in Indonesia, local government units in Thailand have continued to rely heavily on central government subsidies,[14] although the Decentralisation Act of 1999 intended that the share of government expenditure under the jurisdiction of local authorities was to have increased gradually from 20 to 35 per cent (Shatkin 2003: 20–21; Charas n.d.). By 2006, the 35 per cent level was far from being reached,[15] and this was at least partially reflective of a tug-of-war between Bangkok and local coalitions of power, much like what has developed in Indonesia.

The situation is not very different in the Philippines, where the Local Government Code 1991 'mandated an automatic transfer of 40 per cent of internal revenue collections and widened the taxing powers of local governments,' although this has not been achieved. Nevertheless, according to Rocamora (2004), decentralisation has meant significant increases in local government revenue. Even in the Philippines case, however, central subsidies to local governments remain crucial.[16] This displays the limitations of most local revenue bases, especially outside major municipalities,[17] and also provides the central government with an economic instrument to control sub-national governments in spite of decentralisation. As in Indonesia and Thailand, the implementation of the internal revenue-sharing scheme has not always been in accordance to the written law; in Rocamora's view, it has not kept up with functions being devolved to the local level.[18]

In Indonesia, besides the necessity of ensuring that the central state coffers remain adequate to carry out such tasks as debt servicing, it has been a matter of concern to maintain some kind of economic parity among the different provinces and regions, in spite of ideas expressed about the necessity for local governments to compete with each other for a greater part of the economic pie. The same official data mentioned above show that 20 per cent of regions in Indonesia could be considered very poor, while another 20 per cent were well off. The richest 10 per cent of localities, however, had more than six times the revenue per capita of the poorest 10 per cent (Turner and Podger 2003). The World Bank, for its part, estimates that the richest local government in Indonesia today has fifty times the revenue per capita of the poorest one, and the richest province has 10 times as much revenue per capita as the poorest province (World Bank 2003b: 34). Lewis and Chakeri (2004) find that central government spending in the regions has helped to mitigate such inequalities, but only to a limited extent.[19]

It is in this context that the *kabupaten* of Kutai Kertanegara, in previously peripheral East Kalimantan, have become the most prominent beneficiary of decentralisation. A major producer of oil, gas and coal—and with a population of only about 500,000—the Kutai Kertanagara local government recently worked on the basis of a budget that was four times that of the entire nearby province of West Kalimantan (Hill 2006), which has a population of roughly four million.

Given the resources at his disposal, it is no coincidence that the *bupati* of Kutai Kertanegara, a New Order-era Golkar stalwart named Syaukani H. R. (van Klinken 2002.), came to be in a position to sponsor the formation of the Apkasi (Asosiasi Pemerintahan Kabupaten Seluruh Indonesia)—the main lobby group of *kabupaten* chiefs vis-à-vis Jakarta policy-makers. Under his leadership, Apkasi attempted to fight the central government's 2004 amendments on the 1999 set of legislation for fear that these would rein in the powers of local governments (*Kompas* 27 May 2004). It was supported in its endeavour by other groups representing local power interests, including Adeksi or the Association of Indonesian Municipal Parliaments (*Kompas* 31 January 2002). These associations clearly aspire to play a role in the future that is as prominent as that played by the various 'leagues' of local government officials in the Philippines, and play them far more effectively than the relatively tame Thai associations.[20]

Much of the impetus for the amendments in Indonesian law had to do with the widespread perception that local governments were abusing their newfound powers when dealing with local revenue collection. Significantly, the realities of budgetary constraints have induced local governments, with the approval of local parliaments, to develop new ways of collecting revenue; these are usually in the form of the controversial new levies and taxes mentioned earlier, which by now number in the thousands. Supporting the argument of local officials is the fact that approximately 2.6 million of 4.2 million civil servants who were employed at other levels of government were transferred to the local level (*Jakarta Post* 24 October 2000). This placed the burden of responsibility of paying these civil servants' salaries squarely on the shoulders of budget-constrained cities and *kabupaten*.

It is interesting, however, that the World Bank suggests that in aggregate terms, local governments should not claim to be facing such a struggle. According to its calculations, 'more than enough revenues were devolved in 2001 to match the transferred expenditure responsibilities'. This is so even when one accounts for the salaries of re-assigned civil servants, and the maintenance of former central government offices (World Bank 2003b: 32).

Whether driven by budgetary imperatives or simply by the impulse to carve out new economic niches or predatory practices autonomous from Jakarta politics, local officials routinely accuse Jakarta officials of not having a real political will to wholeheartedly implement decentralisation. Thus, local officials are particularly aggrieved at, and feel threatened by, central constraints on their taxation capacities. Many also argue that authority over a number of areas of governance, legally stipulated to reside at the sub-provincial level, has in reality never been transferred to them by Jakarta.[21]

It must be recalled that some statements from the very top of the Jakarta political hierarchy would have strengthened this perception among local officials of a lack of real intent to implement decentralisation. Indeed, no less than Abdurrahman Wahid and Megawati Soekarnoputri were known as only reluctant supporters of decentralisation. During their respective presidencies, both expressed themselves as staunch supporters of the unitary state structure who were concerned about the evolution of any decentralisation framework that would be federalist all but in name. Indeed, Megawati—whether unwilling or unable to distinguish between national disintegration and federalism— once pronounced her fear that Indonesians from different parts of the country will 'have to raise our own flags, sing our own anthems and may well have to have our own militaries' (*Jakarta Post* 17 July 2000). The commitment of the Abdurrahman Wahid presidency to decentralisation was also questioned when it abolished the Office of the State Ministry for Regional Autonomy (Brodjonegoro 2003) in August 2000, leaving decentralisation matters to be absorbed into the responsibilities of the Ministry of Home Affairs.

Considerable controversy also erupted over the effective annulment of a local government right as stipulated by the legislation, that of borrowing from overseas sources. As a result, foreign borrowing continues to be negotiated and managed centrally from Jakarta, in spite of the greater role that sub-provincial units of government should theoretically have had with decentralisation. This appears to contradict the regional autonomy laws that in fact allow local governments to borrow abroad, albeit through the central government. They are unable to make use of this privilege, however, because Rizal Ramli, the coordinating minister for Economic Affairs under former President Abdurrahman Wahid, had banned local administrations from seeking loans from both domestic and foreign sources as early as February 2001 (*Jakarta Post* 13 February 2001). Significantly, the International Monetary Fund (IMF) had asked the Indonesian government not to allow provincial administrations to obtain loans and issue bonds, fearing that these could eventually burden the central government.

The above shows that the controversy around the scope and design of local autonomy is indicative of contests among competing interests that have a concrete, material basis. This has been fairly consistently demonstrated in tussles around the rules of the game governing the power and jurisdiction of officials at the local, provincial and national levels.

In a nutshell, the politico-bureaucrats in Jakarta obviously have a vested interest in maintaining control over local financial resources while attempting to balance this against aspirations for greater local autonomy. On the other hand, local elites want to wrest direct control over these same resources, and they typically cite the injustice of past practices that allowed Jakarta to exploit Indonesia's vast riches at the expense of locals—this despite disparities in wealth among Indonesia's various regions. Thus, the contest has clearly been about control over resources, though it is also often expressed in terms of local pride, or ethnic or regional identity versus national unity (e.g. Schulte-Nordholt and van Klinken 2007).

It is important to note that the stakes involved will vary from place to place. They may be relatively limited in poor areas but not so for rising political entrepreneurs in resource-rich places like Kutai Kertanegara. The *bupati* of Bantul in Yogyakarta, who governs an area that is inclusive of the popular Parangtritis tourist site, spoke in 2000—just before the formal implementation of the decentralisation laws—of setting up new local state enterprises that would take a leading role in a variety of endeavours.[22] Interestingly, though obvious rent-seeking opportunities are much scarcer here than in cash-rich Kutai Kertanegara, the same *bupati* allegedly has been involved in such activities as forcing businesses to make pay-offs when undertaking new projects and utilising public resources to fill his own electoral campaign war chest (Savirani 2004: 48–49). In any case, for this *bupati* and many like him, it is clearly better to have direct control over relatively scarce resources than to have no control over more abundant resources that are under Jakarta's jurisdiction.

Nevertheless, neo-institutionalist authors like Turner and Podger are inclined to view the reforms in Indonesia described above as primarily 'driven by democratisation'. They suggest that the institutional changes are but the 'logical extension of the overthrow of authoritarianism and the introduction of democratic politics at the local level.' The decentralisation legislation in particular, therefore, constituted no less than 'further demonstration of the strong impetus to promote and establish democracy' (Turner and Podger 2003: 27) that existed in the immediate period following the end of Soeharto's stifling rule.

Yet proponents of such a fairly straightforward relationship between decentralisation and democracy have had cause for discomfort. Interestingly, Turner and Podger complain that Law no. 22/1999 does not provide an 'explicit rationale' for decentralisation. They point out that there are only 'fleeting references to its purpose' in 'emphasising democracy, promoting community participation, being guided by popular aspirations, and introducing a range of accountability measures'. Thus, they warn against 'one of the dangers of political decentralisation'—the mere substitution of elites with the result that 'local populations fail to reap the benefits of local democracy' (2003: 70). Obviously, there are strong grounds for such fears.

One of their other laments is quite revealing of how the technocratic and managerialist world view dictates neo-institutionalist accounts of decentralisation and social change. A major flaw in the laws, as Turner and Podger see them, is the absence of 'Managerial and economic arguments extolling the efficiency advantages of decentralised governance' (2003: 27). Apparently, the fear is that without the unambiguous proclamation of such arguments, decentralisation would proceed aimlessly and fail to generate the intended institutions of good governance. But of course, the problem is much more complex than just the absence of such overt proclamations—decentralisation in Indonesia has morphed into something that is quite alien to the 'good governance' worldview because of the kinds of social interests that have presided over it.

The hopes, complaints and fears expressed by such authors encapsulate very neatly the dilemmas of the neo-liberal and neo-institutionalist understanding of decentralisation. On the one hand, decentralisation is viewed as part of the broader good governance agenda that is supposed to create the institutions necessary for the operations of the market. On the other hand, it is difficult to deny that the good governance agenda can be usurped by social forces and groups that constitute strong sources of resistance to neo-liberal market reforms. Though the formal rules of the game governing decentralised governance were mainly designed by domestic and international technocrats, the case studies to which the book now turns reveal why they have not been able to run the local show at all.

Chapter Four

A Political Sociology of Local Elites

This chapter examines the social and political bases of elite dominance in the context of the localisation of power in post-authoritarian Indonesia. It pays particular attention to the cases of North Sumatra and East Java, for reasons discussed below, though references are also made to other regions, notably Yogyakarta, which has a diversity of societal organisations and richness of intellectual life,[1] and has long been considered an alternative centre of politics to Jakarta. Among the key issues examined are those that revolve around identifying local elites and their interests and the institutions and vehicles through which they attain or secure their positions within the institutions of governance of Indonesia's decentralised democracy.[2] Many of these same questions occupied Shiraishi (2003) soon after the first electoral contests were held in the post-Soeharto period in June 1999. Shiraishi's survey, significantly, found that the majority of local parliamentarians have backgrounds in New Order-era political parties and youth and mass organisations.[3]

The picture that emerges from this chapter is one of local elites who have little abiding interest in good governance reforms in the neo-institutionalist vein. In fact, it may be argued that reforms involving transparency and accountability run diametrically opposed to their largely predatory inclinations. However, the groups that comprise these local elites have a large stake in the localisation of power, thus in decentralisation and democracy, and would be among those with the most to lose from any slide back to centralised authoritarianism, regardless of political genealogies that frequently can be traced back to the New Order. What these local elites have learned to do, effectively, is to safeguard their interests while negotiating with neo-liberal reformist impulses emanating from pockets of technocratic power in Jakarta and from within influential international development organisations. An observation can be made also about some similarities in terms of the attributes of rising Indonesian local elites in relation to their counterparts elsewhere. As in post-authoritarian Thailand and the Philippines, successful local elites in contemporary Indonesia tend to be those who already have access to substantial material resources as well as some degree of control over instruments of political intimidation, though the role of political violence in electoral politics remains much less salient in Indonesia than in the other Southeast Asian cases.

Terrains of Local Politics: North Sumatra and East Java

It should be noted that the geographically uneven nature of the development of capitalism, and therefore of integration with the world economy, often means that different parts of the same country will have experienced economic globalisation in diverse ways. This is perhaps most evident today in the rising economic behemoth that is China (Breslin 2000), where the coastal provinces in the southeast have far outstripped the rest of the country in terms of growth and the intensity of social change. It is for related reasons that North Sumatra and East Java are of particular interest in terms of understanding tendencies toward the localisation of power within the broader processes of economic globalisation.

Both North Sumatra and East Java have long been vibrant urban and industrial centres, through which links between the Indonesian national economy and global markets have been forged back to colonial times. North Sumatra, for example, was a centre of the vital colonial-era plantations sector, while East Java is home to the major port city of Surabaya—now regarded as a gateway from the western to the eastern parts of Indonesia—as well as to vast rural and agricultural hinterlands. East Java is also the site of oil and natural gas fields in Cepu and Bojonegoro, respectively. During the New Order, North Sumatra and East Java benefited from the national economic development policy; for example, both were locations for sprawling and quickly expanding centres of light manufacturing industry in the 1980s and 1990s. Like the heavily industrialised areas in and around Jakarta, portions of East Java and North Sumatra were sites of growing unrest and independent organisational activity by industrial workers during the late Soeharto years (Hadiz 1997; Kammen 1997; Ford 2003). In a nutshell, North Sumatra and East Java have long been among the parts of Indonesia in which integration with the world economy has taken place most intensively.

East Java and North Sumatra are also among the most heavily populated provinces in Indonesia. The population of East Java is 34.8 million, making it the second most heavily populated of Indonesia's provinces. This is second only to West Java, which is exceptional because large portions of it are but extensions of the gargantuan Jakarta economy. North Sumatra's population is considerably smaller, although its 11.7 million people make it the most heavily populated province outside of Java, which is one of the world's most densely populated islands. The capital city of East Java, Surabaya, is inhabited by about 2.6 million people while Medan, the capital city of North Sumatra, has close to 2 million citizens; this makes Surabaya and Medan the second and fourth largest cities in Indonesia, respectively.[4] These statistics mask the fact that sprawling industrial, urban and peri-urban formations, with a substantial number of inhabitants, surround these two cities to make up a Greater Surabaya and Greater Medan with much larger total populations. Any brief visit to these cities will confirm the existence of massive peri-urban formations that are in reality inextricable from the economy and society of both cities. In this regard, they are but smaller versions of Jakarta, which spilled-over into neighbouring Tangerang, Bekasi and Depok a long time ago; the vast urban sprawl that is Metro Manila, which made incursions into such regions as Cavite; and the Thai behemoth that is the Extended Bangkok Metropolitan Region.

As in many other parts of Indonesia, in both North Sumatra and East Java, those who inhabited the lower layers of the system of patronage on which the New Order was premised have been the greatest beneficiaries of the opening of political space. They have since latched on to political parties and parliaments at the local level, which they now populate and typically dominate, to further their growing ambitions (Hadiz 2003, 2004a, 2004b; Malley 2003). As mentioned, this has raised the issue of the emergence of new, decentralised systems of corruption that are at least equally rabid as the New Order's but, undoubtedly, less predictable—to the chagrin of business.

One major East Java-based businessman in the real estate sector calculates that official and unofficial levies make up to 20 per cent of his operating costs.[5] In 2002, the leaders of two North Sumatran business associations claimed that 'some 70 percent of development projects in the North Sumatra provincial administration were tarnished by the practices of collusion, corruption and nepotism' (*Jakarta Post* 23 September 2002). Echoing a fairly commonly held opinion in the general public, Indonesian political scientist Indria Samego laments that 'People got nothing out of autonomy, while local officials got rich' (*Jakarta Post* 21 August 2002).

As elsewhere in Indonesia, electoral politics have become lively in North Sumatra and East Java since the departure of Soeharto from the political stage. In North Sumatra and the rest of Indonesia, the PDI-P was the clear victor in the 1999 elections. It won 10 of the 24 North Sumatran allocated national parliamentary seats, 30 of the 85 provincial parliamentary seats and 228 of the overall 690 seats scattered across the sub-provincial parliaments in the province.[6] Altogether, the PDI-P won over 2 million of the 5.1 million votes cast in North Sumatra, while in second place was Golkar, the former state party of the New Order, with around 1.1 million votes. The fortunes of the PDI-P in North Sumatra were to change in 2004 as a reflection of its dwindling popularity nationwide after several years of the Megawati presidency, during which she failed to fulfil the high expectations of, especially, the poor among her supporters. In 2004, the PDI-P only managed slightly more than 825,000 of the over 5.5 million votes cast in North Sumatra. This was well behind the result achieved by Golkar, which won more than 1,130,000 of the votes,[7] thus winning first place in the province, as it did nationally this time around.

In East Java, the PDI-P came second in 1999, winning 6.7 million of the approximately 19.8 million votes cast. The victor in East Java in 1999, not surprisingly, was the PKB led by former President Abdurrahman Wahid; the party is particularly strong in the province's rural hinterland. Here, the PKB won more than 7 million votes although, significantly, the PDI-P was victorious in the capital city of Surabaya.[8] Not coincidentally, rural East Java is also the mainstay of the Nahdlatul Ulama, the traditional Islamic organisation with a reputed membership of 30 to 35 million nationally, and which is mainly organised on the basis of networks of Islamic boarding schools or *pesantren*. In 2004, the PKB maintained its first place position in the province, winning 6.3 million of the votes cast out of a total of just over 20.5 million.

The PDI-P and Golkar mustered a little over 4.3 million and just under 2.7 million of the votes, respectively.[9]

The ups and downs in the political fortunes of political parties are highly suggestive of a vibrant democratic life in Indonesia today. While it is true that decentralisation has been accompanied by democratisation in North Sumatra and East Java, as it has elsewhere in Indonesia, this is not the complete story. The present and following chapters will illustrate in some detail how predatory elites have appropriated Indonesia's institutions of decentralisation and democracy.

The Arena of Struggles

A few basic propositions need to be put forward at this juncture about Indonesia's local elites. First, former New Order elites have learned to dominate democracy at the local level through the use of money politics and various instruments of selective political mobilisation and intimidation. Insofar as relatively new players have entered the game, including those with at least nominally reformist credentials, they have also been largely drawn into the logic of money politics and rent-seeking to ensure their political survival.[10]

Second, among these New Order elites are old bureaucrats who now wish to transform their longstanding hold on the bureaucracy into direct possession of political power, and they have sought to do this mainly by cobbling together local coalitions that would support their forays into elected office. Third, also among these increasingly salient elites are local entrepreneurs, commonly presiding over only small- or medium-level businesses—for example, in contracting, trade or a range of services—whose ambitions have similarly been on the rise. Although many are content to participate in the new democratic arena as unofficial financial backers of candidates[11]—more than a few in the hope of obtaining access to contracts and gaining other forms of preferential treatment from local government—a growing number have directly plunged into electoral politics by contesting local elections. Thus many local entrepreneurs now seek to reinforce their economic position through possession of direct political power. In this regard, comparisons with post-authoritarian Thailand in particular are instructive, where Arghiros notes, citing Withaya, that 'around 61 per cent of councillors in office between 1990 and 1995 were merchants or owned their own business' (2001: 24).

Significantly, many such local entrepreneur-politicos in contemporary Indonesia have backgrounds in business associations that were linked to Golkar
and the state during the New Order. Among the most notable are Gapensi
(the Indonesian National Contractors Association), Kadinda (branch of the
nationally-organised Indonesian Chamber of Commerce and Industry), REI
(Indonesian Real Estate Association), HIPPI (The Indonesian Indigenous
Entrepreneurs Association) and HIPMI (The Association of Indonesian
Young Entrepreneurs). These were all organisations through which businesspeople forged political alliances, advanced their business fortunes and
sought access to state projects and patronage. Though clearly always playing
in a league much lower than the Jakarta-based conglomerates of the Soeharto period, these businesses were no less distinctly a part of, and nurtured
within, the network of patronage that extended down to the local level during the heyday of the New Order.

Fourth, an array of goons and thugs that had played the role of local enforcers during much of the New Order has also been seeking to establish a
niche within Indonesia's democracy. Given the scrutiny placed on the human
rights record of Indonesia's military and police forces following the demise of
the New Order, they have been well-positioned to provide muscle when political actors and groups require instruments of coercion, intimidation or selective mass mobilisation.[12] Even though their fortunes, collectively, have not
been consistently good, many among their ranks have grown in ambition and
have actively tried to wrest control of local political party instruments, as well
as contest local office. Here, lines of comparison with the Philippines—where
'goons and guns' (plus gold) have 'traditionally' featured prominently in local
political life—can be drawn to some extent, as they can be with Thailand. It
should be pointed out that levels of gross acts of political violence in Indonesia
have yet to reach those associated with post-authoritarian politics in either the
Philippines or in Thailand, where politically motivated murders, for example,
are more regular occurrences.[13] In fact, as discussed in Chapter 6, many local
elites in Indonesia are lately developing an interest in ensuring that violence
in local politics is curtailed as much as possible during election time.

Finally, usually scattered within the other groups are political operators
who have emerged out of student and mass organisations that were either
considered to be amenable or tolerated by the New Order. Among these are
the HMI, the Islamic Students Association; the GMNI, the association of
'nationalist' students with traditional affinities to Soekarnoist populism;[14]

the GMKI, an association of Christian students; and the KNPI, the New Order-era state-sponsored corporatist youth organisation. Such organisations had traditionally been a major recruiting ground from which the New Order replenished its supply of political operators and apparatchik; thus, they were rather important conduits to power. It should be remembered that members of the HMI and other non-communist student organisations, perhaps most notably the small but well-connected PMKRI (Association of Catholic Students of the Republic of Indonesia), played a major role in the destruction of the PKI and its affiliate organisations and in the early process of the New Order's institutional development.

It should be noted that the above 'list' of local elites is not exhaustive nor is it mutually exclusive in nature, as individuals can straddle more than one of the categories. Easily added to this list, for example, are local aristocrats and assorted nobilities (Dwipayana 2005), strewn across many parts of Indonesia, who see decentralisation as an opportunity to press their claims for a privileged place in the post-authoritarian system. They will do this by latching on to decentralisation demands that are made in the name of protecting local identity and culture or religion (Faucher 2007: 443); the enactment of customary law, for example, would almost anywhere largely benefit pre-capitalist ruling elites. Many of them might overlap with what van Klinken (2002) calls new 'ethnic elites'.

Van Klinken (2004) also notes that long-dead sultanates and mini royalties are being revived all across Indonesia, and many members of old royal families see democratisation and decentralisation in Indonesia as a window of opportunity for regaining their social and political standing. Clearly, populist sentiments, partly consisting of the call to return to old traditions— and of the type discussed in the Introduction—are an important part of the ideological weaponry of these kinds of social actors as they seek to carve out a niche for themselves in local politics after 1998. Their predictably atavistic pretensions have often had negative effects on inter-ethnic relations in areas characterised by the presence of an 'indigenous' people and significant migrant populations.[15]

Local nobilities and other traditional elites are not rank outsiders who are only now trying to gain a foothold on local power with the demise of authoritarianism. As Magenda's (1991) study of East Kalimantan elites in the 1980s showed, one dynamic of the New Order involved the absorption of local nobilities into the local state apparatus, and so many of them will have been endowed with considerable local bureaucratic power. In other words, some 'royalist' social actors may actually represent entrenched local bureaucratic interests pursuing new strategies of social and political ascendancy.

Whatever a more 'complete' list of salient local elites would actually look like,[16] an important point to make is that local politics today also offer teasing glimpses of Indonesia's possible near future. It is interesting, for example, that even local politicos sometimes speculate that only the rich will soon be able to win political office. What this kind of speculation actually throws up is the real possibility that parties and parliaments will sooner than later, and much less ambiguously, become vehicles for the distribution of the spoils of power among the wealthy and the ruthless.[17] Thus, Indonesia's democracy could increasingly exclude those unequipped to play the game of money politics, and to a lesser extent thuggery, in spite of the widening of political participation through elections and the stated intentions of decentralisation policy. In other words, the localisation of power may continue to produce domains within which local elites preside over contests to control institutions and resources without significantly empowering local citizenries.

Of course, the rich are especially well positioned in most functioning democracies in the world today—the United States is one of the finer examples of a democracy whose workings are dominated by the moneyed and propertied. Such an observation clearly would not have surprised Karl Marx. Nevertheless, the observation pertaining to Indonesia takes on a different importance in relation to the logic of a particularly predatory mode of politics, whereby control over public institutions and their resources becomes a major means for private accumulation as well as the forging of corrupt networks of patronage, including through non-transparent and illegal forms of distributing largesse. Thus, as to be expected, local officials in Indonesia are finding their positions quite profitable, as the rent-seeking possibilities offered by decentralisation are enhanced, and new alliances with local business interests are forged. One former member of the Surabaya legislature openly confesses to receiving regular kickbacks from businesspeople to facilitate their projects; he considers this to be 'normal' practice.[18] In the same vein, Savirani speaks of entrepreneurs giving kickbacks to the *bupati* of Bantul in Yogyakarta, who some consider a reformer, as a matter of course when doing business in his area of jurisdiction (2004: 48–49).

The new rent-seeking opportunities provided by decentralisation clearly make up the fuel for the often intense levels of conflict that surround contests for control of key institutions of governance at the local level. In places like North Sumatra and East Java, especially in the more economically advanced and industrial areas that surround the capital cities of Medan and Surabaya, respectively, much is to be gained by local elites through their levy-making prerogatives and control over local budgets. Through the control of these local budgets, officials are able to approve or reject projects, for example, and are able to be involved in the widespread practice of marking up their actual costs. In this regard, the Indonesian experience does not depart substantially from that of the Thai, as documented by authors like Arghiros. He notes that Thai local politicians have stood to gain much from approving development budgets and infrastructure projects through which businessmen can make huge profits from skimming and overstating costs (Arghiros 2001: 23–24).

Clearly, it is quite easy in a world such as this for would-be reformers to be either marginalised or simply sucked into the logic of rent-seeking. The late Yogyakarta provincial parliamentarian, Ryadi Gunawan, talked about gradually reforming his party, the PDI-P, through an internal gradual process. A former academic and NGO activist who had been active in the GMNI, he expressed disappointment at the same time with the fact that he had to regularly deal with corrupt practices as well as goons and thugs within the party, though he had come to accept this as being unavoidable.[19] Marin Purba, a former critical student figure based in Bandung in the 1980s and active in the Christian student organisation, the GMKI, somehow managed to win the mayoralty of the town of Pematang Siantar in North Sumatra through complex deals with a number of political parties in the local legislature.[20] Though keen to project an image of technocratic rationality and professionalism, he was to be ousted from office because of his implication in a corruption scandal.

The advent of direct popular elections for heads of local and provincial governments (discussed in Chapter 6) also provided the stimulus for the creation of some peculiar political bedfellows. For example, some well-known representatives of predatory elites, and NGO and other reformist activists have sometimes converged in supporting particular candidates due to peculiar local exigencies. In such cases, the activists often become quite acutely aware of the strains being placed on their self-perceptions of personal integrity as they are forced to engage in the ruthless game of money politics.

Interestingly, local politicos have sometimes been placed on the defensive in the public discourse by having to rationalise what appear to be policies that repel investment and place a burden on ordinary citizens—the exact opposite of what decentralisation is supposed to achieve according to neo-liberal/neo-institutionalist prescriptions. Despite the growing criticism of local levies, for example, Medan parliamentarian and *Pemuda Pancasila* prominent figure Bangkit Sitepu suggested in 2001 that it should not be problem for businesspeople to give back to society some of the profits they have been allowed to enjoy.[21] This is an opinion not dissimilar to that often voiced by representatives of locally powerful groups latching on to populist notions of justice, especially those laced with racist sentiments against members of the ethnic Chinese business community.[22]

Such an opinion is obviously worrisome to international development organisations like the World Bank, which have invested resources as well as a significant measure of prestige into the Indonesian decentralisation process, and for whom decentralisation itself is a major pivot of good governance and markets. Thus, World Bank economists in Indonesia came to characterise decentralisation here as a 'flawed process'—one that still opens up immense opportunities to improve the lives of ordinary people but is marred by a host of 'nuisance taxes' imposed by local governments that adversely affect the climate of business (*Jakarta Post* 16 July 2003).

It should be emphasised that local predatory interests are not entirely homogenous in their make-up. Thus, there also can be important tensions and contradictions insofar as local interests are concerned: businesspeople like Yopie Batubara, elected in 2004 as a member of the DPD representing North Sumatra, or Medan-based ethnic Chinese entrepreneur Surya Sampurna echo then KADIN chief Aburizal Bakrie's concerns, voiced in Jakarta, that the barrage of new, formal and informal levies will burden business and discourage investment.[23] Yet, in spite of such locally-rooted tensions and contradictions, distinct politico-business alliances at the sub-national level are clearly emerging; these are concerned about gaining a measure of autonomy from the dictates of Jakarta. This is particularly so given that rent-seeking opportunities at the local level can be quite enticing, as the divide between the realms of politics and business, and the public and the private, remains as hazy as during the heyday of the New Order. Local NGO activists in North Sumatra, for example, have characterised the provincial parliament there as a 'boxing ring', in which parliamentarians slug it out with one another to further the interests of powerful business groups with which they have respectively forged alliances to pursue rent-seeking opportunities.[24]

One major area of controversy insofar as business interests are concerned relates to which level of government actually has the jurisdiction over investment approvals. Officials at different levels regularly give conflicting accounts of the formal procedures of foreign investment and how much real autonomy sub-provincial authorities have with regard to approving new projects. Whatever the actual written rules spell out, the reality of uncertainty does not bode well for Indonesia's efforts to attract foreign investors after the debacle of the 1997–1998 economic crisis. Furthermore, according to one researcher, it would be difficult to get approval for many new investment projects if members of local legislatures were not approached and somehow remunerated.[25] The consequences of this situation is investor lack of confidence in the state's ability to uphold and enforce legal contracts and the requirement that they seek out the instruments through which politically-connected racketeers can be dealt with, for example, in the form of non-transparent deals with local politicos.

Conscious of the newfound power and authority of heads of local governments, and because 'the paradigms on doing business' have now changed, a 'Meet the Bupatis' Forum was organised in Jakarta as early as May 2002 by no less than two leading international firms operating in Indonesia—PT Harvest International and PT Microsoft Indonesia. During the forum, the chief executive officer of Harvest International, Harvey Goldstein—who has had years of experience in Indonesia and often acts as an unofficial spokesman for foreign investors—proclaimed that as most business activity takes place outside of Jakarta, doing business in the regions required 'a firm and committed relationship with the Bupatis' (Guerin 2002). Clearly, international investors have become increasingly aware of the importance of forging alliances with local officials.

In this connection, many central government officials openly suggest, however, that local officials lack the skill and ability to negotiate complex contracts, for instance with large multinational mining companies, and that this responsibility should remain with Jakarta (*Jakarta Post* 30 October 2000). Much of this notion stems from the belief that local politicos are poorly educated, which is supposed to explain the poor performance of many local legislative bodies. The failure of local parliamentarians to live up to the standards of 'good governance' is better explained, however, by their innate interests rather than poor education. Indeed, Shiraishi (2003) discovered in four provinces he surveyed (North Sumatra, East Java, Bali and East Kalimantan) in 1999 that the vast majority of local parliamentarians were university graduates, though of course there is a large number of tertiary education institutions in Indonesia with questionable reputations.

Thus, on the basis of a viewpoint directly opposite to that frequently stated by Jakarta-based technocrats, the *bupati* of Deli Serdang in North Sumatra in 2001—at the time a retired military officer—expressed his annoyance at what he saw as Jakarta's underestimation of the capabilities of local officials. In his view, local officials and politicos are more than capable of carrying out the burden and responsibilities of decentralisation. For him, this was merely another excuse not to devolve power and authority to the local level. He was equally adamant that investment plans within his area of jurisdiction would have to go through his office though this was denied by the then provincial governor, the late Teuku Rizal Nurdin. The latter insisted that the right to approve investment projects was a prerogative of government at the provincial level.[26] Given the preponderance of kickbacks related to investment approval procedures, the lack of clarity regarding the jurisdiction of each level of government is undoubtedly troublesome for potential investors.

In response to such a problem, the central government has made initiatives to simplify investment procedures and update the existing legislation governing foreign investment. In April 2004, President Megawati Soekarnoputri signed a decree on investment procedures that aimed to 'end confusion about which authorities investors should approach, following the implementation of a huge regional autonomy programme in 2001' (*Jakarta Post* 16 April 2004). This did not seem to solve the problem, however. According to the same newspaper report, 'The decree said regional officials as well as ministerial offices may transfer their authority for issuing permits to the [National Investment Coordinating Board]. But it did not say whether they must do so'. Such ambiguity displays the continuing tug-of-war between officials at different levels of governance.

Investment procedural issues will take particularly sticky forms in industries that are resource-based. Gellert notes, for example, that during the Habibie and Wahid presidencies, governments at the level of the *kabupaten* were given the authority to issue 'timber utilisation permits', as well as 'timber extraction permits'. This was of course in line with the decentralisation agenda that was running at full speed at the time. The outcomes, however, were a boom in the issuance of such permits and the effective legalisation of lucrative illegal logging activities. A struggle ensued whereby the central government under President Megawati Soekarnoputri attempted to restrict the authority of local governments over logging. Gellert remarks as well that the *kabupaten* continued to issue small-scale logging permits and impose local fees for quite some time, while the collection of central fees remained minimal. He also adds that the *bupati* of Berau, in forestry-rich East Kalimantan, was brought up on charges of embezzling US$9.4 million in relation to the tax obligations of companies engaged locally in lucrative logging activities (Gellert 2005: 154–155).

On occasion, local predatory interests will collide spectacularly with those of foreign investors, as was the case in the controversial sale of 25.5 per cent shares of the state-owned cement producer, Semen Gresik, to the Mexican concern, Cemex. A Semen Gresik subsidiary named Semen Padang, a cement producer in West Sumatra, was also involved in the purchase by default. The problem that ensued was that the management of Semen Padang and local politicos in West Sumatra adamantly opposed the deal and were eventually able to win the support of some members of the central government in Jakarta. Frustrated with the protracted wrangling over its purchase, Cemex brought the government of Indonesia to arbitration after the latter failed to abide by a 1998 investment deal that was supposed to allow the company to gradually become the majority shareholder of Semen Gresik (*Jakarta Post* 26 May 2006). On the other hand, through a different company called PT Andalas Tuah Sakato, the government of West Sumatra stated its intent to purchase the shares in dispute (*Tempo Interaktif* No. 38/VI/May 23–29, 2006) and was opposed to an alternative arrangement whereby the exasperated Cemex would sell its stake in PT Semen Gresik to an Indonesian private concern, PT Rajawali, owned by New Order-era businessman Peter Sondakh, or to PT Bosowa, a company seen to be linked to Vice-President Jusuf Kalla.[27] Though the stand-off was finally resolved by the sale to Rajawali (*Jakarta Post* 25 July 2006), the issue has been both very emotive in West Sumatra, where local politicos have successfully used populist and atavistic sentiment to cast Semen Padang as a source of pride of the people, as well as exceedingly messy. In a damning indictment of opponents of Cemex, the journalist Vincent Lingga (Lingga 2006), characterises them as:

> vested interests, narrowminded nationalists and various groups of rent seekers [who] have tried since 2001 to spin off SP [Sement Padang], one of three SG cement subsidiaries, from the SG [Semen Gresik] group. Leaders of the West

Sumatra provincial legislature, the then governor of West Sumatra and top SP executives in mid-2001 passed a decree expropriating SP until such time as it is separated from SG. But would the campaign to spin off SP from SG to make it a stand-alone state company really benefit the West Sumatra people? Not likely, if the findings of the special audit on SP by PriceWaterhouseCoopers in 2004–2005 is any indication.

According to Lingga, in the same article:

The rent seekers simply want to retain SP as their cash cow as they did in 2000–2003. The forensic audit that was made at the order of SG shareholders and completed in May 2005 found almost all types of bad corporate governance practices rife in SP. They were notably rampant between 2001 and September 2003, when it was controlled by the then renegade management with the full support of local rent seekers within the legislature and local administration. Auditors estimated tens of millions of dollars in outright and potential losses due to bad practices or even blatant fraud in procurement, inventory and marketing management.

Local Elites, Local Ambitions

Following up on the points made in the previous chapter, special attention will now be devoted to local elites who have dominated Indonesia's party politics and electoral contests—conducted from 2005 on the basis of the popular vote, and before that on the basis of voting confined to local parliamentary bodies. These contests are intricately related to the emergence of still shifting and mutually competing local systems of patronage, cemented by money politics, and at times, instruments of political coercion involving youth/gangster organisations and civilian militia.

Significantly, competition among different groups of enforcers has become more intense and less regulated than it was during the New Order. Although typically revolving around turf disputes, inter-gang conflict has also been more directly related to the dynamics of inter-political party competition. This is unlike the previous New Order era, during which state-sponsored henchmen and enforcers would characteristically find protectors within the local Golkar leadership or military and police commands. It is in the context of this new, unpredictable and frequently rough-and-tumble world of local politics that conflict and competition within a diverse array of local elites will be examined, with particular consideration given to the New Order-era entrepreneurs, bureaucrats and henchmen who have now re-invented themselves as democratic actors.

It is interesting that many of the examples of conflict among players in lo-cal politics are often presented by the actors themselves, at the one extreme, as having to do with lofty conceptions of political morality or community inter-est. At the other extreme, they are also often presented as boiling down to ba-nal rivalries between local individuals and personalities, as animosities among different political actors may indeed run very deep for a variety of reasons.[28] These kinds of self-presentations are often quite misleading. Whether or not banal, underlying these conflicts is almost always the scramble for power and control over key institutions and resources. The crux of the matter is that con-trol of local political offices and machineries, and the resultant access to rent-seeking opportunities, provide the concrete basis for some of the most intense of electoral and political party conflicts at the local level in post-authoritarian Indonesia. Furthermore, many of these conflicts instructively involve the growing schism between local coalitions of power and those based in Jakarta.

In connection with the previously mentioned example of central and lo-cal conflict over the issuance of highly lucrative logging permits, Obidzinski (2005: 199) notes how the framework of decentralisation had made the *bupati* very powerful and, therefore, predictably encouraged businesspeople in that industry to heed local governments at the expense of Jakarta. Such conflicts are no less than the concrete manifestations of a continuing tug-of-war among powerful coalitions of interests at different levels of governance that have a tangible, material basis. They have considerable impact as well on the way in which the formal institutions of decentralisation, and of democracy, continue to be forged and reshaped in Indonesia, and the modes in which they actually operate. McCarthy (2007), in particular, in his study of Central Kalimantan, offers a grim picture of how illegal logging involves conflict in which a range of people, from gangsters to officials at various levels of government to busi-nessmen and traditional local notables, all play an integral part.

BUREAUCRATS AND POLITICAL POWER

As was noted earlier, not long after the fall of the New Order, Malley had shown that old New Order bureaucrats tended to already dominate and prevail in local electoral contests. The significance of this observation is that it indicates how individuals endowed with bureaucratic power, as career bureaucrats, have successfully sought to transform themselves into holders of political power proper. Again, the Indonesian situation is not exceptional when developments here are placed in the context of broader global developments. In post-Soviet Russia, for example, it has been noted that prominent members of the old communist-era bureaucracy had taken control of many local governments even in the context of the early Yeltsin reforms, and were able to use their incumbency to good use when having to face electoral contests (see Slider 2001).

What Savirani has called the 'bureaucrat model' (Savirani 2004: 73) of powerful new local politicos is perhaps best represented in the person of Syaukani H. R., a controversial *bupati* of Kutai Kertanagera. The area, as mentioned previously, is particularly wealthy due to its natural resource endowment. As head of, undoubtedly, the richest local government in Indonesia, Syaukani was also chairman of Apkasi, the Indonesian District Governments' Association. This group has played a leading role in protecting the interests of local governments in the face of threats of some degree of re-centralisation.

As Savarani notes, Syaukani started his career as a civil servant in 1973 and only transformed himself into a major politician at the very end of the New Order when he headed the local parliament in the former *kabupaten* of Kutai resulting from the 1997 election—the last of those highly orchestrated by the New Order. Not surprisingly, he was backed by powerful Golkar political machine. Elected as Kutai Kertanegara's first *bupati* following the division of Kutai into three *kabupaten* after the fall of Soeharto, the ambitious Syaukani was re-elected in 2005 (*Tempo Interaktif* 2 June 2005). Armed with huge amounts of readily available funds, he has built his popularity on a number of local semi-welfarist programmes. He has also displayed a penchant for supporting financially dubious, high prestige 'white elephant' projects (van Klinken 2002). Interestingly, one of Syaukani's actions was to revive the long comatose Sultanate of Kutai Kertenagara, no doubt in a bid to further bolster his populist credibility and make claims of being a defender of the allegedly indigenous cultural heritage. However, this was not enough to hinder corruption charges being laid on him for misappropriating public funds earmarked for constructing an airfield (*Tempo* 1–7 January 2007: 36–37) and a subsequent conviction involving a jail term.

The general observation made by Malley mentioned earlier would appear to hold true as well in North Sumatra, where a considerable number of local heads of governments have been former New Order-era bureaucrats; sixteen of the twenty-two elected since the fall of Soeharto till 2002 were such individuals (Hadiz 2003). Thus, representatives of Savirani's 'bureaucrat model' are easily found here. The rise of bureaucrats with growing political ambitions arguably offers strong evidence of continuities with the New Order at the level of dominant interests in spite of the incredible changes that have occurred at the level of institutional frameworks of governance since 1998. Still, it is important to point out that longstanding entrenchment as a bureaucrat will not always ensure victory in the electoral arena.

For example, in the Medan mayoral election of June 2005, former deputy mayor and long-time local career bureaucrat Maulana Pohan was defeated by his erstwhile boss, the incumbent Abdillah, a businessman in the contracting industry with huge political and economic resources who had the support of both Golkar and the PDI-P. In contrast, although a Golkar functionary during New Order times, Pohan was in fact nominated by an Islamic party, the PKS.[29] Ironically, the PKS had achieved notable success in the 2004 national legislative elections by exploiting its image as a party of outsiders, untainted by corruption. This was not the first time the businessman Abdillah had defeated a noted bureaucrat in a mayoral election. In 2000, Abdillah was also able to muster the resources necessary to defeat another longstanding local career bureaucrat, Ridwan Batubara. This was achieved in a controversial process that, as we shall see later, involved blatant displays of both political intimidation and money politics.

Not surprisingly, the 'bureaucrat model' of rising local politico is to be readily found elsewhere in Indonesia. In East Java, one finds individuals like Wien Hendrarso, the *bupati* of Sidoardjo, who as 'regional secretary' (*Sekretaris Daerah*, or Sekda) was previously the locality's senior career bureaucrat. Hailing from a line of local officials stretching back to colonial times,[30] he was first elected in 2000 before being overwhelmingly re-elected in 2005. Instructively, as another New Order-era career bureaucrat, he was a long-time Golkar stalwart and functionary, but his re-election was secured through the support of a coalition of political parties that consisted of the PKB, the PKS and PAN. One of the defeated rival candidates on this occasion was supported by a notionally powerful coalition consisting of Golkar and the PDI-P (*Republika* Online 12 September 2005)—two entities that formed the major rival blocs in the national parliament in Jakarta; although in the specific East Java context, PKB has been traditionally regarded as the strongest party.

Such outwardly 'strange' political party alignments in Medan and Sidoarjo are particularly instructive, even as they are replicated ad infinitum elsewhere in Indonesian local politics. They provide just two of numerous examples of the fluidity and temporality of party affiliations, which increasingly has little to do with official ideologies or programmes. They provide examples also of how old New Order elites—in these instances based in the bureaucracy— have repositioned themselves in Indonesia's competitive democratic system, and attempted to transform their long hold on the bureaucracy into a direct grasp of local political power. A key aspect of such a transformation involves latching on to political party vehicles, which increasingly function as key instruments through which the modes of distribution and allocation of political and economic largesse are being defined through intricate behind-the-scenes wheeling and dealing, characteristically involving monetary transactions.

A noticeable related development is that, in spite of their origins in and long association with Golkar, bureaucrats will not necessarily turn to it as their chosen electoral vehicle when contesting public office. Though this may be attributable to the availability of other options in a democratised environment, it is also because local branches of Golkar have in specific instances championed other kinds of key local elites, especially from within business circles, over those bureaucrats who used to provide its major pillar of support during the New Order. Given such competition for the endorsement of Golkar—still well-endowed and comparatively impressive as a political machine many years after the demise of the New Order—formerly obedient and rigid local bureaucrats who harbour rising political ambitions have had to be extremely agile and creative in their attempts to thrive in the newer democratic political arena. Given that bureaucrats' loyalties to Golkar were once cast in stone, they have been remarkably successful in finding new, accommodating vehicles through which they can forge new alliances and strategies of survival and advancement. Thus, it is common to find former New Order bureaucrats strewn across all kinds of post-Soeharto political parties, all over the vast Indonesian archipelago, regardless of their professed political platforms and philosophies.

ENTREPRENEURS AND POLITICS

Businesspeople entering the arena of local politics directly have frequently emerged as the main rivals of former New Order bureaucrats in the battle for political ascendance, and they deserve some extra attention. In North Sumatra, an obvious example of the businessman-politician is offered in the person of Rudolf Pardede, the scion of a family business empire based on hotels, property, textiles and other industries. As the PDI-P boss in North Sumatra he was elected deputy governor in 2003 in a pairing with then incumbent governor Teuku Rizal Nurdin, a New Order-era appointee and retired general who managed to retain his position after the old regime's demise. Pardede, whose father was one of the most well-known figures of the non-ethnic Chinese North Sumatran business community that goes back to the 1950s and 1960s, notably ascended to the post of governor following Teuku Rizal Nurdin's death in a plane crash in September 2005, in spite of some strenuous opposition from the provincial parliament. Subsequently, however, Pardede was involved in decidedly ugly wrangling with the central leadership of his own party in Jakarta. In spite of the stature that he attained in the North Sumatra party branch since Indonesian democratisation, the PDI-P in Jakarta refused to endorse him for the gubernatorial elections-proper of 2008—and opted for a New Order-era general and party outsider instead (Detik.com. 25 January 2008).

Before such developments, the combination of Teuku Rizal Nurdin and Rudolf Pardede had been a particularly striking one for it appeared to perfectly synergise local political and business power. The former, as one-time chief of the military command in North Sumatra and with close family ties to the old Melayu Deli aristocracy based in Medan and its environs, had good claims to being a true New Order-era local notable who had risen to national prominence. While Pardede is a good representative of the rising ambitions of locally-based businesspeople, fuelled by the opportunities presented by political and administrative decentralisation, he was in fact no newcomer to politics. Pardede was no less than a member of the national parliament of Indonesia in the 1980s, representing the PDI-P's direct ancestor—the politically inconsequential PDI, the New Order-era party of so-called 'secular-nationalists.'[31]

Although no one as aggressively ambitious is immediately noticeable within the East Java business community, we encounter individuals such as Ridwan Hisyam, a real estate developer and former chairman of the East Java Branch of HIPMI, an association of 'young' Indonesian businessmen. Also no newcomer to politics, he sat in the Majelis Permusyawaratan Rakyat, or People's Consultative Assembly (MPR), from 1997 until 2004 representing Golkar, thus straddling the very late New Order and early post-Soeharto periods as a national politician.

Pardede and Hisyam are obviously examples of a more established stratum of local businessmen who had managed to cross over into national politics during the New Order, latching on to vehicles like Golkar and the old PDI. With political bases beyond the sub-provincial, individuals such as these can be expected to be critical of decentralisation's emphasis on the level of cities and *kabupaten*. As chair of the East Java chapter of Golkar and an unsuccessful contender for deputy governor in 2003, Hisyam openly questions the idea that local autonomy, in the way that it had been framed by the 1999 legislation, has actually made business investments more practical or less costly.[32]

It is notable, however, that before being discarded by his superiors in the party hierarchy in Jakarta, Pardede had come to be deeply entangled in conflicts over the control of sub-provincial political machineries with PDI-P local bigwigs in North Sumatra. In these conflicts, Pardede was usually perceived as representing the interests of the Jakarta leadership of the party against those of local political operators (an irony given his subsequent abandonment by Jakarta). What is interesting here is that his political ambitions, which were once channelled through national-level political institutions, have since been diverted to regional and local level political arenas, where the potential prizes have been enhanced due to decentralisation. Thus the trajectory of Pardede's political career from the national to the regional/local is indicative of the growing importance of contests over local power in post-authoritarian Indonesia.

Only a notch or two below individuals like Pardede in North Sumatra's political ladder, we come across individuals such as Ali Umri, a local businessman/contractor and former Golkar parliamentarian. Mayor of the town of Binjai since 2000, he was re-elected in 2005 with Golkar support, after defeating, among others, fellow businessman Herman Manan, himself the son of a police lieutenant colonel who had served as a New Order-era mayor of the town.[33] Another defeated contestant on this occasion was private businessman Indra Bungsu, who received the backing of the staunchly Muslim PKS, even though he is not a party cadre and in fact hails from a family of local aristocrats and supporters of 'secular-nationalist' Soekarnoism.[34] The only non-business candidate in this particular race was Abdul Gani Sitepu, a long-time local career bureaucrat who was able to cobble together support from a range of diverse parties with very little ostensibly in common by way of official platforms or ideological positions.[35] Subsequently, the fast-rising Ali Umri made an unsuccessful bid for the North Sumatran gubernatorial election of 2008.

In nearby Serdang Bedagai, we find Helifizar 'David' Purba, a contractor whose base has actually been in the local branch of the New Order-era youth/gangster organisation, the Pemuda Pancasila. A feared and respected local notable, he was instrumental in the establishment of Serdang Bedagai as a new *kabupaten*, separating from the economically strategic Deli Serdang, which envelopes the North Sumatran capital city of Medan. It is arguable that, spending more than billions of rupiah of his own money by his own estimate to lobby for the establishment of the new *kabupaten*,[36] Purba had always cast his eye on the post of *bupati*. In fact, he was even the contractor for the erection of the new, quite impressive *bupati* office building in the main town of Tebing Tinggi.

In this connection, it should be reasserted that many local business figures who engage in politics have emerged from the contracting/construction industry, from which illicit profit could be readily made given the opportunities for skimming and marking-up the value of public projects. As pointed out earlier, Arghiros notes the same phenomenon occurring in Thailand (2001:24). This is likely to be more than mere coincidence; it strongly suggests that decentralised politics in the Southeast Asian post-authoritarian context is particularly appealing to those businesspeople who are at least partly dependent on access to public projects and funds. Kasian Tejapira, too, characterises businessmen-cum-local criminal bosses in Thailand who flourished initially in businesses where access to government was crucial to their success, and an environment in which non-transparency and even illegal activity were distinctive features (2006: 13–14).

Significantly, Serdang Bedagai is merely one of many new *kabupaten* that has been established in Indonesia since the fall of the New Order, creating ever newer arenas of contestation over local power and resources. By the end of 2003, there were 32 provinces as well as 416 *kabupaten* and municipalities in Indonesia, with the latter increasing in number at an annual rate of 10 per cent (Brodjonegoro 2003) before the scheduled legislative elections of April 2004 brought this development to a halt by virtue of administrative necessity. Today, new provinces like that of Banten, Bangka Belitung, Gorontalo, Riau Archipelago and North Maluku can be found on a map of Indonesia.

Typically, local notables like Purba in Serdang Bedagai would have been instrumental in the establishment of such new administrative entities as they seek to carve out a more independent niche for themselves in the new struggles between competing with typically predatory local coalitions of power. Yusril Ihza Mahendra, leader of the Islamic-oriented Crescent and Star Party, as well as a former Soeharto speech-writer and member of several *reformasi*-era cabinets, is known to have been a major supporter of the establishment of Bangka Belitung as a separate province from South Sumatra. Erwiza Erman (2007) notes how in these tin-rich islands, local business interests, colluding with local officials and gangsters, have sought to wrest control of the tin industry from the state-owned tin company, and have profited from illicit trade. Likewise, Banten was established as a province separate from West Java with the support of a Banten native who served in the national parliament for Golkar. According to Syarif Hidayat (2007), 'project racketeering', especially in the area of construction, involving one of the area's leading entrepreneurs, as well as local thugs traditionally called *jawara*, has since become more pervasive.[37]

Instructively, in the case of Gorontalo, on the island of Sulawesi, the new governorship was to be filled by the Jakarta-based, Soeharto and Habibie-linked businessman Fadel Muhammad, who has strong family ties to the region. The initial victor in North Maluku's first ever gubernatorial election in 2001, in a controversial process marred by accusations of money politics, was the Soeharto-era former minister and parliamentary leader Abdul Gafur. The latter's victory, however, was overturned when the central government of then President Megawati Soekarnoputri intervened on behalf of Thaib Armayn (Smith 2006), who had close links to the local military (and Golkar). A subsequent and even more hotly contested election pitting the same two descended into farce when no victor could be named by the authorities, although at one stage Gafur seemed to have finally attained the post he coveted (*Antaranews* 11 February 2008). Yorris Raweyai, part Papuan and long-time number two man in the national Pemuda Pancasila, also made a highly publicised but unsuccessful bid for a newly created governorship (with Golkar support)—on this occasion in the controversially created province of Irian Jaya Barat, carved out of the resource-rich province of Papua.

It is interesting as well that such Jakarta-established political and business actors as Abdul Gafur, Yorris Raweyai and Fadel Muhammad have chosen to abandon Jakarta politics and move 'down' to a seemingly 'lower' arena. This shows too that the prize offered in lower arenas of politics may in some cases be more tantalising than those at the national level. In Thailand, Nelson notes as well that 'the decentralisation process has increased the prize of local executive positions to such a degree that some current and former MPs [members of Parliament] have their intention' of running at the level of the so-called PAO or Provincial Administrative Organisations. Nelson suggests that success at such a lower level may be better than 'languishing on the opposition benches' of the national parliament or of being completely subordinated to the prime minister (Nelson 2003: 8). Achakorn Wongpreedee (2007), studying Buri Ram and Pathum Thani provinces, sees another dynamic emerging from decentralization in Thailand: already powerful and wealthy local politicians are increasingly being provided with patronage and resources by the more powerful of national MPs who seek to expand their local vote base. The process frequently includes the securing of projects for local-level politicians who are often also contractors.

In Indonesia, individuals like Yorris Raweyai, Fadel Muhammad or Abdul Gafur (who is married to a well-known New Order-era businesswoman) are able to simultaneously exploit 'sons of the region' (*putera daerah*) sentiment, while harnessing considerable material resources to pursue success in their chosen new terrain of political conquest. In terms of the discussion in earlier parts of this book, such individuals are precisely the kind that could be best exploit localist populist sentiment at the same time that they selectively carve out niches through which local or regional engagement with external economic actors could be forged.

It should be pointed out that governorships will probably become increasingly attractive to individuals such as these, given the struggles over the institutional arrangements of decentralisation that have now resulted in more actual authority being shifted back to the provincial level of government, as opposed to the *kabupaten* and town. Nevertheless, there is a wealth of anecdotal evidence suggesting that less nationally known *putera daerah* of all sorts—formerly well-ensconced in Jakarta as politician, businessman, bureaucrat or political operator—have tested their fortunes as candidates in numerous elections for local office, most typically those of *bupati* or mayor. Many of these so-called *putera daerah* would actually have little intimate knowledge of local development issues, but a large number of them have been enticed by the new personal opportunities arising locally from political and administrative decentralisation. In other words, many are effectively Jakartans who would have very little to offer in terms of real claims of affinity and closeness to local communities.

Returning to the case of David Purba, his path to the top in Serdang Bedagai was to be obstructed. He was to lose the election for *bupati* in June 2005, despite considerable financial investment, to a formidable opponent, local businessman Tengku Erry Nuradi. The latter is no less than the brother of the late Rizal Nurdin. Displaying an interesting new pattern of forging alliances, the latter candidate was to join forces with sections of the NGO community by choosing as his running mate, Soekirman, a highly regarded, senior local NGO activist. Soekirman had failed in an earlier attempt to win a seat in the Regional Representatives' Council (DPD) representing North Sumatra.

It may be said that while Tengku Erry Nuradi provided the necessary political connections and funds for this political pairing, Soekirman provided the populist touch, supplemented by his ability to garner the support of grassroots-based organisations. It should be remembered that large sections of the Indonesia NGO community had gotten onto the decentralisation and good governance bandwagon because it appealed to their sense of local community and social justice (see Introduction and Chapter 1). On the other hand, Soekirman had also served as an advisor to his running mate's brother, the late provincial governor, so he was well connected to local elites. Though mindful of the possibility of being politically compromised, and expressing discomfort with money politics, Soekirman, like many of his NGO colleagues, expressed the belief that joining Tengku Erry Nuradi would help ensure a local administration more responsive to people's needs, despite the latter's business and aristocratic background and sensibilities.[38] The combination of money, access to well-established local networks of power and populist credibility turned out to be too much even for the powerful Purba, who later challenged in vain the electoral results in court.

In East Java, one also comes across individuals like Masfuk, the *bupati* of Lamongan, who owns seven companies engaged in such diverse areas as the production of jewellery, and automobile and furniture parts. A leading member of the East Java branch of the Indonesian Chamber of Commerce and Industry and of HIPPI, Masfuk joined PAN after the fall of Soeharto and was elected *bupati* in 2000 with the support of a coalition of parties that included Golkar and the PDI-P (*Kompas* 15 July 2003). Re-elected in 2005 on the basis of popular vote, Masfuk had to repel a formidable challenge from a new coalition comprising the PKB and, this time, Golkar—again showing the highly fluid nature of political party allegiances. During the campaign, his supporters had to dispel claims that he had misappropriated large sums of the Lamongan local budget (*Indo Pos Online*, 18 June 2005), an accusation that incumbents routinely faced across Indonesia during their re-election battles.

Other businessmen-politicians in East Java notably include small- and medium-level businessmen like A. Wachid, son of a former soldier, small-scale businessman and NU activist; he describes his business as that of a 'supplier' for the hotel industry. A member of the New Order-created Islamic political vehicle, the PPP, since 1974 and also an Ansor and Nahdlatul Ulama (NU) activist, he was only to enter the political big time in 1999 when he was elected to the Surabaya parliament. His main concern in relation to decentralisation, like that of many of his colleagues, is to ensure that it provides greater control on the part of local government over money-making economic activities and over such enterprises as the harbour at Surabaya. Full of ideas to increase local revenue, he suggests that Surabaya ought to be able to get a cut of the tax on cigarette sales collected by the national government, as there are several cigarette companies headquartered in Surabaya.[39] Staving off arguments that this would only help fuel local corruption, he idiosyncratically insists that there has been no corruption in the local Surabaya parliament; this is in contradiction to widespread reports in the local press in 2002 and 2003 about the misappropriation of billions of rupiahs of the Surabaya government budget by members of its parliament.[40]

Again, similar developments are easily recognised elsewhere in Indonesia. In Bantul in Yogyakarta, for example, we come upon Idham Samawi, twice elected *bupati* in the post-Soeharto period under two different electoral systems. This particular local politician hails from a prominent family of newspaper publishers whose purview includes the daily *Kedaulatan Rakyat*, which is regarded to be Indonesia's oldest. The media tycoon turned politician is also well-connected to the family of the Sultan of Yogyakarta, whose father served as one of Soeharto's vice-presidents in the 1970s (Savirani 2004: 44). As mentioned earlier, Idham Samawi's tenure has been marred by claims of corrupt practices involving business kickbacks, though he is eager to project an image of technocratic professionalism underpinned by plans of raising local revenue, spearheaded by a number of new as well as reorganised local state enterprises.[41]

In Yogyakarta as well, one encounters individuals such as ethnic-Chinese businessman Budi Setyagraha, who became a member of the provincial parliament in 1999 for PAN. This was at first glance an odd vehicle for a Chinese businessman: locally in Yogyakarta as well as nationally, PAN is filled with Muhammadiyah activists who often quietly express anti-Chinese business sentiments. The Muhammadiyah is widely regarded as an organisation

representing the 'modernist' stream of Indonesian Islam, traditionally underpinned by urban-based Muslim traders and businessman who, since the
early twentieth century at least, often found themselves in competition with
ethnic Chinese rivals. Setyagraha, however, was a convert to Islam and is
in fact a leading figure in a national organisation of Muslim Chinese. More
crucially, he was an activist of ICMI,[42] the Association of Muslim Intellectuals once headed by Habibie and which functioned in the late Soeharto era
to mobilise support for the New Order from the growing Islamic middle
class and intelligentsia (Hefner 1993). Indeed, ICMI became a key conduit
to power and patronage and a source from which New Order operators and
apparatchik would be recruited in the 1990s. PAN was established in 1998
in the context of the fall of Soeharto by Amien Rais, a scholar-politician
who was leader of the Muhammadiyah, from which ICMI garnered many
key personnel during its heyday. Though he came to be known as a leading opponent of Soeharto in 1997 and 1998, Rais was in fact a key ICMI
leader until he was ousted from the organisation. Thus, Setyagraha's ascension to a position of local political prominence expressed a particular kind
of dynamic—that of the repositioning of those who had latched on to the
all-pervasive New Order system of patronage, in this case through its ICMI
element, in new 'reformist', post-authoritarian political parties.

It is certain that businesspeople will become increasingly involved in contests over local political office out of sheer necessity; thereby making the
Thai model of businessmen-politicians increasingly relevant to Indonesia in
many respects.[43] For one thing, the process of being elected to local office
has become increasingly expensive with the institution of direct polls.[44] The
well-known North Sumatra-based businessman and politician, Yopie Batubara, already estimated in 2001 that it was necessary to have a war chest of
tens of billions of rupiah to successfully win a local election, referring quite
specifically to the city of Medan where his brother, Ridwan Batubara, had
been a defeated candidate the previous year.[45] Another defeated candidate for
electoral office in the immediate post-Soeharto years, this time for *bupati* of
nearby Tapanuli Selatan, estimated that a successful bid there would require
an investment of just Rp 2 billion.[46] If these figures are to be accepted—given
before changes to the electoral system were subsequently implemented—
they indicate that the costs of waging a successful election bid will vary considerably even in locations of relatively close geographical proximity, partly
depending on the economic stakes that are locally involved in relation to

possession of political power. Similar observations are put forward by local political actors in East Java.[47]

Just as bureaucratic power does not guarantee electoral success, a background in the business world also does not ensure victory in electoral contests even if the proliferation of election-time money politics should be advantageous to businessmen-turned-politicians. In Sleman in Yogyakarta, Hafidh Asrom, a well-known businessman in the furniture industry who was able to garner the support of the local branches of several Muslim-oriented parties, lost a bitterly contested race for *bupati* of Sleman in 2000[48] against the PDI-P supported Ibnu Subiyanto; this defeat was repeated in 2005. According to Hafidh Asrom, his first loss, which was a particularly controversial affair that involved a bomb scare at the local parliament building, was attributable to intense pressure exerted on members of the NU-based PKB to desert him. Strangely, this pressure, which he says took the form of kidnappings and beatings directed at members of the local parliament, was supposed to have been exerted by Banser. This is the militia group also linked to the NU,[49] thereby providing yet another seemingly inexhaustible illustration of the fluidity of party politics and allegiances. This kind of fluidity again raises questions about the basic nature, social role and functions of political parties in post-authoritarian Indonesia, especially because the same observation, as has been mentioned, has been applied to post-authoritarian Southeast Asian societies like Thailand (see Ockey 2003; Shatkin 2003) and the Philippines (see Abinales and Amoroso 2005).

POLITICAL ENFORCERS IN THE NEW LOCAL POLITICS

As mentioned, also among the local elites of post-authoritarian Indonesia are the former enforcers and henchmen of the New Order, who had always straddled the criminal underworld and 'legitimate' economic, political and social activities. According to Ryter, members of organisations like the Pemuda Pancasila, which was feared despite the demise of the New Order that it had served so well, have pursued a twin strategy of survival in post-authoritarian Indonesia. The strategy has included involvement in party and parliamentary politics as well as efforts to 'maintain or expand' control over 'sectors of the informal and illegal economy' (Ryter 2002: 195) that provide their main sources of income. Clearly, their experiences under the New Order would have given them ample experience in pursuing these aims.

The case of David Purba in Serdang Bedagai in North Sumatra was already referred to in relation to the rise of political power and ambitions of local entrepreneurs; indeed, it is often difficult to extricate the goons and thugs of the New Order completely from its strata of local businessmen, who are often engaged in such activities as construction and contracting for government projects. Today, many who were nurtured within the structures of the New Order's state-supported youth/gangster organisations remain active in organised crime activities. Insofar as many of these were incubated within the state authoritarianism of the New Order, parallels can be found with some of the experiences of post-Soviet Russia. There, as Shelley notes, 'the origins of crime lie deep in the Soviet period', and it is the individuals who had 'access to the resource of the Russian state' that make up the most significant part of organised crime in Russia today (Shelley 2001: 249). As in post-Soeharto Indonesia, many of the most powerful Russian criminals get themselves elected to political office, including at the local levels of politics (Shelley 2001: 252), thus acquiring new levels of legitimacy and social status that they could not have previously enjoyed.

In North Sumatra, organisations of goons and thugs like the IPK and the Pemuda Pancasila have traditionally been dominant players in the underworld (Ryter 2002) and in the private business of providing 'security'. However, they have been challenged in the post-Soeharto era by the emergence of the militia arm of the PDI-P, known as the *satgas* or literally, 'task force', which nevertheless has been notoriously ridden with internal rivalries and conflicts.[50] Members of the PDI-P *satgas*, moreover, appear to have been recruited from within such organisations as the Pemuda Pancasila (Ryter 2002: 196). Perhaps given its disparate components, the PDI-P *satgas* has been particularly conflict-prone internally; its different branches have been known to fight with one another in support of different political protagonists within the party. This was the case, as we shall see, during the period of conflict within the PDI-P over the mayoralty of Surabaya in 2002. Moreover, a number of 'rival' militias with claimed, if informal, links to the PDI-P have also emerged here and there[51] to become immersed in intra-party conflicts. The most obvious role of organisations such as these is to provide muscle power and mass mobilisation services when they have been needed in some of the more intense cases of conflict.

In North Sumatra as well, Syamsul Arifin, who is a veteran of a number of New Order-era youth/gangster organisations, provides one of the better examples of those who rose from the ranks of regimist enforcers but who now thrive in the post-authoritarian environment; he was successfully elected *bupati* of Langkat in 1999, re-elected in 2004—and finally won the North Sumatran governorship in 2008. Admitting to adolescent dreams of becoming a 'godfather', he has had a curious personal history in both the Pemuda Pancasila and the Forum Komunikasi Putera-Puteri Purnawirawan Indonesia, or Communications Forum for Sons and Daughters of Indonesian Retired Servicemen (FKPPI), which have traditionally been rivals, and claims to be the son of a colonial-era intelligence operative. Indeed he is well connected: having risen through the ranks of various state-connected 'youth' groupings, he was also the head of the North Sumatra branch of the Komite Nasional Pemuda Indonesia, or Indonesian Youth National Committee (KNPI), the New Order's peak youth organisation. Not surprisingly, Syamsul Arifin was already a member of the Langkat local parliament during the rule of the New Order. With a range of business interests to boot, including in the timber industry, he boasts that eighteen generals attended his first inauguration ceremony in 1999.[52] Given the history and political background of this particular individual, it is not surprising that his tenure has been, albeit not uniquely, coloured by allegations of violence and intimidation instigated against political opponents, as well as corruption and abuse of power.[53] Interestingly, the staunchly Islamic PKS, which likes to project an image of political integrity, backed Syamsul Arifin in his eventually successful bid for the governorship of North Sumatra in 2008 (*Republika Online* 25 January 2008), after which he replaced Rudolf Pardede.

In East Java, the constellation of organisations of goons and thugs is rather different from North Sumatra. There, it is the Banser, the long-present and feared militia force linked to the NU, which is the dominant provider of services related to political muscle power and coercion. The IPK, largely a North Sumatran phenomenon, does not exist in East Java, though the Pemuda Pancasila and assorted gangs, including that of Madurese migrants, make up the rest of the constellation of gangland, especially in the bustling port city of Surabaya.

Individuals whose social base essentially lies in the array of organisations that provide muscle power and 'security' have not been so uniformly successful in the post-authoritarian context. In East Java, for example, the New Order's former enforcers have notably thrived less in their forays into local politics than their counterparts in North Sumatra. In fact, it is difficult to find an individual approximating the power and stature of Syamsul Arifin or

David Purba in the East Java context, though one does encounter people like Lutfilah Masduki, a provincial parliamentarian and, simultaneously, head of the PKB *satgas*.[54] One Pemuda Pancasila leader and contractor in Surabaya calculates, for example, that its cadres control less seats in local legislative bodies in East Java than they did under Soeharto, attributing this to a lack of swiftness on the part of local members in abandoning Golkar for other parties in the 1999 elections, in which the former New Order state party came second to the PDI-P. He claims this was different to the situation in North Sumatra, where Pemuda Pancasila members were more politically adroit and quickly latched on to new alliances. Nevertheless, he suggested in 2003 that the Pemuda Pancasila had a still considerable 10 to 15 members in sub-provincial legislative bodies in East Java but none in the provincial parliament, and around 400 across parliaments all over Indonesia. He also admits that no Pemuda Pancasila cadre had been able to make it to the level of *bupati* or mayor anywhere in East Java up to then.[55]

It is clear therefore that political gangsters and the like have only really encountered a mixed level of success in their efforts to reposition within Indonesia's democracy and local politics. This is in spite of the previously mentioned opportunities that they have been able to exploit as providers of muscle power. The challenges they face, and which may place a ceiling on how high their fortunes can rise, will be scrutinised further in Chapter 6.

In the meantime, what the present chapter has done is to identify some of the more salient types of elites in post-authoritarian local politics in Indonesia. It has presented some personalities who provide a good gauge of the kinds of social backgrounds and interests that are readily associated with such elites and the strategies they employ to maintain their political ascendance and to secure further advancement. These strategies invariably involve control of such newly important institutions of local governance as the offices of mayors and that of the *bupati*, as well as local parliamentary bodies. Also important has been access to material resources, and sometimes, instruments of coercion and selective mass mobilisations, especially in an increasingly rough-and-tumble world of local politics and of electoral contests.

Yet, the road to local power is hardly a smooth one. Contests for control over local institutions and their resources, over elected positions, party branches and militia groups are intense, costly, and more than occasionally violent. In itself, this ensures that the types of local elites identified above are especially well-placed to contest the arena of post-authoritarian local politics. Significantly, as discussed in the next chapter, such contests are also becoming increasingly costly, not in the least in straightforward monetary terms, thereby providing the impetus for officials and politicos to recoup their investment during their terms in office. The logical implication is that these contests also invariably pave the way for the further proliferation of predatory forms of power at the local level. As social and political ascendance are built on the success of shifting alliances and networks, they become contingent as well on the capacity to generate private accumulation on the basis of control over public institutions and resources.

Essentially, this has been a major problem for advocates of social change through institutional reform and engineering. The reality is that the 'right' institutions can hardly ever be supplied as a matter of policy choices only, no matter how seemingly 'enlightened' or well-intentioned. These institutions will have to operate within an existing context of social power and interests, which may drive them in directions that have little directly to do with the original intent.

This observation forms an important component of an explanation for the puzzle of 'unintended outcomes' of institutional reforms. In the gritty world of local politics in post-authoritarian societies like Indonesia—and quite clearly also in Thailand and the Philippines—it matters little that the originators of reform packages are state officials imbued with technocratic rationality or professional consultants and advisers perched in the mighty offices of international development organisations. Such is the case so long as the institutions, reformed or newly created, can be penetrated and appropriated by interests pursuing a wholly different kind of logic of power.

Chapter Five

Money Politics and Thuggery in New Local Democracies

This chapter focuses on the processes and mechanisms through which predatory local elites maintain and secure their position in the post-authoritarian context. As in the previous chapter, much attention is paid to the conflicts that have surfaced within arenas of electoral contests, or as epiphenomena, in the form of friction within political parties or between individual actors. But what are some of the more deeply-rooted, underlying social bases for such friction and conflicts, and how are they ultimately related to contests over the localisation of power? In answering this question, the chapter necessarily highlights the role of money politics, the selective use of political thuggery, and the changing position of an array of often uniformed gangster/youth organisations and civilian militia in the mechanics of electoral democracy. As in the previous discussion, the empirical material here is mainly taken from the contemporary experiences of North Sumatra and East Java, especially their capital cities of, respectively, Medan and Surabaya.

Local Money Politics

It has been noted by numerous observers that money politics and violence play a big part in local contests over power in the Southeast Asian societies of Thailand and the Philippines. In Thailand, the practice of money politics had already begun in earnest by the 1970s but became increasingly prevalent with the parliamentary politics and gradual democratisation of the 1980s. Demonstrating the appeal of possessing local political power here, the price of being elected into local office has been constantly rising for some time. Arghiros, for example, notes a local Thai politician's estimate that during the course of three elections, taking place between 1985 and 1995, his personal campaign expenses had grown by no less than twenty-five times (2001: 209). Clearly, such a development has had a distinct impact on the actual operations of democracy, nationally as well as at the local level. Much of this money goes to outright vote-buying; Shatkin (2003: 16) cites an estimate by one prominent Thai NGO that US$4 billion (at the time about 100 billion baht) was spent on vote-buying in the 1996 elections, and there is no reason to think that the amount has not been continuously rising, even with the recent turmoil in Thai democracy. In other words, the elections industry is one of considerable size, especially for a country of Thailand's socio-economic profile, as it is in the Philippines and lately in Indonesia too. In the Philippines, the operations of illegal lotteries known as *jueteng*—which can involve astronomical sums under the non-transparent control of politicians—play a critical role in funding especially local level contests (Philippine Center for Investigative Journalism 2001: 86–89; Co et al. 2007: 171). These effectively help to finance escalating campaign costs that could involve expenditures such as expensive television advertisements in the case of major politicians (Co et al. 2007: 157).

In post-authoritarian Indonesia, money politics—taking on a variety of forms—has become the main political game in town and village. In an analysis of legislative elections of April 2004, the daily *Media Indonesia* reported that the PDI-P charged individuals between Rp 200 and Rp 300 million to be included in the official list of candidates for provincial parliamentary seats and Rp 400 million for national parliamentary seats, as did Golkar (*Media Indonesia* 21 December 2003). One local parliamentarian from Medan claims that each prospective candidate for the April 2004 legislative elections had to personally allocate at least Rp 150 million just to ensure formal registration while describing, with notable exasperation, the growth of a financially-draining semi-underground elections 'industry'.[1] It has now become accepted widely that prospective candidates for political office need to make hefty payments to party officials at various levels to ensure their presence on such lists. It is partly because of these payments that the issue of allowing non-party, independent candidates to contest local elections became a topic of public debate.

In fact, the practice of charging candidates for official political party endorsement was to occur with greater impunity in 2005, when the first batch of local elections for governors, mayors and *bupati* by popular vote took place. As Choi (2005) observed, the new electoral system, based on Governmental Regulation no. 6/2005, effectively transferred some of the money politics occurring in the institution of local parliament, formerly vested with the power to elect local government heads, to that taking place more patently in relation to political party branches and their executive bodies. According to the 2005 Regulation, only a party or coalition of parties in control of 15 per cent or more of seats in the relevant parliament has the right to nominate candidates for governor/*bupati*/mayor and their deputies, thereby making the executive bodies of local political party branches very strategic gatekeepers to power. Thus, large sums of payment from potential nominees to political party branches were typically necessary before any aspiring politico could even take to the electoral field in 2005.[2] Rinakit (2005: 2) estimates that one-fifth of candidates' campaign funds go toward paying for their nomination. What in fact emerged, therefore, is a veritable auction house-like system where the highest bidder would likely win a party nomination—one that is obviously bereft of any mechanism of public accountability.

The revamped electoral system, moreover, helped to induce the monetary price of winning local office to spiral almost out of control, as the kind of mass vote-buying typically associated in Southeast Asia with elections in places like rural Thailand has become a more pervasive feature of local election contests. How much so is difficult to estimate with precision for obvious reasons, though Rinakit (2005: 2) suggests—on the basis of observations on ninety elections—that successful gubernatorial candidates would have to spend, on average, US$10 million dollars, and those for *bupati* and mayor, up to US$1.6 million. Again, such generalised figures must be approached with caution—in major cities like Surabaya or Medan, winning the mayoral position will likely cost much more than that, as discussed below.

Nevertheless, there were clearly good reasons—from a strictly technical, institutional reform point of view—for shifting to a system of popularly-elected heads of local government. In theory, the new electoral system would more likely result in local governments that are closer and more accountable to the ordinary people of local communities. Furthermore, the reform was also in keeping with the populist aspirations of local NGO activists across Indonesia who had been critical of the flaws of Indonesia's democracy and who wanted a system that would provide the conditions for more transparent practices of governance. In other words, direct local elections satisfied the good governance dispositions of state and international technocrats, while simultaneously satisfying the local community empowerment ideals of populist NGOs. So, what actually has been the problem?

Again, it is the broader terrain within which the electoral reform took place that needs to be taken into account, which ensured that the objective of curbing money politics, or of creating local governments that are more accountable and responsive to the needs of local communities, would not be achieved by this reform. Not only were the changed rules hijacked again by still-ascendant local predatory interests, they broadly conformed as well to the need of heads of local governments to free themselves from over-dependence on local legislative bodies, particularly at the onset of their tenure—and thus NGOs later pressed for the idea of independent, non-party candidates.[3] It is well known that relations between mayors or *bupati* and local legislatures can frequently get strained (e.g. Lay 2002). The former typically accuse the latter of lacking in individuals with the required skills and intellect to monitor the workings of local government.[4] Even this sort of friction has a more tangible, material basis; it is often alleged that heads of local government have to provide kickbacks to local legislators to ensure approval for new policies as well as acceptance of their all-important annual and end-of-term financial reports (see Kurniawan et al. 2003: 23). The system, however, effectively enhances the authority of local heads of government vis-à-vis local legislative bodies. Of potential importance for the longer term is that, freed to some extent from their previous over-dependence on parliament, the emergence of the kind of local 'strongman' or 'notable' more closely resembling that which Sidel (2004) associates with Thai or Filipino experiences may yet be facilitated in Indonesia.

In fact, contests for offices such as *bupati* and mayor in today's Indonesia have become ever more feverish and costly. This is not surprising as the potential economic gains to be accrued from heading local governments remain tantalising, as are the opportunities to build more personalised instruments of power and networks of patronage through control of local administrative and political machineries. Thus, it may not be necessary for ambitious local politicians to aspire to partake in 'higher' level politics and political struggles. What is on offer locally can be enticing enough and sufficient to form the building blocks for local coalitions of predatory power and to sustain them materially.

Not surprisingly, the first truly intense local election in post-Soeharto Indonesia occurred in North Sumatra, which even during the days of the rigidly-controlled New Order had a reputation for comparatively rough politics. Indeed, before the New Order, North Sumatra was a major site from which military-sponsored mass and youth organisations would begin to enter into open conflict with those affiliated with the Indonesian Communist Party; this foreshadowed the open violence that would take place across many parts of the country during the military-led anti-communist pogroms of the mid-1960s.[5]

The election in question involved the mayoralty of the particularly tough North Sumatran capital city of Medan held in March 2000—the city's first after the fall of Soeharto. It was on this occasion that Abdillah (see Chapter 4), a former official of the North Sumatra branch of Gapensi, the Association of Indonesian Construction Businesses, reportedly paid off sixteen parliamentarians belonging to the PDI-P—the dominant faction in the Medan legislature—to ensure success in his first foray into electoral politics. Each of these parliamentarians, including local PDI-P notable and then head of Medan parliament, Tom Adlin Hadjar, was believed to have received a relatively meagre Rp 25 million for his or her support (*Kompas* 23 March 2000). This caused acute embarrassment for the national party leadership under Megawati Soekarnoputri, which had supported the aforementioned career bureaucrat, Ridwan Batubara.[6] Though it is unclear why the choice of Batubara was made in Jakarta and whether it involved monetary transactions, what is certain is that the Megawati leadership's overlooking of party apparatchik and activists at the local level caused a great deal of discontent within the PDI-P's Medan branch.

One may already notice in this case the beginnings of a now growing impulse emanating from local coalitions of power to carve out a niche relatively free from the dictates of those based in Jakarta. Local PDI-P politicos went on to explain that they had refused to back Batubara as a mark of protest against the Jakarta leadership's perceived intrusion into local power contests, which in this case took the form of backing a bureaucrat who had little direct ties to local party cadres[7]—a decision that would conceivably have ramifications on the way that the spoils of power would be disbursed. Indeed, the scent of money politics in this particular occasion had been so strong that prior to voting day the Medan media had published admonitions from local notables that the election should be postponed, with one stating that the process was going to be akin to that of choosing between different 'mafias'.[8]

Subsequently reprimanded for not sticking to the official party line, the Medan legislators in question were in fact also the victims of physical intimidation carried out on behalf of Abdillah, the nominee of a Golkar-led coalition, by a motley group of supporters. The colourful and brazen Martius Latuperisa, then a Medan parliamentarian with close links to the military as well as leader of the local FKPPI, confesses to having abducted and threatened the PDI-P legislators into casting their vote for Abdillah. By his own admission, he made them choose between accepting 'the money or the gun'.[9] The scandal that ensued caused a delay in the inauguration of Abdillah and his then-running mate Maulana Pohan. Their official inauguration (by governor Teuku Rizal Nurdin) as mayor and deputy mayor, respectively, only took place in April under circumstances that have been described as abrupt and secretive (*Edison* 24–31 May 2000).

Although well publicised, the events in Medan that have been described were hardly exceptional. In truth, reports proliferated at roughly the same time throughout many parts of Indonesia about the deployment of violence during local elections following the fall of the New Order, combined with monetary incentives, geared to influence the vote of local parliamentarians. In North Sumatra alone, thirty-seven local parliamentarians from different towns and *kabupaten* were investigated for involvement in scandals of money politics in 2000; this really should be viewed as only the tip of the iceberg (*Media Anak Bangsa* 7–8 September 2000). The intimidation and bomb threats in Sleman were already noted but in the *kabupaten* of Karo in North Sumatra, mass mobilisations by competing candidates were compounded by the mysterious razing of the local parliament house during the 2000 *bupati* election, in a prolonged conflict that lasted no less than eight months between the nominees respectively advanced by the PDI-P and Golkar.[10]

One particularly spectacular mass mobilisation in the early post-Soeharto period on behalf of the PDI-P was believed to have been orchestrated by Rudolf Pardede himself (see Chapter 4), in a move to stamp his authority over the party in North Sumatra soon after having taken over leadership of the provincial branch.[11] The election of the *bupati* of Sampang in East Java in the same year was also a grim affair by any standard (see *Tempo Interaktif* 14

September 2000; *Jakarta Post* 8 October 2000; Lay 2002; Malley 2003: 113) and pitted the defeated supporters of then President Abdurrachman Wahid's PKB against a candidate backed by the PPP (Nurhasim 2005: 27–78). It must be remembered that rural East Java is the main stronghold of the PKB, and so the defeat was a particularly hard slap on the face. The Sampang election dispute took a full year to resolve but not before the local parliament house was destroyed in a mysterious fire similar to that in Karo.

One of the consequences of such tactics was that it became difficult for central party leaderships in Jakarta to force local politicos to hold to official party lines as demarcated from above during periods of crisis. This was evidently a particularly bad problem for the PDI-P, which had grown so rapidly within the first few years of Soeharto's fall and was the party 'in power' nationally during Megawati Soekarnoputri's presidency between July 2001 and October 2004. In July 2003, the party announced that it would replace twenty of its local legislators across the country for lack of discipline. Interestingly, the right of central party leaderships to recall 'rebellious' legislators had been reinstated in 2003 after it had been scrapped in 1999, when it was considered an undemocratic mechanism that had been used many times during the Soeharto-era to curtail parliamentary independence (*Jakarta Post* 16 July 2003). The re-instatement of the recall mechanism indicated the high level of tension emerging between central party leaderships and local politicos in the context of decentralisation.

Moreover, also in July 2003—at a time when many gubernatorial contests were being fought—the PDI-P central leadership fired the party chairman in the province of Central Java for having dared to announce his intention to contest the gubernatorial race that year, even though the party had formally endorsed someone else. This was merely a repeat of actions taken slightly earlier in the context of provincial-level elections occurring in Jakarta, Lampung and Bali (*Jakarta Post* 22 July 2003; *Jawa Pos* 28 July 2003). What this kind of development showed, in fact, was that central leaderships of parties—most obviously in the case of the PDI-P—were unable to 'trust' their local political operatives given the unpredictability of political contests where money politics and political thuggery were thrown into the equation. At the same time, local politicos who had made their careers and reputations by developing strong bases and networks of patronage at either the provincial or sub-provincial levels were getting increasingly aggravated that, again especially in the case of the PDI-P, non-party cadres were being promoted because of deals believed to have been made by such individuals with the central party leadership. As suggested earlier, such a tendency had potentially severe implications for the way that the spoils of political power were to be disbursed at sub-national levels.

Returning to the case of Medan, once in office in April 2000, Mayor Abdillah was to rule quite flamboyantly but adroitly as well. Given his background in the construction industry, it was no surprise that Abdillah was known to favour expensive though popular projects involving new lights to brighten up the city, as well as the development of flashy new shopping centres. So successful was he in placating potential rivals that for his re-election bid in 2005 the mayor was able to cobble together an impressive coalition of otherwise mutually hostile parties, including Golkar, the PDI-P and the PPP. Abdillah's social standing was further lifted when he was granted the traditional Malay noble title of 'Datuk' by the local notables of that community (*Medan Bisnis* 17 June 2005). He was only seriously challenged by the Muslim-oriented PKS, which had been emphasising, nationally and locally (*Analisa* 17 June 2005), a platform that placed importance on integrity and incorruptibility, as well as its image as rank outsiders in the electoral process.

Abdillah's re-election campaign in 2005 was said by insiders to involve a war chest of approximately 50 billion rupiahs,[12] a royal sum that would have considerably dwarfed the resources available to career bureaucrat Maulana Pohan, the incumbent's own former deputy and rival for the top position in town.[13] Pohan's running mate, Sigit Pramono Asri, a former HMI activist, was head of the PKS faction in the Medan parliament. From Pohan's point of view, the PKS connection and support provided the credentials for integrity that was obviously calculated to divert voters' attention from the fact that he was part of the same Abdillah administration of 2000–2005 that he was criticising for financial mismanagement. Indeed, the dividing line between the allegedly corrupt and the supposedly virtuous was much more blurred than would appear at first glance, in this particular case as well as often across Indonesia. Pohan and Sigit were in fact joined by low-ranking members of the PDI-P (*Sumut Pos* 15 June 2005), and some of its militia (*Medan Bisnis* 17 June 2005) who went against party discipline partly as a result of mobilisation by local political figure, Marlon Purba.[14] A former North Sumatra provincial parliamentarian, he was also once head of the feared North Sumatra PDI-P *satgas* before he fell afoul of Rudolf Pardede. Rather less than an icon of incorruptibility, Marlon Purba was in fact a former policeman *and* convicted murderer, who admitted to having run illegal gambling rackets, and whose current businesses included the sale of firearms 'obtained from the police'.[15]

Contests over control of the mayor's office in the East Java capital of Surabaya have been only slightly less controversial. In fact, while the election of the mayor of Medan in 2005 proceeded relatively smoothly in the context of the new system of direct elections, in Surabaya it descended into a particularly bitter wrangle over the validity of results, which favoured the incumbent, the PDI-P's Bambang Dwi Hartono. Perhaps part of the reason was that the candidates in Medan were so obviously unequally matched; Abdillah's resources, for example, meant that he was able to 'buy' the support of the local press according to local media watchdogs,[16] as well as engage the services of the city's gangs and militia groups to undertake mass mobilisations of support on his behalf.[17] Furthermore, during his first term in office, Abdillah the businessman had stamped his authority over officialdom in Medan and procured the support of a disparate range of local politicos, in a way that Bambang Dwi Hartono was never able to do; the latter was to face constant challenges from within his own party relating to intense competition for control of the local party machinery. Still, Abdillah's freewheeling ways would eventually land him in trouble; he was to be the subject of a corruption investigation by the Indonesian Anti-Corruption Commission in early 2008 for alleged budgetary misappropriations (*Waspada* 7 January 2008) and was subsequently convicted.

Significantly, both Abdillah and Bambang Dwi Hartono had been regarded as virtual political party outsiders upon their initial ascension to power, though the latter was in fact already a junior pro-Megawati activist in 1995 (Nurhasim 2005: 104) and later served as an official in the PDI-P Surabaya branch. Still, Bambang Dwi Hartono hardly ceased to be seen as an imposition from 'above' by many local party cadres, especially within his own PDI-P. Many such cadres had grown ever keener to break free of the shackles imposed by the Jakarta leadership to take advantage of the local opportunities presented by decentralisation. As a result, the mayor was constantly under siege by the local parliament, in which his own party was the dominant force. For, example, Bambang Dwi Hartono was accused by a parliamentary commission of improprieties in the sale of land owned by the city to private investors (*Surya* 27 March 2002). He was also stridently opposed in his efforts to replace senior city government officials with new ones (*Surya* 24 August 2002).

Though he would not have likely survived for long if many local PDI-P politicos did not in fact tow the party line to support him,[18] the Surabaya mayor was regarded for many years by a great number of his colleagues as either a relative lightweight or a Johnny-come-lately who did not suffer the worst of the repression the party had to withstand during the latter years of the Soeharto period. They refer therefore to the long bygone days when Megawati was considered by the New Order a dangerous possible rallying point for opposition groups due to her Soekarno family lineage. Indeed, the experience of having 'defended' the party against Soeharto's repression seemed to have become a 'badge of honour' among PDI-P local politicos, and not just in East Java or Surabaya, especially in view of the number of 'migrants' the party came to accommodate as soon as political circumstances had changed with the fall of Soeharto.

Given the internal dissent to his leadership in Surabaya, Bambang Dwi Hartono was later to be much assisted by the elevation of a distinctly non-party cadre as his running mate in 2005, Arief Affandi, chief editor of the flagship daily of the giant media conglomerate based in Surabaya, *Jawa Pos*. Arief Affandi was in a position not only to provide material resources but also, given the number of publications controlled by *Jawa Pos*, to secure a valuable instrument of election propaganda in a contest that was undertaken on the basis of direct popular elections (*Jakarta Post* 16 February 2005; *Jakarta Post* 27 June 2005).

In any case, it should be noted that Bambang Dwi Hartono's initial ascension to power took place under rather bizarre circumstances even in the context of the vagaries of Indonesian local political alliances. His immediate predecessor Sunarto Sumoprawirno was initially a New Order-era Golkar appointee (in 1995) better known as Cak Narto[19] and had gone to Australia for medical treatment in October 2001. For reasons that remain unclear, he ended up being away and neglecting the responsibilities of his office for a prolonged time. It is widely believed that the mayor had in fact made a deal with Bambang Dwi Hartono that he would hand over power to the latter within two years as part of an effort to split the PDI-P vote and win re-election in early 2000 in the new post-Soeharto context. The alleged deal had already caused much bad blood within the local PDI-P, with rumours of bribes being paid to some PDI-P local parliamentarians also being rife (Nurhasim 2005: 100–112).

Upon Cak Narto's 'disappearance', the PDI-P faction in Surabaya's parliament then led an effort to topple Cak Narto, finally succeeding in January

2002 when local parliamentarians voted to appoint Bambang Dwi Hartono, then the deputy mayor, as replacement. In a move reflective of the continuing tug-of-war between nationally and sub-nationally based interests, the Indonesian minister of Home Affairs annulled the decision, stating that local parliaments could elect executives of local government but could not dismiss them, as that power was his. As a means of overcoming the impasse, the minister appointed the governor of East Java, retired general and New Order appointee, Imam Oetomo, as acting mayor. In June 2002, the governor appointed Bambang Dwi Hartono as the new mayor, a decision that was supported by the minister of Home Affairs under the Megawati government of the day, another New Order-era senior general named Hari Sabarno.

Even though the local parliament's original decision was in effect now upheld, albeit through a rather circuitous route, this was not to be the end of the highly unsavoury episode. Soon enough, the same parliament that had appointed him started new impeachment proceedings against Bambang Dwi Hartono, under the pretext that he was responsible for the unsatisfactory status of his predecessor's financial report to the legislature (*Surya* 12 July 2002). What had actually transpired behind the scenes was another major split within the Surabaya PDI-P. The rival groups were led by Armudji, head of the PDI-P faction in the Surabaya parliament, and Mochamad Basuki, speaker of the Surabaya parliament as well as the PDI-P branch in the city—backed by parliamentarian Isman, who laid claim to Armudji's post (*Surya* 23 March 2002, 2 April 2002).

Backed by party bigwigs in Jakarta, Armudji supported Bambang Dwi Hartono's appointment, while local party boss Mochamad Basuki viewed it as a manifestation of Jakarta's intrusion into the affairs of the local party branch.[20] In other words, as local party boss, Basuki effectively wanted the right to have a major say in who would be mayor. Given the strategic position of mayor in such a major city as Surabaya in relation to the potential economic opportunities presented by decentralisation, this was to be expected. Basuki, moreover, laid claim to having been at the forefront of PDI-P efforts to defeat Golkar in Surabaya in the 1999 elections. Exasperated by incessant party bickering, however, Megawati Soekarnoputri put Basuki in his place and ordered the dismissal of the whole board of the Surabaya branch of the PDI-P. She also threatened local legislators that they would be written off the party list for the next elections if they did not behave (for details of the entire affair, see SCTV at www.liputan6.com 16 January 2002, 15 July 2002, 10 October 2002, as well as *Gatra* 18 July 2002).

This particularly extraordinary episode in Surabaya local politics would continue to have repercussions on patterns of conflict between local and central PDI-P officials over the control of local institutions and resources. Indirectly at stake were the real and material, rather than merely legal-formal, parameters of decentralisation and local autonomy. The outcome of the conflict would entail the political downfall of Basuki and his imprisonment for corruption as well as charges of corruption laid against a number of his parliamentary allies (*Jawa Pos* 17 July 2003: 25; *Kompas* 22 April 2003). The process also involved violent clashes between rival units of PDI-P militia forces[21] for and against Mayor Bambang Dwi Hartono, thereby vividly illustrating the volatility of a system of power run by money politics and, when necessary, political thuggery.[22] In the end, however, it was plain that the local politicos had in fact lost with the fall of Basuki and his allies. The centre had therefore asserted its authority over the local.

Notwithstanding the physical clashes involved in the case above, money politics rather than overt political thuggery has tended to be a more overt part of the political game as far as East Java is concerned, at least until the advent of local direct elections in 2005. It must have helped that the local business community, certainly in Surabaya, had been able to utilise money to buy security in exceptionally effective ways in the past. In May 1998, when many major cities in Java were rocked by racial riots while security forces mysteriously disappeared, the predominantly ethnic Chinese business community was reportedly able to guarantee relative peace in Surabaya by paying generous sums of money for the services of the local military (Dick 2002: 475).

The case of the gubernatorial election in East Java in July 2003 offers a good window into the workings of money politics and electoral contests in post-authoritarian Indonesia, particularly prior to the institution of direct popular elections in 2005.[23] The run-up to this election—confined to voting within the chambers of the provincial parliament as under the old system— was not marred by any real outbreak of violence or demonstration of prowess through mass mobilisations, which had often accompanied the most controversial of recent local and regional elections by that time. Indeed, the entire process seemed almost anachronistically peaceful and orderly, though fraught with the kind of tension that suggested that the environment could have precipitously changed. The activists of youth/gangster organisations and civilian militia were actually largely conspicuous due to their absence; indeed, one suggested that they were paid *not* to create trouble on this occasion and told to remain as inconspicuous as possible.[24] The underlying tense political atmosphere was revealed, however, as the 'safety' of the 100-member legislature was clearly in some doubt until the last minute. Most were holed up in hotel rooms and kept incommunicado for several nights before Election Day, protected by an assortment of goons and thugs employed to roam the hotel lobbies and surrounding areas. The fear was evidently that parliamentarians aligned to one candidate would be abducted by the toughs of another and then intimidated or bribed into changing their allegiance; this was the case, for example, in the race for the mayor's office in Medan in 2000.[25]

If more overt political violence was somehow avoided in this particular case, it is widely believed that money politics was instead especially rife and blatant. Subsequent to the election, some local political actors suggested that provincial legislators tasked with electing a governor were accepting financial bribes offered by both candidates.[26] In fact, rumours had proliferated wildly in Surabaya just prior to Election Day that one legislator's vote was valued at between one to three billion rupiahs by each of the two rival candidate's camps.[27] Months before the elections, a top NU executive in East Java explicitly stated that money would speak loudest in the election and that the winner would be the candidate with the most money (*Kompas* 7 March 2003). Moreover, the gossip mills were kept busy by additional rumours that the candidates' respective war chests were filled by, among others, two infamous ethnic Chinese gambling czars. One was allegedly a local businessman known locally as Wei Fan, while the other was reputedly none other than Tomy Winata, a notorious Jakarta tycoon with close links to major New Order elites; he was also allegedly by then the capital city's dominant force in the underworld.[28] Some sceptical locals even went so far as to view the governorship contest as partly a proxy battle between racketeers for control of the lucrative illegal gambling industry in and around Surabaya.[29]

It should be noted that the eventual winner, retired general and incumbent Imam Oetomo, was backed by the PDI-P at the insistence of the Jakarta party leadership, in spite of vocal protests from East Java cadres who instead supported one of the local party bosses (*Tempo Interaktif* 7 May 2003). Significantly, General Oetomo had been commander of the Brawijaya Division based in East Java (*Kompas* 13 January 2003) during the New Order. His running mate notably was the top provincial bureaucrat, Soenarjo (*Surya* 27 March 2003), regarded as a long-time Golkar rather than PDI-P cadre.

The losing candidate was no representative of any reformist impulse in Indonesian society either; tellingly, neither was he well-rooted in local party machineries. He was Ahmad Kahfi, yet another retired general whose running mate was still another Golkar functionary, the real estate developer Ridwan Hisyam, who had earlier harboured ambitions of running for governor (*Kompas* 6 March 2003). This pairing was strenuously supported by the central leadership of the PKB in Jakarta loyal to Abdurrahman Wahid, at the expense of local cadres who regarded Kahfi, a former deputy governor of Jakarta (*Kompas* 10 March 2003; *Surya* 11 March 2003) as an intruder.[30] He was also viewed as one without an obvious background either in the NU, the East Java-based Muslim organisation that gave birth to the PKB, or the party itself.

Interestingly, Imam Oetomo earlier had failed to secure the support of Abdurrahman Wahid, the chief patron of the PKB, partly because the latter was reportedly displeased with the incumbent governor's interventions in a prior election for the *bupati*-ship of Probolinggo, which a rebel PKB candidate—Hasan Aminuddin—eventually won in what was supposed to be an area in which Gus Dur commanded loyalty (*Kompas* 19 March 2003; *Surabaya Pos* 19 August 2005). Hasan Aminuddin was a PKB functionary and local parliamentary figure whom Gus Dur had dismissed from the party, but who was still able to cobble together local support from party activists to win the election.

The overall composition of candidates in the case of the East Java gubernatorial contest—generals, top bureaucrats and Golkar functionaries, and the parties they had latched onto—is just one reminder of how difficult it is to draw the line between simple 'status quo' and 'reformist' interests in Indonesia today, and of the vagaries of local political alliances and coalitions. As pointed out in Chapter 4, all the major political parties in Indonesia today are inhabited to a significant extent by variations of old New Order elites who have now claimed reformist credentials (Robison and Hadiz 2004). They constitute fragile and tentative alliances that, in a sociological sense, draw on the same pool of predatory interests that had survived the demise of the New Order. This is the case nationally as well as locally, and it explains why two self-proclaimed 'reformist' post-New Order parties, the PKB and the PDI-P, are comfortable in backing old Generals and bureaucrats in major political contests.[31]

There is an underlying dynamic at work as well, which comes replete with new tensions and contradictions. One of the opportunities that came up in the current context is for deals to be made by particular powerful individuals with Jakarta-based coalitions of interests as represented in central party leaderships. A distinctive outcome has been the emergence of tensions *within* the often tenuous alliances that make up formal political party vehicles, as local cadres come to perceive that their entry into the gates of power in the towns and *kabupaten*, or even provincial government, is being blocked from above despite the supposedly rewarding opportunities offered by decentralisation. This was seen in Medan in 2000, Surabaya in 2002, the province of East Java in 2003, and replicated in numerous other cases.

Instruments of Coercion: Gangsters and Militia

If money politics is the cement that holds together political activity in post-authoritarian Indonesia, the use of political violence also became a notable part of the workings of Indonesian democracy, though so far not at levels often associated with Thailand or the Philippines—where political conflicts and electoral rivalries have cost the lives of democracy activists and local politicos alike. Goons and thugs associated with youth/gangster organisations or an array of civilian militia groups have played the role of providing muscle power and security-related services for contending elites. They have also been utilised in organising selective mass mobilisations when required by the exigencies of local contests over power.[32] Still, as shown in Chapter 6, limits seem to be appearing in relation to the usefulness of muscle power, especially during election time, and therefore on the political opportunities open to goons and thugs.

In any case, political violence is far from new in Indonesia; indeed, its selective deployment was part of the way that the New Order maintained political stability for decades—through intimidation and the inculcation of fear. As is well known, from the promulgation of martial law in the late 1950s in the face of separatist rebellions in parts of Indonesia until the demise of the New Order in the late 1990s, the military played a formal, entrenched part in the social, economic and political affairs of local communities in the name of the so-called military dual-function doctrine. As Ryter (2000, 2002) has noted, the maintenance of political order and stability was not undertaken solely by the military/state security apparatus proper, but more typically in-volved the mobilisation of 'youth' gangs whose activities often blurred the difference between legal and criminal activity. In turn, as many have pointed out (see Lindsey 2001; Ryter 2002), the operations of these gangs could not be separated from the interests of the Indonesian military itself, whose local commanders provided the patronage, sponsorship and protection required by members of crime organisations to thrive in a rigidly controlled authoritarian environment.

The most important of New Order-nurtured youth-gangster organisa-tion has always been the nationally-organised Pemuda Pancasila (PP) with its origins in North Sumatra in the 1950s. It was here that the military first decided to mobilise youths and local toughs to confront pro-communist party youth organisations in the context of escalating rivalry with the PKI.[33] The PP was even instrumental in the election of a military-backed mayor of Medan in 1966 soon after the anti-communist pogroms that followed events in Jakarta the previous year and which accompanied the obliteration of the PKI (Ryter 2000). In Jakarta, the national PP is led by long-time chief Yapto Suryosumarno: a lawyer by profession, he is the son of a general and a close associate of the Soeharto family, and was a distant cousin of Soeharto's wife (Ryter 2002: 157). His own ascension to power within the organisation in the 1980s in many ways represented a process of more closely integrating the op-erations of the organisation with the political and business requirements of the Soehartos and other elite families of the New Order. Significantly, these families were then already beginning to actively colonise and appropriate the instruments of state power to further their own interests, which included the building of huge private business empires (Robison and Hadiz 2004). In this context, PP members under Yapto were effectively the personal henchmen and bodyguards of the elite families of the New Order.

Other important New Order-era 'youth' organisations include the FKPPI, the 'communications forum' of the children of retired military officers. It has since splintered badly between those with family ties to the military and those with ties to the police force. Once linked closely to the Soeharto fam-ily as well, this organisation still has a considerable presence throughout the country, including in North Sumatra and East Java. Its long-time leading figure in Medan in North Sumatra was Martius Latuperisa, who was once a Golkar operator and Medan parliamentarian for that party. He later joined the military-sponsored PKP (Unity and Justice Party) following the demise of the New Order and again managed to claim a seat in the local legislature.[34] Circumstances, however, forced Latuperisa to attempt another transformation; in 2003 he joined the Medan branch of the PKB but failed to wrest control of it.[35] As has been mentioned, he had played an important if controversial role in the initial rise to power of Medan's powerful mayor, Abdillah, in 2000.

Notwithstanding the status of the Pemuda Pancasila in Indonesia, the most important youth/gangster organisation in North Sumatra remains the IPK, the Association of Functional Group Youths (Ikatan Pemuda Karya). It is widely believed to dominate the lucrative illegal gambling industry in the city of Medan. The origins of the IPK lie in a split within the PP in the early 1980s, in which the soon to be dominant splinter group was supported by local Chinese businesspeople (*Tempo Interaktif* 14 October 2002) and sections of the local military command, which had developed an interest in organised crime activities and grown wary of the PP's then untrammelled dominance over the underworld.[36] Interestingly, the supreme leader of the IPK, Olo Panggabean, simply known all around Medan and North Sumatra as 'Bang Olo',[37] is often cited by residents as the city's 'night-time' or 'real' mayor—a testimony to his social and political stature in Indonesia's fourth largest city.

It should be noted that local security forces currently still have a strong presence in organised crime activity, as evidenced in a highly publicised gunfight between military and police units in Binjai, North Sumatra, in October 2002 that resulted in at least eight fatalities. The cause was allegedly competition between these forces over illegal drug trafficking in the area (*Jakarta Post* 2 October 2002). It would not be surprising, therefore, to find continuing links between the activities of local military or police commands and existing youth/gangster organisations.

Political gangsters, known by Indonesians as *preman*, arguably can no longer rely completely on military and police patrons of the past in the context of the changes that have occurred in the country since 1998. They have thus been forced to seek new strategies of survival, including providing political parties with a well-oiled apparatus of violence especially when necessary during election periods. Many have observed that the ranks of the PDI-P *satgas* had swelled, particularly during Megawati's tenure as president, from an influx of 'migrants' from organisations such as the PP (Ryter 2005: 22–23). These new members were looking for new patrons within the dominant political power at the time.[38] By now, many leaders of such organisations have come to run local branches of political parties and/or hold important local and even national offices (see Ryter 2002: 195–196). PDI-P officials even admit that all kinds of unsavoury elements were admitted into the party because of the perception that it required muscle power to compete successfully in the new democratic politics of Indonesia. Indeed, one PDI-P national leader admitted that many have now taken up politically important positions within the party (*Tempo Interaktif* 5 April 2003). So bad was the reputation of the PDI-P members of the Surabaya parliament, for example, that they were ordered by their faction leader to undergo urine tests to prove that they did not consume illicit drugs (*Surya* 31 May 2002).

As a consequence, goons and thugs can play a substantial role in the process of settling political disputes and turf wars, including within political party machineries. In Medan, they played a major part in a protracted struggle over control of the local PDI-P branch, which pitted Rudolf Pardede—who had the support of the central party leadership—against an alliance put together by rebellious local politicos. This provided yet another example of local-central conflicts of the kind witnessed over the mayoralties of Surabaya and Medan. In this case, a local figure named Usaha Ginting, who was actually a former minor Golkar functionary and bureaucrat who had migrated to the party[39]— was forced to defend his leadership of the PDI-P branch in Medan against his rival, long-time party activist and operator, Doni Arsal Gultom. Interestingly, Pardede favoured the ailing Ginting over Gultom, whose own controversial election to the disputed post in 2000, involving the mobilisation of goons and thugs, was annulled by the party central leadership in 2003. This prompted a response in the form of a concerted campaign to oust Ginting, which included legal proceedings that were highly publicised in the Medan press.

More dramatically, Gultom's supporters failed to wrest control of the party's provincial branch office in an open show of defiance against both Pardede and the Jakarta central leadership when their 'invasion' was repelled in a bloody confrontation that left two people dead (*Jakarta Post* 27 September 2003). Significantly, given the previous discussion on local strongmen in Southeast Asia (see Chapter 2), Gultom claims that Pardede had him ousted because of his opposition to the businessman's attempt to build a political dynasty by promoting close friends and relatives in the party ranks and as legislative candidates.[40] The failed attack itself was commonly understood to be at least partly the work of then provincial parliamentarian Marlon Purba, who had earlier been pushed out by Pardede as well as the head of the PDI-P's feared North Sumatran *satgas* in favour of a former Pemuda Pancasila thug.[41] Thus, Pardede's retaliations were to be directed not just at Gultom but at Marlon Purba as well, through orchestrated mass mobilisations against him in the provincial parliament house.[42]

Essentially, however, while previously dependent on Golkar and the security forces for their social position, the *preman* have had to be flexible and agile in the current post-authoritarian environment. In this, the political gangster has been no different from the bureaucrat or the businessman. While providing their services, *preman* have simultaneously repositioned themselves and crossed over to various political parties according to local exigencies while abandoning past exclusive political loyalties. According to Ryter, the PP Congress of April 1999 decided that members would be free to join any political party vehicle they liked (Ryter 2002: 196). Thus, gangsters were instrumental in organising rallies for a variety of political parties they joined in the 1999 and 2004 elections (Ryter 2005: 22–23). It is for this reason that such individuals as long-time Pemuda Pancasila and Golkar notable in Labuhan Batu in North Sumatra, Haji Enteng, contested the *bupati*-ship there in 2005 as a nominee of its New Order-era competitor, the Partai Persatuan Pembangunan, or United Development Party (PPP).[43]

More recently, the Pemuda Pancasila has even set up its own Pancasila Patriot Party to contest elections on its behalf, making use of its well-established national organisation and networks.[44] According to Wilson, the cause was a sense of disenchantment with a lack of reward for loyalty to Golkar; he quotes Yapto Suryosumarno proclaiming the better choice of forming a new party compared to the option of sticking to a party that 'doesn't care' (Wilson 2006: 290)

Proof of the agility of the *preman* can also be seen in their forays in the media. It should be noted that since the fall of Soeharto, Indonesia has had one of the most liberal press scenes in Southeast Asia, and the number of print publications and electronic media has grown impressively in just a few years (see Sen and Hill 2000; Heryanto and Hadiz 2005). Moreover, the importance of the media is enhanced in the context of a changed political environment that emphasizes elections and political parties, as has been already alluded to in the above discussions on recent electoral contests in the cities of Medan and Surabaya.

In this connection, it is relevant that gangsters have developed an interest in wielding control over press publications, as well as associations of journalists. In both North Sumatra and East Java, for example, *preman*, who go back and forth between formal business and political spheres, and the shadowy underworld of organised crime, produce tabloids that appear only irregularly for extortion purposes and in connection with competition over contracts or local office.[45] On the other hand, intimidation of the media by politically-connected goons has also become commonplace, replacing the New Order-era practice of muzzling the press through censorship, closures and rigid laws.

In all of Indonesia, it is undoubtedly North Sumatra and particularly Medan and its environs that display most clearly the presence of political gangsterism in post-authoritarian Indonesia. With their camouflage uniforms of distinct colours and regalia, they represent private armies that can be mobilised on behalf of the rich, the powerful and the ruthless. There is probably no other Indonesian city in which the signposts of these organisations are so prevalent and obviously placed, as if designed to demarcate territorial boundaries. Nevertheless, even here the situation can get quite unpredictable, as some of the organisations seem to lack the kind of discipline that is sometimes, though not always correctly, associated with the Nazi and fascist goons of Europe from an earlier time, which they might be compared to in some respects. We see this, for example, in the conflicts pitting members of the same civilian militia against one another. Some observers of gang activity in North Sumatra claim that members seem to literally change uniforms at will, and in spite of the efforts of local leaders, don the colours of whichever organisation is willing to mobilise them at any given time. This has given rise in everyday conversation to the notion of the PS, or *pemuda setempat*; essentially, this refers to local thugs available for hire by anybody and who do not have a particular sense of allegiance to any single organisation.[46]

Ostensibly, 'Islamic' hooligans have also emerged as organised under the banner of the Islamic Defenders Front (FPI) into which, according to Ryter, New Order-era members of youth/gangster organisations were recruited. Such thugs attack places of entertainment in the name of morality but are probably interested as well in turf struggles for the right to collect protection money (Ryter 2005: 22–23). Interestingly, the FPI has been linked strongly in the media with a range of top national political figures, from former Vice-President Habibie to retired General Wiranto to PPP leader Hamza Haz to PAN's Amien Rais. Another 'Islamic' group, which makes a special appeal to the ethnic sentiments of the 'indigenous' Betawi people of Jakarta, is the Betawi Brotherhood Forum (FBR).[47] Engaged in similar activities as the FPI and populated by a number of well-known hoods based in the capital city, it also has links to New Order-era elites (Wilson 2006: 289). Indeed, the genesis of both the FPI and the FBR, and their subsequent development, appears inseparable from connections with the military and/or the police forces (YSIK 2004: 15; Wilson 2006: 285–286)—institutions that have been struggling to maintain their political relevance, as well as economic interests, in the post-Soeharto period.

Groups like the FPI, FBR and the individuals who serve as their leaders and patrons, have been able to bolster their populist credentials by making atavistic and vague references to Islamic morality. In the same vein, regional autonomy has been used as an opportunity by politicos in a host of localities to support bylaws that enforce adherence to a very conservative interpretation of appropriate Muslim dress and public behaviour (especially for women) (*Pelita* 26 May 2006). This is the case even though the decentralisation legislation stipulates that religious affairs continue to be the purview of the central government. Activists from Indonesian women's organisation recognise how the claimed return to local traditions of morality, citing culture and religion, can be severely detrimental to the freedom and rights enjoyed by women (Noerdin et al. 2005: 36-41). The case of such bylaws, therefore, provides a good example of how localism can be appropriated to further socially reactionary projects and agendas in some instances, as discussed earlier. Vulnerable to accusations that they regularly exercise power 'immorally', some local politicos have appeared to take the high ground on public morality issues, not in the least because it conveniently deflects attention from ongoing corrupt practices they may be implicated in. It should be pointed out that these local politicos are not necessarily members of political parties with Islamic or any other religious identity; thus the 'pragmatic' aspects of the call for stricter public observance of claimed Islamic precepts should not be underestimated.

As mentioned, in comparison to North Sumatra, groups of organised thugs have generally been less of a feature of struggles over local office in East Java, though prominent outbreaks of violence were to occur in the latter province upon the implementation of the system of direct elections in 2005. This is the case even in the harsh urban sprawl that is the provincial capital city of Surabaya, where the political enforcers and henchmen of the old

New Order were once also cultivated, typically in close association with the military. The contrast with Medan/North Sumatra is partly reflective of the inability of organisations like Pemuda Pancasila to establish clear dominance over the underworld even during the New Order. In fact, the constellation of gangs appears to be somewhat 'egalitarian' and dispersed in Surabaya, a city renowned for the role of its street toughs in Indonesia's war of Independence in 1945–49, and in which small, diffuse criminal outfits are not clearly beholden to larger, nationally-established organisations. Moreover, it appears that the state security apparatus proper in East Java had come to develop a somewhat different kind of relationship with the underworld to that in North Sumatra—the original 'home' of the youth/gangster organisations (Ryter 2002). Largely bypassing the 'youth' organisations here, the military is said to have more direct links, for example, with lucrative ethnic-Chinese-controlled illegal gambling operations, acting as their immediate protectors and bodyguards.[48] Not surprisingly, military and police units in the province have also been known to fight over control of criminal activity, as they did over the gambling industry in the town of Madiun (*Gamma* 12 October 2001). Moreover, the Indonesian navy and marine forces in the city of Surabaya are believed to have a direct stake in the city's illegal prostitution industry.[49]

In a nutshell, compared to the New Order era, the constellation of politico-gangster organisations in Indonesia has now become exceedingly complex; each of the major parties is equipped with a paramilitary arm that often interlinks with the criminal underworld. The most prominent of this type nationally is undoubtedly the paramilitary arm or *satgas* of the PDI-P, though smaller parties like PAN also come equipped with a small militia. As is well known, the PKB relies on Banser forces traditionally linked to the wider NU organisation that provides the party with its social base, especially in the rural hinterland of East Java. It also comes equipped with an ostensibly separate *satgas* of its own, as well as a special outfit made up of martial arts experts, the so-called *Pagar Nusa*.[50]

In his brief but useful analysis of the gangster and militia organisations in post-authoritarian Indonesia, particularly the array of *satgas* linked to political parties, King (2003) observes that: 'Essentially, *reformasi* was a liberalisation of both party politics and underworld criminal activities. The *satgas* have been the most astute beneficiaries of both processes'. Furthermore, according to King, the *satgas* 'are little more than private armies' serving the needs of the political parties and have an internal structure that 'replicates military orders of hierarchy from the regional commander down to the platoon'. Many *satgas* even have 'logistics and intelligence wings, fatigues and jackboots, and training drills'. King then suggests another strong link with the military and with the New Order: 'Commanders are often former military men or veterans from New Order mass organisations'.

Even in comparatively calm Yogyakarta, where locals are proud of the area's 'high' local traditions and culture, goons and thugs grouped under such organisations as the 'Islamic' Gerakan Pemuda Ka'bah operate under the co-ordination of elements of the local PPP leadership.[51] Moreover, what appear to be newer gangs have emerged in economically and politically strategic places like the capital city of Jakarta (Wilson 2006). In spite of the military's general retreat since 1998, most of these will still benefit from close association with 'backers', especially from within the formal state security apparatus, including the police force.

Nevertheless, in what could be a sign of things to come, brakes have already appeared that have at least temporarily stalled the further rise of the *preman* and which may reveal the potential limits of political gangsterism as a base of social power in the future. Specifically, the self-confidence of activists of youth/crime organisations and of civilian militia group members seems to have dwindled somewhat as a result of being partly marginalised in the direct local electoral contests first held in 2005. By this time, competing political figures had developed an apparent interest in curbing instances of violence during election time. In 2004, many of their leaders failed to win seats in legislative elections, which must have also sapped morale.[52] In general, individuals who are mainly hooligans and thugs appear to have found it difficult to find a niche in the context of a new electoral system based on the popular vote. No longer carrying out the vital role of coercing and intimidating legislators during elections for local heads of government, they are struggling to find new ones to remain relevant in the continuing jostle over power.[53]

Thus, in spite of the overwhelming authority of a towering figure such as Olo Panggabean, internal schisms have appeared even within the more centrally-organised IPK, in which tradition dictates that few subordinates are able to make major initiatives without the approval of the supreme patron.[54] Rank-and-file IPK operatives now speak of the need for regeneration and change within the organisation, comments not directed at the irreproachable Olo, interestingly, but at the generation that had taken over the day-to-day activities and operations. They point to friction between supporters of a more 'professional' model of organisational activity based on engagement in more overtly legitimate business ventures that would provide employment opportunities to the rank-and-file, rather than one primarily based on the old-style model of racketeering and thuggery.[55] The IPK also notably encountered problems in the immediate post-Soeharto period when its chief rival in Medan/North Sumatra, Pemuda Pancasila, apparently encouraged local police to crack down on Olo-controlled gambling operations, which are widely believed to be backed by the local military command. This instigated events in December 1999 that involved the shooting up of the IPK headquarters and even its supreme patron's private residence by members of the local elite police mobile brigade (Ryter 2002: 196).

Nevertheless, the more general rise of the former New Order's echelon of local apparatchik, operators, enforcers and entrepreneurs in post-authoritarian Indonesia could not contrast more starkly with the fortunes of those who were already politically marginalised during the rule of Soeharto. For example, in spite of the new freedoms concerning the right to organise, and successful demands for wage increases, labour remains largely a poorly organised social force. The legacy of systematic disorganisation of mass-based social groups and movements, like that of labour, during the New Order persists in spite of these new freedoms. As has been mentioned, labour activists and organisers are often the victims of goons and thugs, linked to youth-gangster organisations or civilian militia, hired to ensure industrial stability by local businesspeople. With such issues in mind, Chapter 6 will deal more closely with processes of political ascendance and marginalisation associated with the localisation of power in Indonesia.

Chapter Six

The Politics of Inclusion and Exclusion

It has been shown that the localisation of power in Indonesia, as expressed institutionally in decentralisation policy, has frequently resulted in outcomes unintended in the good governance blueprints drawn up by neo-liberal and neo-institutionalist technocrats. It has also proven not to be the bastion favoured by populist NGO activists who tend to seek local sites to produce genuine grassroots social organisations that empower local citizenries. Indeed, local citizenries have only been ambiguously empowered by decentralisation more generally in post-authoritarian Southeast Asia, whether in terms of having a greater presence in and influence over the operations of markets or from the vantage point of successful protection of local communities from the supposed corrosiveness of globalised markets (see Appadurai 2000).

What is less uncertain from the foregoing is that decentralisation in Indonesia has helped to further entrench the position of predatory local elites. The localisation of power has in fact provided a lifeline to a range of New Order-nurtured local elites who were, albeit temporarily, threatened by the unravelling of the centralised authoritarian regime that had fostered them. These have been provided with new opportunities to reinvent themselves according to the exigencies of change and to survive and thrive yet again. In the process, they have selectively latched on to the language and aspects of neo-liberal good governance, as well as localist populism, including the latter's atavistic tendencies when necessary, to carve out a measure of autonomy in relation to Jakarta.

The question that is to be examined further now has to do with how social forces with little access to power and resources, by contrast, have fared under decentralisation and democratisation. Even if there are more avenues for political participation, why are they not consequently better equipped to contest power and challenge the dominant social position of predatory local elites? The discussion strongly suggests that governance reforms technocratically designed to widen the scope of political participation have ironically provided even newer avenues for local elite interests to insulate themselves from challenges from broader civil society. In other words, another quandary has emerged in decentralised, democratised Indonesia: greater scope for political participation has resulted in little discernible empowerment of people who had already been marginalised under centralised authoritarianism.

This is not to say, however, that the unravelling of centralised authoritarianism in Indonesia has not benefited lower class-based social movements in ways that are otherwise quite tangible. Danzer (2006) as well as Affif et al. (2005) and Jeon (2005) firmly argue that democratisation has had noticeably positive effects on the organisational capacities of the peasantry and industrial workers in Indonesia. The main benefit of democratisation for marginalised and formerly politically suppressed social groups is that they can now organise more freely and with less fear of direct repression from the state's security apparatus. During the New Order, as is well known, attempts at independent labour organising or even the slightest hint of labour militancy was often met with the full force of the feared security apparatus of the state (see Hadiz 1997). These sorts of changes should not be taken for granted, as most on-the-ground activists who experienced New Order repression, no matter how disillusioned they may be with the outcomes of *reformasi*, would no doubt concede.

To gauge the situation more closely, along with the attendant tensions and contradictions, this chapter assesses the labour movement in Indonesia in the period of *reformasi*—following the end of the systematic suppression experienced under the authoritarian New Order. The chapter then goes on to take a brief look at social movements based on peasant or 'indigenous' land rights to ascertain whether there have been qualitatively different developments in areas outside labour organising.

The analysis in this chapter continues to go beyond the formal and institutional aspects of power in order to examine the underlying social basis for the further entrenchment of elite predatory interests in post-authoritarian

Indonesia, on the one hand, and the continuing marginalisation of other social interests, on the other hand. It does so by further scrutinising the deeper significance of the advent of direct local elections in 2005. The latter could be held up as a prime example of how *reformasi* has produced a revamp of the institutional makeup of local governance in the direction of greater public participation, but with socio-political outcomes that are at best ambivalent, and at worst, contrary to the expectations of technocrats and localist-populists alike. The contrast between the fortunes of predatory elites and of social movements representing marginalised social interests within Indonesia's decentralised democracy underlines many of the arguments that have been put forward in this book thus far. It constitutes no less than a statement about the actual winners and losers in contests over power in post-Soeharto Indonesia.

Organised Labour and Local Politics

Developments in the area of organised labour are instructive in many ways of the ironies of Indonesia's democratised and decentralised politics. Even after the demise of authoritarianism, labour has been inhibited as an effective social force by the lingering legacy of repression and rigid controls exercised for over thirty years by the New Order, during which labour activism and militancy were often unhelpfully equated with communist resurgence.

It must be recalled that as a consequence, a particular kind of labour activism was induced during the New Order, even that which was oppositional in its stance. As a strategy for coping with authoritarianism, labour was often only very informally and rather amorphously organised throughout the late 1980s and 1990s. When Indonesia's export-led industrialisation strategy on the basis of low-wage exports was proceeding at full speed, many workers who rejected state-sponsored trade unionism were organised through an array of disparate NGOs (Ford 2003) and other labour-based organisations that did not necessarily take the form of trade unions. In order to overcome institutional controls over independent organising, many such vehicles largely concentrated on organising activities at the community level rather than predominantly in the workplace, to steer clear of the state's repressive arm (Hadiz 1997: especially chapter 7). It is in this way that the trajectory of the labour movement in Indonesia has diverged much from that which is commonly associated with the historical experience of workers in the West or some important cases in Latin America.

Thus, the late Soeharto years saw the proliferation of small, often community-based labour-organising vehicles with no formal place in the official industrial relations system, and many of which worked in conjunction with labour-based NGOs (Hadiz 1997; Kammen 1997; Ford 2003). Notably, several independent, though technically illegal, unions were also established during this period; this represented a daring if largely ineffective challenge to the institutional arrangements then in existence that precluded unions apart from the state-sanctioned Federasi Buruh Seluruh Indonesia (All-Indonesia Labour Federation, FBSI)/Serikat Pekerja Seluruh Indonesia (All-Indonesia Workers' Union, SPSI)/Federasi Serikat Pekerja Seluruh Indonesia (Federation of All-Indonesia Workers' Unions, FSPSI). Among the most important of these were the Setiakawan (Solidarity) Labour Union, the Serikat Buruh Sejahtera Indonesia (Indonesian Labour Prosperity Union, SBSI), and the left-wing Front Nasional Perjuangan Buruh Indonesia (Indonesian National Front for Labour Struggles, FNPBI), which had close links to the radical stream of the student movement. All were established in the first half of the 1990s and were almost immediately greeted with harsh reprisals from the authoritarian state. In spite of their endeavours, rigid controls were continually imposed on labour organising, legitimised ideologically in part through the past association of labour militancy with the banned Indonesian Communist Party and the claimed 'indigenous' cultural predisposition to eschew class conflict (see Hadiz 1997). Throughout the New Order, independent labour organising at the workplace level remained both difficult and dangerous.

The fall of the New Order resulted immediately in some positive changes for workers and labour organisations. Among the first steps that the Habibie government took to establish its reformist credentials, and distance itself from Soeharto's, was to annul a wage freeze enforced by the New Order's last minister of manpower (*Jakarta Post* 1 July 1998: 1). Thus, in Jakarta, the minimum monthly wage was set at Rp 198,500, although this was only US$ 14.10 according to exchange rates current at the time. Similar increases were to take place throughout Indonesia but against the background of a national inflation rate of around 80 per cent due to the ongoing deep economic crisis. Since then, labour organisations have been able to press for periodic minimum wage increases; this in itself is notable given continuing high unemployment and the protestations of employers against this form of state intervention in the workings of the labour market.

In 2006, the minimum monthly wage in Jakarta was about Rp 819,000, or roughly US$82, according to prevailing exchange rates. North Sumatra had a minimum wage of around Rp 737,000 while East Java's was a rather low Rp 390,000. It should be recalled, however, that these wage increases took place in relation to constant price hikes and the lifting of government subsidies on various basic services and goods that continually eroded their real value. The official inflation rate for 2005, for example, was in excess of 17 per cent (*Waspada* 17 December 2005; *Jakarta Post* 11 January 2006), when the Indonesian economy had for several years showed signs of partial recovery. Thus workers continue to claim, surely quite understandably, a lack of improvement in their general welfare, and to begrudge the perceived lack of responsiveness to their plight by those in authority.

In terms of the right to organise, it was significant that the Habibie government also ratified seven International Labor Organisation (ILO) conventions on basic labour rights, including Convention 87 on Freedom of Association and Protection of the Right to Organise. These were implemented through presidential executive decisions as well as by regulations set up by the minister of manpower soon after the fall of Soeharto. Later, a law on trade unions was passed that, remarkably given recent history, allowed as few as ten workers to form a union as well as the existence of more than one trade union in any single workplace. The government still maintained the right to withdraw official recognition of unions for administrative reasons, however, and the courts were empowered to dissolve unions whose activities were regarded as threatening to national security (Ford 2006: 4). In spite of such caveats, the institutional framework governing state-labour-capital relations had quickly become substantially different from that which had characterised the New Order.

It may appear to be another puzzle that the dramatic growth of labour-organising activities and vehicles after the fall of Soeharto has not translated into a significantly more effective labour movement than that which currently exists under the new democratic environment. A valid question to ask is why the labour movement has not been able to influence contests over power that take place within a much more participatory institutional framework than existed in previous times. In this connection, it should be pointed out first that workers continued to be constrained by massive unemployment levels produced by the 1997–1998 Asian Economic Crisis and its aftermath, and therefore were almost organisationally paralysed during many of the key struggles that took place in the early post-Soeharto period. During this time, only small radical student groupings briefly acted in proxy for the interests of marginalised sections of broader civil society in the absence of coherent movements representing the lower classes.

Over a million manufacturing jobs were lost as a result of the crisis, according to Ford (2006: 4), and the real wages of those who retained their positions actually dropped by 38 per cent in that economically devastating period. Unemployment (10.3 per cent) and especially underemployment (31 per cent) remained at excruciatingly high levels (*Media Indonesia* 2 July 2005) years after the height of the Asian Economic Crisis. Furthermore, in many large cities, the unemployment rate remained very high after almost a decade had passed; in Medan, it stood at above 19 per cent at the end of 2005 (*Waspada* 17 December 2005). The prevailing economic milieu alone goes a long way in terms of explaining the painfully slow development of labour's organising capacities in spite of the ostensibly more hospitable social and political environment.

There have been other equally important factors at work. While locally-organised, often community-based, semi-formal organising vehicles without clear structures may have been advantageous in avoiding the full brunt of state repression during much of the New Order, they are not necessarily ideal for the emergence of more sophisticated and effective vehicles in a post-authoritarian context. Attempts at developing nationally organised labour movements since 1998 have only met with limited success, partly due to the legacy of a highly fragmented labour movement. At the national level, though dozens of labour federations and a number of confederations were to be registered at the Department of Manpower within several years, a good many of these existed in name only and had a limited level of sustained activity at the level of workers' communities or the workplace.

Therefore, a different route that many organisers quickly adopted after 1998 was characterised by the establishment of what they termed 'local' labour movements or unions that operated in specific localities. This was in itself a tacit admission of the limited capacity to effectively organise nationally. As might be expected, the localities concerned were usually within or around the more industrialised cities of Java and Sumatra, and also on islands like Sulawesi, in which the city of Makassar had grown into a major industrial hub by the 1990s. Thus, in urban formations like Surabaya, locally-organised labour unions such as the Serikat Buruh Reformasi (SBR; Reform Trade Union) emerged within the first years of the post-Soeharto period, together with the Serikat Buruh Independen (SBI; Independent Trade Union); some workers in the Greater Jakarta-West Java area formed the Serikat Buruh Jabotabek (SBJ; The Jakarta-Bogor-Tangerang-Bekasi Trade Union). In Medan, the Serikat Buruh Medan Independen (SBMI; Independent Medan Trade Union) was established in 2003. These organisations were arguably the new institutional expressions of already existing local networks of labour organising that had been forced to keep a low profile during the Soeharto years.

Some of these local unions would prove to be rather militant in nature despite the generally inhospitable socio-economic terrain on which they operated. The SBMI in Medan, for example, was involved in September 2004 in a violent dispute with the management of PT Shamrock, an American-owned producer of rubber gloves for medical use that employed 1,700 workers, mostly young females. The situation became so serious that no less than 200 police personnel were eventually sent in to quell the unrest arising from various labour demands, including that the company adhere to the officially stipulated minimum wage level and improve work safety conditions (see http://www .umwaelzung.info/shamrock/shamrock-en.html.). With the dispute still unresolved a full days days later, it was reported that protesting workers were attacked yet again, this time by a gang of thirty thugs, under the direct gaze of police (see http://www.pkps.org/hotnews/detail.php3?itemid=h_1095488868). According to Wilson and other reports, these thugs were likely hired directly by the factory management (Wilson 2006: 27; also see *Waspada* 12 August 2004, 19 August 2004, and 11 September 2004).

As mentioned earlier, the tactic of hiring goons associated with youth organisations or party militia to intimidate workers during protests and at their homes has become quite prevalent, although workers sometimes report that state security forces will also be directly involved in labour disputes.[1] It is alleged that there is even a *satgas* SPSI for hire in North Sumatra, believed by local workers and labour activists to be made up of moonlighting members of other organisations specialising in the service of intimidation.[2]

In spite of such developments, Jeon (2005) argues that labour's organisational capacities have been steadily rising after democratisation in Indonesia. He makes this contention on the basis of fieldwork from 2001 in East Java, especially on trade union-organising activities at Maspion, a giant, highly diversified company based in the province that is well known for producing household goods.

Owned by the family of Chinese-Indonesian entrepreneur Alim Markus, known to be well connected to local and national political elites, Maspion's array of factories has been notorious as a site of labour disputes since at least the early 1990s. Displaying the fact that the state security apparatus at times still involves itself in quelling labour unrest on behalf of business interests, a 2003 strike at one of Maspion's factories was accompanied by the abduction and assault of three workers by East Java police (*Kompas* 11 June 2003). Focusing on the recent experience of a specific Maspion factory in Sidoarjo, a major industrial enclave just outside of Surabaya, Jeon maintains that labour-organising activities and the experience of labour disputes are now giving rise to a generation of more solidly grassroots-based and competent leadership than ever before. For Jeon, the labour activism in the New Order, while often dramatic, took place with poor organisation and leadership. In contrast, the organisational capacities of workers are improving quietly at the factory level today as a direct result of the erosion of the authoritarian state.

Jeon's favourable prognosis may be supported by some notable, though still rather exceptional, achievements on the part of organised labour, nationally.[3] One such instance was demonstrated when the central Indonesian government dropped its plans to enact labour 'reforms', reportedly due to fierce opposition from unionists to suggested stipulations regulating the firing of workers, outsourcing, and the setting of wage rates (*Financial Times* 13 September 2006). This case is particularly interesting because no less than vice-president and top businessman Jusuf Kalla had been brandishing the labour 'reforms' as essential in attracting foreign investment in resuscitating Indonesia's economy, which is still not yet fully recovered from the Asian Economic Crisis of the previous decade. Kalla was driven to lament, in what amounted to a huge exaggeration, that the power of unions in Indonesia was comparable to that of 'France or America'. He also suggested in apparent exasperation that democracy had gone too far in Indonesia and 'had come too early' (*Financial Times*, 13 September 2006), reflecting dismay that in this particular instance, Indonesia's 'reformed' governance institutions had failed to keep distributional interests at bay.

Senior business figures like Kalla have an interest in overstating the power and influence of Indonesia's labour movement. At the very least, their misrepresentations, which often go widely reported in the mass media, provide added legitimacy to any act designed to pre-empt its real emergence as a social force. In spite of Kalla's complaints, a study of labour relations in two localities, the highly industrialised Tangerang (in the new province of Banten and just outside of Jakarta proper) and Pasuruan in East Java show that workers do have a legitimate reason to be concerned with the increasingly pervasive practice of outsourcing and short-term contracts (Akatiga, TURC, Lab Sosio-University of Indonesia 2006). This is particularly so because the practice is taking place in the context of already widespread unemployment and underemployment.

Notwithstanding the publicised grievances of businesspeople, whether foreign or domestic, the labour movement remains essentially constricted in its capability to influence the fundamental agenda of social and political reform in Indonesia. Typically ignored at the national level, workers' organisations have been marginal in local contests over power in the context of decentralisation and local autonomy, where the reform agenda has been largely shaped by political and economic interests unconnected, and even hostile, to that of the labour movement. Apart from some well-coordinated mass mobilisations, notably those conducted on Labour Day on 1 May, cross-class alliances involving labour continue to be restricted to small segments of middle-class-based NGO and student movements. This was exactly the case before Soeharto's fall (Tornquist 2002). There are also few overt signs of sufficiently coherent working-class organising, or social alliances that prominently include workers, which would seriously trouble local elites and governments anywhere.

It follows that none of the newly salient coalitions of interest contesting political change in Indonesia, most overtly expressed in the form of political parties and the shifting alliances within and between them, has as yet seriously accommodated the interests of organised labour. In other words, organised labour has largely been left out of the hurly-burly world of post-Soeharto party and electoral politics, nationally and locally. Although including labour sections or 'departments', parties like PAN or the PKS have not shown serious interest in developing strong labour constituencies; thus, still no organic links exist between them and working-class organizational vehicles. At the level of local branches, for example, one would be hard pressed to find the functionaries of major political parties with interest and expertise in dealing with labour issues, even if they are located in industrial areas with large numbers of industrial workers and labour vehicles. More significantly, one would be even more hard-pressed to find major local political party leaders and functionaries with a serious background in labour organisations.

As in the national level, the representatives of labour remain excluded from leadership of parties and parliaments locally, although one minister of manpower hailed from the formerly state-sanctioned FSPSI. There is also no record of local elections that have produced candidates with overtly pro-labour platforms anywhere. Not surprisingly, a recent study found little difference in the attitudes toward labour of a local government controlled by Golkar (in Tangerang) and one controlled by the reform-era PKB (in Pasuruan) (Akatiga, TURC, Labsosio-University of Indonesia 2006). Such a situation is of potentially great importance if one takes into consideration the role posited for organised labour in democratisation processes as described by Rueschemeyer, Stephens and Stephens (1992) and Therborn (1977).

The problem at the core is that organised labour remains too organisationally weak and fragmented to be regarded a significant enough social force for elites to seriously co-opt, in spite of the occurrence of substantial Labour Day demonstrations and the like. Nevertheless, there has been some limited presence of elite interests in a few labour organisations with only dubious links with the mainstream of the emergent post-Soeharto labour movement. These, like the NU-linked Sarbumusi or the Persaudaraan Pekerja Muslim Indonesia (Brotherhood of Indonesian Muslim Workers, PPMI) appear to be no more than part of strategies of selective mass mobilisations related to narrow exigencies. The PPMI, for example, was closely aligned with ICMI leader and Soeharto successor B. J. Habibie, whose short-lived presidency was embattled and precarious.[4] Its function during Habibie's tenure was to help demonstrate the muscle power of the then president's supporters and to provide the Soeharto protégé and long-time engineer-technocrat with simultaneously reformist and populist credentials.

Again, the Indonesian case is not entirely exceptional within the broader Southeast Asian context in terms of both relative marginalisation of labour in the midst of the rise of electoral democracy and the growing power of local elites. In 1990s post-authoritarian Thailand, Brown shows that 'lacking a strong organised voice, workers were isolated in a developing electoral political system dominated by big money, vote-buying and the entrenching of links between crime bosses and local and metropolitan business' (Brown 2004: 105). Similar to the Indonesian case, Ungpakorn notes the absence of a political party of the working class in Thailand in spite of the objective expansion of the wage labour force due to capitalist transformation (Ungpakorn 2003b: 20–24) and democratisation. He also identifies the emergence of gangster-unionists involved in extortion—a social category that has also made an appearance within the Indonesian labour movement.

In the Philippines, too, the labour movement cannot be said to be a major player in the post-authoritarian context. Like in Indonesia today, workers there have long been at the mercy of unleashed goons attached to paramilitary forces (see McCoy 1991: 131), though in this case such goons are likely to be more directly under the wing of influential political clans. Throughout post-authoritarian Southeast Asia, therefore, organised labour has remained only a marginal and ambiguous beneficiary of the democratisation process and the localisation of power.

How has the localisation of power in Indonesia affected the fortunes of organised labour according to its own activists? According to one such activist, S. Aminah (2005), organised labour has had little clout with local governments that are run by former bureaucrats, entrepreneurs and the like. In fact, she suggests that organised labour has been placed in an especially precarious position in relation to local governments *because* of some of the pressures exerted by the simultaneously expressed requirements of decentralised governance and that of economic globalisation. She argues that local government officials now have a growing stake in forging successful alliances with businesspeople and mobile investors to enhance rent-seeking possibilities. Once again, there is nothing distinctively Indonesian about this development. It has been noted in rapidly growing China, for example, that local governments tend to take the side of capital during labour disputes, because a veiled 'symbiosis' of interests has emerged between local officials and private business (Chen 2003: 57). Such local officials, whether in Indonesia or China, will almost naturally regard organised labour as a nuisance to the pursuit of their material advancement.

Local officials in Indonesia, too, according to S. Aminah (2005), are concerned with ensuring that businesses do not relocate elsewhere because of labour issues; they are therefore prepared to go to some lengths to ensure the continuing weakness of the labour movement. Insofar as this is true, the irony of course is that investors are at least as much put off by the lack of legal certainty that has accompanied decentralisation and local autonomy, as well as by the propensity of local politicos to impose levies on business activities. It has long been easier, however, and more politically convenient, for businesses to place the blame on labour demands for unattractive investment climates than to squarely challenge powerful state bureaucrats and politicians who may make exorbitant claims on their potential profits in the form of rents. The potential for the growth of locally based politico-business alliances opened up by decentralisation would make such confrontations still more costly than skirmishes with an underdeveloped, though sometimes vocal, labour movement.

Perhaps a preferred form of resolution of the situation for business is one that was explored in the Philippines. Here, in spite of national labour laws that uphold labour rights, special economic zones, such as in Subic, are created within which organised labour ceases to exist—leaving investors, domestic and foreign, to just deal with the local bureaucracy (Chan and Kelly 2004). Indeed, Indonesian officials have been speaking about setting up a number of new special economic zones within which national labour laws favourable to labour organisation would not apply.[5]

S. Aminah's contentions are largely supported by a separate study that found that decentralisation has meant that local notables and government officials have more direct dealings today with companies operating within their area of authority. This study especially demonstrates the importance of the informal role of local notables and officials in the actual exercise of labour relations today, notwithstanding the gains that workers have enjoyed in the area of legislation. It states that (Akatiga, TURC, Labsosio-University of Indonesia 2006: 6) 'Companies collaborate with the local elite', some of whom function as 'recruitment agents'. Such elites may also 'help in disciplining the workers' due to their high social standing. However, they can also ostensibly protect workers when disputes with management occur; 'a role which is double-edged because at the same time they prevent the emergence of workers' collective protest'.

This report, however, also points to the probable tensions arising from such collaboration. It notes that the role of local elites as labour recruiters potentially gives them considerable leverage in relation to businesses operating locally. Local officials, for example, might be tempted to make use of this leverage by introducing levies, fees and taxes, many of which may be non-transparent—thus, ultimately causing a new source of financial burden for enterprises. Intriguingly, the same report on Tangerang and Pasuruan suggests that one strategy that companies employ to deal with troublesome local elites is to provide support for their political rivals, thereby identifying one basis for the possible intervention of business into arenas of local power in which money politics have become increasingly prevalent.

There are yet other more historical and sociological reasons for the disinclination of political party elites to 'invite' labour into the formal political fold in post-authoritarian Indonesia. Significantly, the continuing salience

of the interests that had been embedded in the New Order's patronage network re-appears in the worldviews of major political actors, both national
and local. It must be recalled that the political genealogies of the majority
of these actors can be traced to the parties and mass organisations that, in
tandem with the military, instigated the destruction of the PKI, including
its labour arm, Sentral Organisasi Buruh Seluruh Indonesia (All-Indonesia
Central Labour Organisation, SOBSI), and were thus involved directly in
the horrific massacres of the 1960s that continues to scar Indonesia's collective political memory. It is not surprising, therefore, that a range of local elites spread over an array of political party vehicles almost uniformly
replicate New Order-era views about the dangerously subversive potential of
strong labour movements, even today.

Thus, some local parliamentarians display an interesting mixture of
condescension, paternalism and moral outrage when discussing the actions
of 'uneducated' workers who engage in 'troublesome' protest activities. It
should be noted that one form of labour protest has been for workers to demonstrate and express their grievances on the grounds of provincial or local
parliamentary offices. This perhaps is not so surprising, given the context of
decentralisation. In assessing this practice, one provincial-level parliamentarian in Yogyakarta argued that labour unrest is but the outcome of the
self-interested manipulations of NGOs and of the small, Leftist student-led
Partai Rakyat Demokratik (Democratic People's Party, PRD), which mis-
leads 'impressionable young workers'. This is evident, he suggested, in the
kinds of militant songs that workers sing in their demonstrations, which
recall socialist-inspired struggles. The politician, an Himpunan Mahasiswa
Islam (Islamic Students' Association, HMI) activist as a student, argued that
such labour actions may create 'threats' to Indonesian democracy and must
be mitigated by more moderate kinds of labour organising.[6] The HMI, it
must be recalled once again, was at the forefront of the anti-PKI student
movement that aligned itself with the military in the mid and late 1960s. The
politician's comments are interestingly reminiscent of the 'labour activism
equals communism' formula that was favoured by New Order-era state officials, perhaps most notably the communist-phobe Sudomo, a Soeharto-era
security chief and one-time minister of manpower.[7] This parliamentarian's
view was echoed in other comments made by a colleague, who argued that
'psychologically, the Muslim community still felt vengeful toward communists' and that the small PRD, often cited as being behind some of the more

militant outbursts of labour unrest in the immediate post-Soeharto years, had the same 'basic ideas' as the long departed communists.[8]

In North Sumatra, local parliamentarians with links to such organisations as Pemuda Pancasila, which was also active in the military-led campaign against the PKI in the 1960s, exhibit the same dispositions toward organised labour. Speaking of Leftist infiltration of social movements, including that of labour, one such parliamentarian suggests that one should always be 'vigilant . . . because [communists] are shrewd, well-trained.' She adds that 'they do not only acquire this shrewdness from internal organising' but also through 'foreign contacts'.[9] A slightly different slant on the same argument was put forward by one of her fellow Medan parliamentarians at the time, the FKPPI-linked Martius Latuperisa. He suggests that the labour movement can be manipulated by any contending elites, but that the real national threat was that of lingering communist influence.[10]

In East Java, the head of the PKB *satgas*, Lutfilah Masduki, is also concerned about the 'politicisation' and radicalisation of the labour movement. While he claims to have no objection to protests related to strictly labour-related issues, he is convinced that labour demonstrations that touch on open broader social and political controversies such as democratisation exhibit evidence of tampering by remnants of Leftist political forces.[11] Not coincidentally, such a stark de-linking of economic and socio-political struggles was a major feature of New Order official discourse. The PKB is of course the offspring of the NU, which is also the parent of the Banser, the militia that played a leading role too in the massacres against real and imagined communists, especially in Java, in the 1960s. East Java Banser figure Jakfar Shodig, interestingly, admits that Banser forces have been used to apply pressure on striking factory workers on behalf of industrialists—a practice that has been widely reported by labour activists in Central and East Java but that has been, understandably, commonly denied by Banser officials.[12]

Thus, several major factors have combined to ensure the continuing marginalisation of labour in the post-authoritarian era and to inhibit its capacity to engage in local arenas of political conflict. First is the legacy of authoritarian rule, which was particularly harsh on organised labour in the first place—circumventing workers' organisational capacities through systematic, and often brutal, state repression. Quite simply, organised labour has not been able to overcome this legacy and re-learn the skills of effective organising and perhaps still needs to reclaim the tradition of political unionism that was so much a part of labour history before the New Order (Hadiz 1997, chapter 3). Second, the context of chronic massive unemployment and underemployment, especially in the wake of the economic crisis of 1997 and 1998, which Indonesia still struggles to overcome, is not particularly conducive to effective labour-organising efforts, even when their ambitions are confined to the local level only. Third, national and local elites continue to have political and ideological dispositions that are broadly anti-labour, which can be explained on the basis of their political socialisation and backgrounds in New Order-nurtured social organisations. S. Aminah's observations about the link between local officials and business in the context of certain decentralisation and globalisation pressures may also be added to this list.

Yet, it is not just organised labour that continued to be politically marginalised in spite of the widening of the scope of political participation in post-authoritarian Indonesia. Organisations representing the peasantry, for example, have hardly had it much easier. New, albeit sometimes very informal organisations representing local peasantries or 'indigenous peoples' movements had emerged during the first years of the post-New Order period, during the heady days of newfound political freedoms. For example, displaced peasants took unilateral action to gain control over land they believed traditionally belonged to them and from which they were previously banished for development projects, plantations, real estate development activities, golf courses and the like. Such actions clearly would not have been possible if not for the circumstance surrounding the abrupt unravelling of the highly centralised and authoritarian New Order (see Lucas and Warren 2000). Indeed, there were also reports of village chiefs, closely associated with oppressive New Order rule, being unceremoniously toppled in local peasant uprisings.

Peasants were so active in some places that elites momentarily paid attention as renewed debates took place about agrarian reform as a pressing issue. It was under these circumstances that Lucas and Warren speculated that it was possible that the management of agrarian issues might soon take a fairer and more equitable form than ever before (Lucas and Warren 2000: 235). The relatively high expectations that had been raised by largely spontaneous actions were perhaps destined to be dashed in many instances.

Wee, for example, reports that peasant action in Riau to demand proper compensation for land previously confiscated from them for the purposes of business activities has only been partly successful. Though Riau is oil-rich, the post-1999 revenue-sharing mechanism that has appeased local elites, according to Wee, has not guaranteed a 'trickle down' process to satisfy demands at the grassroots level for such things as adequate compensation for land dispossession (Wee 2002: 59). Thus, local peasants have resorted to acts of ransacking the offices of companies such as Caltex, the major U.S.-based oil concern operating in Riau. In Bintan in the Riau Archipelago, thousands of peasants protested to receive proper compensation for land they claimed was virtually stolen from them under the New Order to build an industrial park on the northern part of the island. Their efforts were thwarted by local authorities, however, given that powerful interests have long been entrenched in the tourism and industrial sectors of Bintan, including those of the Soeharto family; their main crony and ally, Liem Sioe Liong; as well as investors from Singapore (see *Kompas* 21 January 2000).

In North Sumatra, a peasants' movement predicated on claiming customary rights for 'indigenous' ethnic Melayu peasants to a huge amount of land formerly controlled by Dutch plantations and then Indonesian state-owned plantations has existed since 1953. Led from 1969 by Abnawi Nuh, an activist of the old Soekarnoist PNI, and before that by his brother, the lands claimed by the community of some reportedly 70,000 peasants span large portions of at least two *kabupaten*, Deli Serdang and Langkat. According to Abnawi, the conflict over the years has involved fighting with the security apparatus and more lately, members of *preman* organisations, resulting in fatalities. For Abnawi, the reality is that democratisation has not produced any progress in the realisation of peasant demands—not surprising, perhaps—given the current value of the lands in question and given that local political elites have offered little more than rhetorical support.[13] To his vexation, local governments endowed with greater powers since 2001 have been no more responsive to the aspirations of his movement than those of the previous authoritarian and centralised era.

On the other hand, movements predicated on 'indigenous' or local cultural identity may be supported at times by sections of local elites. Such movements have had high hopes about regional autonomy's capacity to deliver more rights over land and other natural resources to indigenous, often ethnic minority communities in specific localities (see Nababan 2002). Especially predisposed to support these movements are local nobilities who had been forced to retreat to a position of relative political marginality during the New Order. This, however, creates a new set of problems for those interested in more genuine empowerment of local communities, including NGO activists, partly on the basis of protecting local cultures. Van Klinken's observation on the 'return of Sultans' through local politics has already been noted. Here, the issue is that such nobilities/aristocracies or other traditional elites have been prone to manipulate atavistic sentiments (see Dwipayana 2005) to bolster their bargaining positions vis-à-vis others, and have no abiding interest to alter the basic nature of the allocation of economic and political resources. In fact, Nababan (2002) expresses fear that regional autonomy will hurt the most marginalised of local communities as local governments develop the need to intensify exploitation of natural resources and land in order to boost local revenue.

As noted in Chapter 4, the atavistic turn in some local Indonesian politics frequently relies on calls for the upholding of *adat* (customary law) as a sign of acknowledgement of and respect for local community traditions within the framework of decentralisation. By definition, customary law almost always favours traditional local elites who are in many instances also deeply involved in the post-authoritarian competition for access and control over natural resources. Bubandt's (2004) observation that the resurgence of traditional elites has sometimes sparked ethnically-defined social conflicts, rather than lead to the re-establishment of some sort of idealised, pre-modern, peaceful state of nature, is not surprising when one considers what is at stake in concrete struggles over land and other resources.

In conflict-ridden North Maluku, for example, the Sultan of Ternate and his family have made, though only partly successful, bids to regain the local aristocracy's former position within Indonesia's decentralised democracy. A former senior member of the local and national Golkar political juggernaut during the New Order who had subsequently moved to another party, the Sultan was 'only' successful in winning a national parliamentary seat in 2004, and one for his wife in the DPD in the same year. Unlike in the Philippines, where national congressmen with local political bases often vie with mayors and the like for political ascendance, such positions in Jakarta do not entail access to local resources and institutions that could form the foundation of local networks of patronage. Other bids by the Sultan and his wife to win the governorship of the newly-created province of North Maluku and the mayoralty of Ternate, respectively, failed in the face of opposition from other past and present senior national and local Golkar figures—displaying the salience of actors' old links to the New Order across the board (Smith

2006). In spite of these failures, the Sultan's strategy of reclaiming old powers and privileges was clearly partly based on a call to 'tradition' and the manipulation of local identity and pride.

In a nutshell, the experience of organised labour in general and that of some peasant movements in the post-authoritarian period shows that democratisation and decentralisation have not produced an environment in which the interests of those who had been suppressed in the first place under authoritarian rule can now thrive. Although a certain amount of euphoria accompanied the fall of the New Order, workers and peasants have found that the institutions of decentralisation and democracy—parties, local parliaments and the like—continue to be inhabited by the kinds of powerful interests with few organic links to peasant or labour movements. Instructively, similar to post-authoritarian Thailand and the Philippines, there is no major political party that claims to represent the interest of the working class[14] or the peasantry. Indeed, those presiding over mutually competing local predatory coalitions of power have few reasons to set a course for social and political reforms entailing a substantial degree of redistribution of economic and political resources. Consequently, the new salience of electoral politics has been of only limited use to lower-class interests and social movements in post-authoritarian Indonesia.

Electoral Democracy: More Participation, but Little Contestation?

THE SOCIAL OUTCOMES OF DIRECT ELECTIONS

In contrast, electoral politics have been exceedingly useful for Indonesia's local elites once nurtured within a centralised system of authoritarian rule. This is so even though they have had to adapt quite adroitly to changing social and political circumstances. For example, Law no. 32/2004 and Governmental Regulation no. 6/2005 have created the setting for a new system within which heads of local government are directly elected by the local citizenry instead of by parliamentarians in the closed chambers of parliament house. While the change was broadly in the interest of local politicos who needed to bolster their position in relation to local legislative bodies, the system obviously entailed new political strategies of winning public office. The most tangible change was the dramatically escalating cost of winning electoral contests, as money politics was diverted from a concentration on local parliamentary bodies to the public at large.

Local politicos were obviously not responsible for drafting the legislation that made possible these local direct elections. This task was undertaken in Jakarta, where policy-making is at least partly influenced by ideas of good governance reforms. The institution of local direct elections may have been at least partly premised on the assumption that direct elections, being more participatory in nature, will result in governments more accountable to the local citizenry. According to Mietzner (2006: 17), 'the new system of direct elections was' even 'designed to close the door to excessive money politics in local legislatures and introduce transparency and accountability to the electoral process'. The expectation might have been that local predatory interests would be defeated; thus, the road would be paved for forms of local governance that would be more rational in the technocratic mould. Indeed, Mietzner points out that some observers had hoped that a new crop of leaders would somehow emerge 'to break the grip of entrenched bureaucratic elites on local government' (ibid). Quite remarkably, no less than 248 elections for sub-provincial and provincial heads of government were already undertaken approximately between June 2005 and June 2006, out of a total of 472 that were scheduled until 2008–2009 (Asia Foundation 2006), across the expansive Indonesian archipelago.

There remain strong reasons, however, for being sceptical of this institutional innovation. For one thing, instead of curbing money politics, it has transferred the practice to domains beyond that of legislative chambers. The resultant dramatically rising cost of winning office may, in the long run, help to tighten the grip on local power held by some of the best-positioned of predatory elites, as explained below. This is the case even though nearly 40 per cent of incumbents—elected on the basis of the prior system of voting by legislative bodies—were estimated to have lost office (Gross 2006; Pratikno 2006) in local electoral contests from mid-2005 to early 2006. For reformers within Indonesia, the defeat of so many incumbents was greeted as a positive indicator of potential for change and, importantly, the limitations of the advantage of holding office.[15] The fear, naturally, was that incumbency meant the capacity to influence the workings of a range of local institutions engaged at various stages of the electoral process. Especially where powerful incumbents did win (for example, in Kutai Kertanegara or in Medan), however, there continued to be major questions about the neutrality of local electoral commissions. Equally significantly, there were issues about the neutrality of lower-ranking members of the local civil service, such as the *camat* and the *lurah*, whose own fortunes will tend to be closely intertwined with that of a presiding *bupati* or mayor and, therefore, will have reasons to oppose change. Local activists supporting Abdillah's challenger in Medan, for example, were allegedly assaulted by the underlings of certain *lurah* in the city (*Analisa* 15 June 2005). A particularly thorny issue concerned the integrity of the voter registration process involving lower-level officials.[16]

In fact, there are good reasons to question the above mentioned interpretation of the only mixed success that incumbents enjoyed in local electoral contests, as local elections were invariably tarnished by the prevalence of money politics. Therefore, in spite of the defeats that many individual incumbents suffered, there is little evidence that they have been replaced by essentially different kinds of interests. These remain the sort whose genesis ultimately cannot be separated from the exercise of predatory, albeit much more centralised, power during the New Order. This is indicated in the continued successes of former New Order bureaucrats, and Golkar-linked functionaries and activists almost all in direct electoral competition, and the absence of candidates with organic links to social movements that could represent challenges to such social interests.

Mietzner, for example, estimates on the basis of fifty local polls he analyzed that 36 per cent of the victors were career bureaucrats. Another 28 per cent were entrepreneurs (again showing the increasing appeal of direct hold of political office to many local businesspeople), 8 per cent were retired police and military officers, 22 per cent were party officials and only 6 per cent were academics or civil society leaders. It is likely that a large portion of the 'party officials' cited will include those whose political socialisation had taken place in one of the New Order-era electoral vehicles or through the select number of mass organisations through which the Soeharto regime recruited functionaries and operatives. Although Mietzner sees the broadening of available choice to voters and speculates that voters consciously threw out some local leaders with the worst of reputations, he also observes that 'the direct elections did not facilitate the rise of new political elites; instead, they simply forced the old elites to play by new rules' (Mietzner 2006:17–18).

It is significant that prior to the institution of direct local elections, Indonesian reformers of different political stripes had been grappling with the issue of how to make use of the potential opportunities provided by democratisation and decentralisation. Aware of their inability to challenge political party machines based in Jakarta, some NGOs were supportive of the idea of developing local political parties that would only contest elections in particular localities.[17] In this, they appear to be following the line of thought apparent among Filipino activists such as Rocamora (2000). The belief was that local political parties would allow them to channel activities into building viable, albeit smaller 'genuinely reformist' electoral vehicles on the basis of earlier vast experience in grassroots social work through which access to local communities had been established during the New Order.

Such a strategy, if taken, would have had to address some obvious obstacles. Given the increasingly considerable resources necessary even to win local office, there would have been little guarantee that local parties would not just become the instrument of local notables who fail to win support from the major political parties. This is perhaps a rather moot point, for the plan was pre-empted by other electoral law reforms that were aimed at simplifying Indonesia's political party system.

Interestingly, this system had been long regarded in technocratic quarters as exceedingly unwieldy because of the sheer number of participants in elections. Forty-eight parties contested Indonesia's parliamentary elections in 1999, and while only 24 contested them in 2004, political parties and the hurly-burly of electoral competition have been increasingly portrayed as dysfunctional to technocratic good governance. Because few if any reformers fitting a technocratic profile have been produced by such electoral contests, political parties seem to be increasingly viewed as a necessary nuisance that can get in the way of the stability and predictability that is understood to be required for investment and the flourishing of markets (*Jakarta Post* 22 January 2003; *Kompas* 5 May 2003). In spite of such criticism of party politics emerging from state technocrats (for example, academic and Minister of Defence Juwono Sudarsono claimed that Indonesian democracy was impaired, see *Tempo Interaktif* 19 May 2006), few would be unwilling to put up with them. The alternative would be an even more unwieldy and chaotic system that technocratic reformers dread, characterised by a plethora of local political parties.

This is the case even though it is clear that political parties have not had the 'aggregating' and 'articulating' roles traditionally associated with them but, in the context of electoral democracy, functioned increasingly like auction houses for the rich and powerful. As was described in Chapter 5, candidates for local office have had to pay off political parties to obtain the position of official party nominee. This is partly because a law states that only a party or combination of parties that have 15 per cent or more of seats in any legislature possesses the right to advance candidates for local government head, whether *bupati* or mayor. If the aim of the technocratic restriction was to create a semblance of order in electoral competition, the real effect has been to induce political parties to simply auction off nominations and support to the highest bidder, almost regardless of programme or ideological issues.

The end product has been a very rambunctious system in which prospective candidates negotiate 'prices' with various parties before a 'sponsorship' deal is made, even though they have no connection whatsoever to the party of choice. Even people who are known as cadres of Golkar or the PDIP—the two largest parties with the broadest followings and notionally, therefore, the best possible electoral vehicles in many contexts—would easily jump ship when convenient. This will happen if the asking price of the parties they belong to in a particular locality is too high or if these parties had already made a deal with someone else, not infrequently, a party outsider. Observing local elections in Gowa, South Sulawesi, Buehler and Tan (2007: 65) conclude that 'As a rule, candidates originated from outside the parties that nominated them', and moreover, that relationships between candidates and parties were formed on an ad hoc basis.

Another obvious consequence is that campaigns are never fought primarily according to party programmes or ideology even though candidates typically produce vague statements of their election platforms. Instead, these are done in very ad hoc and opportunistic ways where alleged 'charisma', connections with fellow local notables and capacity for vote buying and influencing media reporting are important factors for success. Anyone remotely familiar with the vagaries of power in Southeast Asia's other major post-authoritarian societies, Thailand and the Philippines,[18] will no doubt find the above description eerily familiar in many respects. Therefore, in spite of its potential contribution to 'messiness', a further reform in the making—already supported by the Indonesian Constitutional Court in 2007—is to allow for independent, notionally non-party affiliated candidates to contest local elections—though strict criteria on eligibility are expected to be applied.[19]

Again, it is necessary to reassess the conventional rendering of what political parties are *supposed* to do and look like in a democracy, as if all democracies operated according to the same principles and served the same kinds of interests. It is hardly useful to succumb to the temptation to label

Indonesia's political parties as 'immature', 'irrational' or not 'modern' on the basis of idealised notions of party roles in Western liberal democracies. In the context of many contemporary post-authoritarian societies like Indonesia, where money politics and, to varying extents, political thuggery are the major games to play, political parties as they are today are quite well-suited for the purposes and aims of the predatory interests that preside over them. In other words, there is an internal logic to political party life and electoral competition in post-authoritarian Indonesia that does not lend itself easily to transformation in a neo-liberal, technocratic mould that have to do with the kinds of social interests that predominate. Indeed, the Western liberal-pluralist model of the political party may be viewed as being increasingly exceptional given the experience of the democracies, such as those in South and Southeast Asia, which have actually emerged in the past decades.

This does not mean that 'successful' elections cannot take place. Local direct elections were on the whole successfully implemented in Indonesia from mid-2005. Most took place quite smoothly in spite of a host of technical problems, and conflicts arising here and there that sometimes led to outbreaks of violence (see Barron, Nathan and Welsh 2005). The level of violence and intimidation, however, was quite minimal in most cases, especially given the emergence of organised groups such as thugs as major players in local politics, as described earlier. Indeed, violence seemed to be less a feature of local elections in general than it had been in the earlier part of the post-Soeharto period, when cases such as the mayoral election in Medan in 2000 came to the fore. Even in areas previously torn apart by ethnic or religious strife, such as in North Maluku, Poso in Sulawesi and in West Kalimantan, elections proceeded in a relatively orderly manner with no fatalities. For a huge, diverse archipelago like Indonesia—often portrayed by Western media pundits and academics alike as a violence-prone, fragile entity following the demise of authoritarianism—this was indeed a significant achievement.

It is a different matter, however, to suggest that the successful implementation of the elections in Indonesia signalled the 'consolidation' stage of Indonesia's democracy, in the sense more or less inherent to the 'democratic transitions' literature more broadly. It had earlier been assessed that the 2004 legislative elections and/or the ensuing direct presidential poll of the same year marked the end of Indonesia's 'transition', thereby suggesting the beginning of democratic 'consolidation' (Aspinall 2005b, 2005c; Barron, Nathan, Welsh 2005). It should be recalled that an otherwise sympathetic analyst like Carothers (2002) has warned against the excessive acceptance of the assumptions of the transitions literature discussed previously in Chapter 2, because these tend to underplay the complex and messy process of political and institutional change. With this objection in mind, perhaps it is better to view the newly instituted local direct elections as a potentially important part of the broader process of development of a distinctly illiberal form of democracy related to the workings of Indonesia's predatory form of capitalism. As put forward by Robison and Hadiz (2004), this predatory capitalism essentially rests on the appropriation of public resources and institutions for the purposes of private accumulation.

TOWARDS LOCAL OLIGARCHIES?

The view put forward by Robison and Hadiz is premised on particular kinds of political participation and contestation far removed from the jargon of good governance often heard from technocrats or of populist politics as espoused typically by a variety of NGOs. Still, the rules of the game by which elites maintain their ascendance have been changing dramatically since 1998—including with regard to those that govern political participation and contestation. These will change again to some extent should independent candidates begin contesting these local elections (*Antaranews* 17 November 2007). The further point to emphasise, however, is that these local elites have been very adept at dealing with changing circumstances, and they have come out on top repeatedly in spite of various governance changes that were supposed to provide opportunities for more genuine reformers to take power in the local arena.

This is the case even if a fairly large proportion of individuals in local office failed to get re-elected under the system of direct local elections first practiced in 2005, which typically bloated the amount of money required to win electoral contests. Nevertheless, it is not true that the candidate who spends the most money will always win. Thus in West Sumatra, PDI-P candidate Gamawan Fauzi, who had built up a reputation for honesty as the *bupati* of Solok, defeated candidates that included a wealthy Jakarta-based businessman supported by a coalition of parties (*Kompas* 10 July 2005). However, it is highly unlikely that a winner, almost anywhere, would have been able to free him- or herself from utilising tactics involving money politics. Mietzner's (2006) conclusions on these direct elections, cited earlier, suggest that—as a rule—they have not produced outcomes that alter the basic nature of the social backgrounds and interests represented by those who have emerged victorious in them.

The increasing importance of money politics could have a direct bearing on the relatively diminishing importance of overt violence and intimidation in winning local electoral contests. It is arguable that local elites have now developed an interest in the peaceful running of elections, in order to safeguard the legitimacy of the political process that ensures their ascendant social position, and that this objective is now best served by emphasising money politics over political intimidation. Thus Barron, Nathan and Welsh (2005: 11) point out that in many places, local elites made public appeals to supporters to refrain from practicing overt violence.

This would appear to substantiate the claim made by political gangsters in North Sumatra that they have been asked by candidates to adopt a lower profile in electoral campaigns, to the point of sometimes being asked not to appear in their menacing organisational colours during public mobilisations of support.[20] The hope was that in this way, large-scale clashes between rival groupings of enforcers and thugs could be averted. Still, if outbreaks of conflict and violence, such as between rival groups of thugs, are essentially detrimental to the interests of many such elites today—the ready availability of instruments of coercion still can be subsequently useful in the everyday business of running the government after election time.[21]

Such developments must be viewed in relation to a basic interest to prevent any return to a centralised authoritarianism that would warrant a larger role for the Indonesian military. Significantly, major outbreaks of disorder would not only damage the standing of Indonesian democracy and the actors presiding over it but could also entice the military to demand a more significant part in the workings of politics, whether local or national, in the name of national stability. As an institution, it is the military that is poised to restore order should the competition involved in electoral contests heat up to levels that give rise to acts of violence and destruction on a large scale. Obviously, civilian politicians who have benefited from electoral democracy do not want a situation where the military's bargaining position could be enhanced—even if military commands are already involved in local business activities—much less a move toward a military-led form of centralised authoritarianism.

Thus, a statement by Indonesian military commander, General Djoko Santoso, on local elections, must have had a chilling effect on local politicos of all stripes all over Indonesia. Commenting on (and rather exaggerating) the violence that accompanied these elections, the general suggested that Indonesians were not truly ready for democracy. More disconcertingly, he added that the military had to take responsible action if national unity and stability were ever threatened by the impact of local elections (*Kompas* 24 January 2008).

General Santoso was evidently referring to some of the more notable eruptions of violence in some places, which did at least indicate considerable tensions brewing beneath the surface of relative calm. In Binjai, North Sumatra, for example, where the incumbent mayor, Ali Umri (see Chapter 4) was victorious, followers of losing candidates contested the poll results of 27 June 2005, and protests on their behalf led to attacks on the offices of the local electoral commission. Moreover, the supporters of all four competing candidates mobilised by youth/gangster organisations came to be involved in violent brawls—something that had been avoided throughout the electoral campaign period. The three defeated rivals, all New Order–era local notables, unsuccessfully brought their grievances to court, pleading that the local electoral commission's twice rescheduling of polling day, which allegedly involved 'pressure and threats' from Ali Umri's camp, was detrimental to them.[22]

Indeed, the rejection of poll results occurred in many areas. In North Sumatra alone, where twelve local elections took place on 27 June 2005, eleven produced disputed poll results (*Republika Online* 18 July 2005). In Sibolga, polling day was also delayed by several days because of alleged technical irregularities. The sole exception was in the North Sumatran capital city of Medan; ironically, an area where politics has been particularly rough-and-tumble over the years. There, the dominant position of Abdillah, as described previously, was unassailable. Another controversial outcome occurred in a later poll conducted in Central Tapanuli, where allegations of 'dirty politics' being practiced were prevalent. In this case, protest actions were directed against the victorious incumbent; he was accused of benefiting from the favouritism allegedly displayed by the local elections commission—whose disqualification of a rival ensured that the *bupati* had run unopposed (*Kompas* 16 December 2005; *Jakarta Post* 18 May 2006).

Of course, it was not only in North Sumatra that disputed poll results emerged. In fact, the most nationally celebrated case was perhaps that of Depok, a town on the outskirts of Jakarta where the prestigious University of Indonesia is located, and from which state technocrats, especially in the area of economics, have been traditionally produced. There, the former national leader of the PKS initially lost to a Golkar candidate in yet another controversial poll before intervention by no less than the Supreme Court finally saved him from a possibly embarrassing defeat in a 'mere' local contest (*Suara Merdeka* 17 December 2005). That a renowned national politician turned to a local level electoral contest provides yet another indicator of the perceived heightened importance of local office since decentralisation.

East Java, however, where politics had been more orderly than in North Sumatra, displayed notable instances of election-related violence—again having to do with disputed poll results. No less than in the provincial capital city of Surabaya, mobs protested under the banner of an ad hoc grouping called the People's Movement for Democracy and Justice against the victory of the incumbent mayor, Bambang Dwi Hartono. The protest took a notably violent turn as supporters of the mayor's rivals inflicted serious damage on the local parliament building (*Suara Merdeka* 14 July 2005). Again, the main gripe was alleged irregularities occurring on Election Day, to the extent that a repeat poll was demanded (*Bali Post* 13 July 2005).

In the case of Banyuwangi in East Java, local parliamentary elites and religious figures tried to oust incumbent Ratna Ani Lestari, another victorious incumbent, who was supported by a host of small parties; they claimed vaguely that her administration was incompetent. Mass rallies were organised by religious leaders tied to the PKB and NU—traditionally dominant in this area and stunned by their defeat—and unsuccessful appeals were made to higher levels of government to annul electoral results that returned her to power.

In Tuban, also in East Java, the situation got particularly ugly when protesters burnt down the local election commission office as well as property belonging to incumbent Haeny Relawati, who won re-election with Golkar backing on top of allegations of vote rigging (*Jakarta Post* 18 May 2006). The violence, instigated by supporters of a losing candidate backed by the PKB and PDI-P, became so widespread that a curfew was put in place along with 'shoot to kill' orders handed to the security apparatus. The Tuban case is particularly interesting because it is an area that has recently been developed industrially and in terms of infrastructural projects, and one which will likely grow because of the Cepu oil field located within its boundaries. It is notable that much of the anger expressed against the incumbent is believed to be actually directed against her husband, a prosperous local businessman who critics accuse of abusing the power of his wife to win business contracts (Marijan 2006).

Though it should be reasserted that direct local elections have been carried out in most cases without violence reaching alarming levels, similar instances to the ones described above occurred in many places across the archipelago, from West Sumatra to Bengkulu to Sulawesi. This is in many ways perfectly understandable given the stakes involved in any single electoral contest. As a result of the high cost of engaging in direct polls, the amount invested in losing candidacies can be quite astounding and financially ruinous. This fact alone will tend to further ensure that local electoral contests will, in the future, mostly be the purview of those particularly well endowed with material resources. In other words, the process of further entrenchment of a class of local politicos over the arena of sub-national politics seems to be well under way.

The further question for the near future is whether this process of entrenchment leads in the direction of the formation of more distinct local political oligarchies centred on individuals and groups of more genuine 'strongmen' or dominant local notables. The experiences of post-authoritarian Thailand and the Philippines, and arguably more distant places as post-totalitarian Russia, show that this is a possibility. A thriving locally-focused electoral democracy—within which coherent and genuinely reformist forces able to challenge the dominance of established predatory elites are largely missing—is conducive to the emergence of local oligarchies. Such local oligarchies have an abiding interest not just to maintain their position vis-à-vis potential challenges, but also to safeguard a substantial degree of autonomy for local arenas of power. It is true that any further erosion of central state authority will likely benefit would-be local oligarchs. In spite of some recentralising tendencies already mentioned, which will impede those already harbouring grandiose local visions, it is highly unlikely that the general shift toward the localisation of power can be fundamentally reversed in the foreseeable future.[23]

Conclusion

Decentralisation, Recentralisation and Globalisation

Contesting the Local

Local politics—just like politics at any level—is an arena of contestation between competing coalitions of social interests. The most contentious aspects of local politics, it should come as no surprise, are commonly those that—directly or not—have to do with struggle for access to tangible, concrete resources. Decentralisation policy thus embodies struggles over the setting of the parameters of local power and the establishment of the kinds of social interests to preside over it. What is at stake is no less than the shaping of the rules and regulations to govern the exercise of local power and allow it to be of service to particular sets of social interests, while erecting barriers to others. In other words, contests over decentralisation policy in Indonesia, so often couched in the apolitical, technocratic language of good governance, represent a protracted and continuing struggle over the *kind of* localisation of power that takes place and its set of main beneficiaries.

The danger thus lies in failing to grasp the nature of the fundamental tensions and contradictions within the localisation of power as they pertain to such issues as development, democracy and political participation and contestation. The conflict over local power in Indonesia, and in the post-authoritarian Southeast Asian cases more generally, has not been about 'rational' developmental technocracy attuned to the requirements of global markets and pitted against the 'irrationality' and insularity of predatory politics. Nor has the conflict been about local communities and citizenries struggling against the purportedly homogenising globalisation juggernaut, thereby somehow resurrecting the 'authentic' or 'indigenous' in the process.

This book has shown that the main contenders in the contest in Indonesia are essentially shifting locally-based coalitions of predatory power rooted in the now demised New Order. Such coalitions have selectively latched on to both the agendas of technocratic good governance and that of localist populism—perhaps infusing the latter with more statist-nationalist elements from time to time—to ideologically legitimise their social ascendance. Interconnected with local conflicts are the interests of Jakarta-based coalitions that otherwise have their own motives for containing local power or shaping it in certain ways—often with considerable success. Such containment may be imposed institutionally in the form of laws pertaining to the exercise and scope of local governance, but also in the form of centralising impulses within such instruments of contestation (associated with electoral democracy) as political parties. As a general rule, what is at stake are access to opportunities for private accumulation on the basis of control over public resources and institutions; such are the foundations for the development of localised alliances of predatory power and patronage.

While general observations about the nature of the localisation of power are useful for analytical and comparative purposes, acknowledgment of difference—in historical legacies for instance, and of the precise ways in which societies are actually integrated into the global capitalist economy—is also necessary. It has been pointed out that the concrete manifestations of the localisation of power can be quite different in some important respects. A salient example given was the different legacies of previously centralised authoritarian rule in the different societies, as well as the divergent social bases and characteristics of what is often dubbed local 'bossism' (Sidel 2004). These differences have had consequences for the specific outcomes of the localisation of power in post-authoritarian Indonesia, Thailand and the Philippines.

But experiences further away from Southeast Asia may also shed some light on what is occurring in Indonesia. In an article on decentralisation and globalisation in China, Breslin (2000: 205–206) observes that the 'dual processes of decentralisation and globalisation are reconfiguring loci of decision making and authority'. Thus, the rise of provincialism and of local power vis-à-vis the centre has resulted in situations where the policies of the latter are not always followed in the way intended at the lower levels of governance. In some ways such developments are reflective of some of the conflicts described in this book between coalitions of power based at different levels of governance in Indonesia.

Breslin also notes the regional differences stemming from the uneven impact of globalisation—so much so that one challenge faced by China's national elites has been to respond to calls from local leaders in less developed areas to redress developmental imbalances (Breslin 2000: 219).[1] In the case of China, the uneven impact of globalisation in spatial terms is clearly linked to its recent history of fairly long seclusion from the world capitalist economy that was followed by a form of reintegration that was focussed on the south-eastern coastal provinces. Sharp regional inequalities exist in Indonesia too, however, which are reflective of the uneven nature of the rapid capitalist development presided over by the New Order. The consequence is that the nature of 'things at stake' in local contests over power will be different according to distinct local socio-economic profiles and levels and ways of integration with the global economy.

In East Kalimantan and many other particularly natural resource-rich regions, it is easy to imagine that the stakes are tangible in terms of opportunities for predatory forms of private accumulation, as they are as well in economically more diversified North Sumatra and East Java. This is not to say that struggles over local power in more economically backward or less strategic parts of Indonesia will *necessarily* be less intense. As mentioned in earlier chapters, even relatively minor kingpins in such areas will have a stake in carving out a realm of autonomous power; given the obvious advantages of more direct control over local budgets or of revenue-generating activities, for example. Vel (2005: 106) observes that all the candidates in the 2005 local election in East Sumba district, on the island of Sumba, were involved in money politics 'to some degree', noting how they all required funds given openly or behind the scenes by businessmen; and that the 'position of district head has become a very attractive and powerful bureaucratic post . . . so that candidates for the post can attract investors who hope to profit from their loyalty in the future'. East Sumba is certainly no Kutai Kertanagara, but there, too, local elections were vigorously fought.

It is in many of the areas where the struggle over local institutions of governance, and their resources and authority that involve the most tangible of possible rewards, however, that the emergence of viable local oligarchies is promised most strongly. In these areas, wars of attrition in the form of future electoral contests could well weed out those with less capacity to mobilise the financial and other resources necessary to fight the battles in a sufficiently ruthless fashion.

The cases of North Sumatra and East Java have been analytically useful for the purposes of this book for a number of reasons. Because of their socio-economic profiles and histories, they have been sites for the emergence of numerous instructive cases of fierce competition among competing local elites who seek to establish local hegemony. The establishment of the parameters of local power in North Sumatra and East Java has been especially marked by strenuous efforts on the part of local elites to carve out a realm of autonomy from Jakarta in ways that from time to time have involved head-on collisions. We have seen these in the wrangling over political party candidates for local office, as described in Chapter 5, and in other instances. Furthermore, North Sumatra and East Java provinces—unlike East Kalimantan, for example—have long been the homes of active, though not consistently effective, civil society-based movements and organisations, including those premised on trade unions and NGOs, thereby potentially providing a further complicating factor. This, too, reflects a degree of social differentiation that is more advanced in these two regions than in most other parts of the immense Indonesian archipelago.

Insofar as the localisation of power was expected to produce the impetus for greater political participation, these two provinces would have been among the prime candidates to deliver on either the promises of neo-liberal good governance or, conversely, that of localist populism. The outcomes associated with either sets of promises, however, would have required a profound transformation in the kinds of social interests that preside over local power; and as has been argued, this is precisely the missing element in the local political equation in both cases. In the absence of such a transformation, the outcomes have been predominantly those described in this book.

The Limits of the Local

Decentralisation in Indonesia as understood in the original 1999 set of legislation provided greater autonomy to authorities at the sub-provincial level: the *kabupaten* (regency) and *kotamadya* (city or town), at the expense of both national and provincial levels of governance. A few years after their implementation in early 2001, the pendulum swung back partially in the direction of the provinces and away from the sub-provincial level, thereby potentially undermining or at least affecting the strategies of ambitious local politicos who had thrived since the advent of democratisation.

Some of these ambitious local politicos would have been put back in their place by attacks taking the form of corruption investigations. No less than ten *bupati* in Kalimantan alone, for example, were prosecuted in late 2005 for alleged involvement in illegal logging and the embezzlement of government reforestation funds (*Jakarta Post* 5 December 2005)—an activity in which interests centred in Jakarta were more prominent players during the New Order. As already mentioned, hitherto successful local politicos like Abdillah in Medan and Syaukani in Kutai Kertanagara have also been embroiled in serious corruption cases. The fact that such local bigwigs were investigated with the approval of the government in Jakarta no less, it is suggested, can be read as a message that local elites would not be allowed to run roughshod in spite of the expanded powers formally accorded by decentralisation.

Powerful individuals at the provincial level also have had to take caution in spite of greater authority headed in their direction. In West Sumatra, almost the entire provincial legislature was convicted of graft (*Kompas* 11 June 2004); at the time, this helped to infuse a measure of credibility to the central government's stated aim to crack down more seriously on corruption. Nevertheless, even this initially lauded move proved to be tentative. Though the legislators were initially convicted in court by mid-2004, none actually landed in prison, at least for quite some time.[2]

In spite of the inconsistent nature of the Jakarta-pushed campaign against local corruption, a large number of cases involving members of legislatures and executive bodies at local and provincial levels has been reported in the national media (see *Jakarta Post* 24 July 2004; *Tempo* 27 February 2005: 26–35). While the widespread reporting is clearly reflective of the freedom of the press in post-authoritarian Indonesia, it is also an indicator of the extent and scope of decentralised corruption today (*Tempo Interaktif* 4 November 2004).

From just 2003 to 2006, 967 local and provincial parliamentarians and some 8.06 per cent of local executive heads in the country were named suspects in corruption cases according to the *Jakarta Post*. Most of the parliamentarians were charged with violating a government regulation on budgetary spending (*Jakarta Post* 11 October 2006)—an act that may involve diverse practices including the tendering of projects, the keeping of fictitious accounts, and outright embezzlement of centrally allocated assistance funds (*Tempo Interaktif* 4 November 2004). It should be pointed out, however, that the government regulation concerned, no.110/2000, was later annulled by the Supreme Court, leaving many corruption investigations potentially in legal limbo.

In spite of this kind of inconclusiveness, anti-corruption campaigns emerging from the centre could be viewed as a useful tool of checking the power of ambitious local political actors. Even in the one-party state that is Vietnam, the much publicised pursuit of corruption cases can be fruitfully understood in terms of the political centre's efforts to maintain control over individuals at the lower levels of the party and state, prone to exercise higher degrees of independent action in the context of *doi moi* (Gainsborough 2003: 71). As in Indonesia, such anti-corruption campaigns are not only about establishing transparent governance but are part of the political dynamics of establishing the parameters of local power. In other words, they are at least partly about the reassertion of the power of the centre over the local.

As alluded to earlier, a process of undermining local power had also taken place in Thailand. Before its sudden fall from grace, the Thaksin Shinawatra-created Thai Rak Thai party (see McCargo and Ukrist 2005) had acted to bring to fruition a stronger and more centralised government, despite the tentativeness of the country's actual process of decentralisation (for example, as indicated in the transfer of budgetary authority and revenues) that is mirrored in some respects in Indonesia and the Philippines. Thus the power and authority of centrally appointed governors—effectively running regional appendages of the central bureaucracy in the Thai model (and in reality, working as little more than the prime minister's personal assistants)—was enhanced in relation to that of elected local officials.[3] These 'CEO-governors', as they were called, for instance, were given more say in important matters like budgetary spending and the signing of contracts (Nelson 2002), which in the exercise of local power could make or break local networks of political patronage.

In the Philippines, in the meantime, legislators appear now to have only a limited interest in further decentralisation initiatives. Thus, new legislation proposed to further the scope of decentralisation—advanced primarily by a group of technocrats associated with long time decentralisation advocate Senator Aquilino Pimentel, Jr.—failed to take off in 2006. According to one 'insider' explanation, the root cause is the growing rivalry between national politicians armed with pork-barrel funds who are so instrumental in cobbling together local alliances and the executives of municipal bodies who have been arguably among the main beneficiaries of decentralisation up to now. This is the case even though many congressmen, senators and local executives are similarly members of local elite families due to the particular nature of so-called bossism in the Phillipines.[4] As Hedman and Sidel note (2000: 89), in the Philippines, a 'multi-tiered hierarchy of elected executive and legislative offices encourages the aspiration to boss-hood of municipal mayors, congressmen, and provincial governors but complicates their efforts through overlapping or cross-cutting jurisdictions, resources, and prerogatives'.

The reversion to centralisation rhetoric or sentiment, moreover, has not been confined to Southeast Asia. Outside of the region, in the case of Russia, the Putin government that took over in late 1999 essentially forced a reversal of the strong decentralisation tendency that characterised the tenure of Boris Yeltsin. It did so when placing governors and 'republic leaders' in a powerful position over mayors and local district chiefs who had been gaining political ascendancy since the break-up of the Soviet Union. Significantly, governors were given the authority to dismiss mayors and district chiefs who refused to obey directives emanating from higher levels of government (Slider 2001: 68), thereby curtailing the relative autonomy they had previously enjoyed. Looming in the background throughout these changes were fights against secessionist rebellions in various parts of the country.[5]

The above are not cases that show the inevitable swinging back of the pendulum toward recentralisation once the decentralisation course had been somehow exhausted, so that some sort of imaginary state of 'equilibrium' or 'ideal' balance is achieved through the innate wisdom of technical decision-making. It is also not the case that 'the degree' of decentralisation can simply be chosen by autonomous actors in a social vacuum. What these cases reveal is that decentralisation, like any other policy agenda, cannot be extricated from existing political topographies, which in some circumstances may induce varying degrees of recentralisation as an outcome of struggle.

Nevertheless, any renewed centralising impulse can be beset by its own internal contradictions. It was mentioned earlier that political parties in Indonesia today represent tactical alliances among actors, national and local, that largely emerged from the much more centralised, but extensive, predatory network of patronage that had been a defining characteristic of the New Order. They are the vehicles through which repositioned predatory interests now maintain their social ascendancy in the context of an electoral democracy. As tenuous alliances these parties would often fracture, as local-level alliances—frequently cross-party in nature—take shape quite independently of any central party directive. Such local alliances are formed on the basis of local exigencies, which is itself an indication of the often distinct imperatives of local power. Central party structures, however, do have an interest in safeguarding local party branches that will have a crucial role when mobilisations of support bases and networks are required during national elections. Such an interest may sometimes override the interest to rein in local politicos.

Thus, the Indonesian National Parliament, in a highly controversial move in 2006, recommended the dropping of prosecution cases against local officials implicated in corruption cases linked to abuse of local budgets. It even suggested that the government 'rehabilitate' the names of regional heads and local parliamentarians involved in these cases. Why was such a blatantly unpopular move undertaken, given the widely-held disdain for corruption on the part of the powerful? The answer is fairly simple. As one Indonesia Corruption Watch activist remarked at the time, the prosecuted members of local parliaments are 'the peers' of national parliamentarians through their political party affiliations (*Jakarta Post* 11 October 2006). To crush these local parliamentarians so unflinchingly would be akin to obliterating the local political machineries and networks that national politicians need to rely upon during such times as national elections. Of course, national parliamentarians would also have an interest in insulating themselves from the snowball effects of a strong anti-corruption campaign.

In fact, local politicos were as often rewarded as they were penalised: a particularly controversial government edict of 2006 was understood to have increased the salaries and perks of local parliamentarians in a particularly obscene way in the context of an Indonesian nation still struggling to economically re-emerge one decade after the devastations of the Asian Economic Crisis. The most contentious parts of this edict came to be withdrawn, though not before they came to be seen as symptomatic of the 'legalised robbery' of the people; in this case, that would have had severely negative repercussions on the finances of many struggling regions (*Media Indonesia* 6 January 2007).

Given the constant tug-of-wars, to what extent will local predatory interests become more successful in the future than they have been so far in carving out greater domains of autonomy from Jakarta to pursue their rent-seeking activities? Or will they have to lower their sights after all? This is an important question that already has been raised in this book. Some observers have suggested that such success is quite unlikely (Choi 2006; Pratikno 2006) given the more recent backlash resulting in calls for a measure of recentralisation. No less than President Yudhoyono, for example, declared that regional autonomy has 'gone too far' in Indonesia, that it has scared off investors rather than attracting them, and failed to result in improved public services (*Jakarta Post* 24 August 2006). His assessment on the quality of public services after decentralisation was supported by a report compiled by a group of NGOs in twenty *kabupaten* and ten municipalities across the archipelago which suggested that local governments did not prioritise spending in areas like health and education (*Jakarta Post* 9 December 2007).

Ultimately, however, those interests that preside over local power are by now so well-entrenched that they cannot be ignored or simply wished away, as such diverse actors as investors and organised labour alike have discovered. Their subjugation would require a struggle that would certainly have some violent and unpredictable consequences given the concrete and tangible interests at stake. Thus, it is necessary to take local power seriously as a longer-lasting post-authoritarian social phenomenon, including its predatory characteristics, even while recognising that local power-holders confront limits to their ambitions.

The Poverty of Technocracy

The empirical analysis of the possible outcomes of the localisation of power provided here shows that, under particular circumstances, the widening of political participation (even through electoral democracy), may not entail a greater scope for more fundamental kinds of political contestation. Some interests are simply better positioned to take advantage of the opening of politics, and these may be the sorts that have nothing to gain from rocking the boat more than is necessary for their immediate and tangible purposes. A fundamental source of challenge, it needs to be reasserted, to predatory power remains absent in the Indonesian case, in spite of technocratic attempts at social engineering through institutional tinkering.

Again this is but an Indonesian manifestation of a phenomenon that has been evident globally, as other experiences in Southeast Asia show. Thus, even Grindle, who writes on local governments in contemporary Mexico from a broadly neo-institutionalist perspective, recognises that the range of incentives that institutionalised, competitive electoral politics was supposed to provide toward the development of accountability have been only ambiguously effective. The institutional crafting of local democracies has frequently given rise instead to highly conflict-ridden local governments pre-occupied with resource distribution and allocation in relation to old-style patronage politics (Grindle 2007: chapter 3).

The problem confronted in all of these cases is that dominant local elites have an abiding interest to resist neo-liberal, good governance reforms, even when they simultaneously have a stake in engagement with some aspects of economic globalisation and marketisation—if only to broaden rent-seeking opportunities with the expansion of markets. The pressures exerted by globalisation, which might induce economic competition among different localities, thus do not seem to inevitably result in the demise of predatory coalitions of local power in any predetermined way. This is so even if local government officials in Indonesia, such as the *bupati*, are now being encouraged by Jakarta technocrats to train in the art of attracting investors, and therefore to exhibit more technocrat-like sensibilities.[6]

The evidence so far suggests that the appropriation of state power by its officials to further their predatory interests will continue to be the main theme of Indonesian political economy albeit in an environment that is more democratised and more localised. Such an observation accords with the conclusions reached by Robison and Hadiz (2004) on the reorganisation of economic and political power in Indonesia after the fall of Soeharto. It does not bode well, however, for the advocates of technocratic good governance (or for the aspirations of localist populists within the NGO community in Indonesia and elsewhere). In particular, there is a huge disjuncture between the theoretical assumptions of good governance as consumed by elites and intellectuals and what is then practiced as a matter of interest (Orlandini 2003) in many societies that have jumped on the decentralisation bandwagon.

This should direct us to consider seriously the diversity of ways in which separate parts of the geographical territory that national states claim authority over can be engaged with the global economy without entailing a radical redrawing of their internal political topographies. It has been pointed out that the shift of focus to the local in neo-liberal thinking on globalisation was premised on the view that larger national states posed a barrier to the efficient workings of the market, as illustrated by experiences with protectionist or rent-seeking oriented national elites. Now, however, we see that particular trajectories may produce such outcomes as local arenas of power that exhibit distinct sources of resistance as well to many aspects of neo-liberal reform and whose strength, ironically, can actually be augmented by efforts to institute them. The homogenising effect that the pressures of economic globalisation impose on socio-political phenomena has, once again, proven to be rather greatly exaggerated by the champions of neo-liberal transformation.

Reference Matter

Notes

Introduction

1. This contradicts Huntington's view (1996: 28) that local politics is about 'the politics of ethnicity', while 'global politics' is a much grander 'politics of Civilizations'. His characterisation is misleading as it is unclear why contests over power at the local level should have primary driving forces and logic that are distinct from those at the national or supranational levels.

2. Though utilising a different approach in her book on decentralisation in Africa, Boone emphasises the kinds of competing social interests on the formation of state institutions governing central-local relations in different countries.

3. Indonesia thus seemed less likely to produce what Tornquist called 'bad guy democracy' (2002), in reference to cases like the Philippines.

4. In spite of the complicating factor of the 2006 coup in Thailand (see Ungpakorn 2007; also see Kasian 2006) and its aftermath.

5. See the World Bank's Decentralisation Homepage Library (n.d.) at http://www1.worldbank.org/wbiep/decentralization/regions.htm#europe.

6. The most influential work on Philippines local politics is arguably Sidel (1999); while the most thorough on Thailand is arguably Arghiros (2001). For Thailand also see the collection edited by McVey (2000), which contains a number of illuminating articles by seasoned Thai experts, though mainly in relation to the *chao pho* or 'local godfather' phenomenon. Also see the recent work by Nishizaki (2002, 2006) and various pieces by Nelson (e.g. 2002, 2003, 2005) on decentralisation. Due to the resurgence of Thailand's 'southern violence' there has been some attention recently devoted to the predominantly Muslim provinces of the restive South. A collection edited by McCargo (2007) offers the best and most well-rounded view of local politics in Southern Thailand. The recent work of the young Thai scholar, Achakorn Wongpreedee (2007), is especially useful in understanding how entrenched local political interests, as in Indonesia, have successfully utilised decentralisation to protect their social power and position. On the Philippines, besides

in Sidel, the phenomenon of 'bossism' is examined in five case studies edited by Lacaba (1995). For a discussion of post–Marcos era political change from the point of view of local politics, see Kerkvliet and Mojares (1991). Abinales's (2000) local political-historical study of the state in Mindanao is useful too. In addition, a fine historical background to the emergence of local oligarchic families in the Philippines is provided in Cullinane (2003).

Chapter 1

1. Some of these questions were raised as well in Hadiz 2004a.

2. The same observation has been advanced with regard to the Philippines. A document produced by the Development Academy of the Philippines (2005: 7) argues that the country's ethno-linguistic diversity and geographical features logically support the advancement of a decentralisation agenda.

3. The authors are staff of the United Nations Support Facility for Indonesian Recovery (UNSFIR), in Jakarta.

4. Interview with Professor Eduardo Gonzalez, former president of the Development Academy of the Philippines, Quezon City, 6 June 2006. Also see Abueva (2005) for a proposal for a federalist structure to help end conflict in Mindanao.

5. Also, interview with Chaiwat Satha-Anand, academic and member of National Reconciliation Commission, Bangkok, 28 September 2006.

6. See the World Bank's 'Decentralisation Net' at: http://www1.worldbank.org/publicsector/decentralisation/Different.htm

7. See the further discussion in Chapter 3.

8. The term *federalism*, however, raised alarm bells among Jakarta's political elites, largely because it is associated with late Dutch colonial efforts to maintain a measure of power in the archipelago and to disrupt the emergence of a unified Indonesian republic.

9. In practice, aspects of the law were also the result of work of another team based at the Ministry of Home Affairs as well as one in the Ministry of Finance. See Turner and Podger (2003: 14–15).

10. Not surprisingly the World Bank and other donor organisations have invested a lot of resources into decentralisation programmes around the world and have an ever-growing institutional stake in their success. According to Litvack, Ahmad and Bird, a growing number of World Bank-funded projects have been in effect supporting decentralising schemes worldwide as part of the neo-liberal good governance agenda. Twelve per cent of Bank projects completed between 1993 and 1997, for example, is said to have involved decentralising responsibilities to lower levels of government (Litvack, Ahmad and Bird 1998: 1). There is no reason to believe that there has been a massive reduction in the intervening decade. In 2003, the German aid organisation, GTZ, which along with the World Bank has been

a leading actor in the decentralisation push in Indonesia, estimated that no less than US$2.9 billion were being expended by funding agencies on decentralisation-related projects in Indonesia, the vast majority of which was accounted for by the World Bank and the ADB (Asian Development Bank) (Turner and Podger 2003: 130). In addition, a UNDP (United Nations Development Programme) report in 2002 estimates that 50 per cent of the organisation's financial allocation in the area of 'decentralisation and local governance' has been to the programme 'sub-area' of 'decentralisation policies', compared to just three per cent for 'alliances by the poor' (UNDP 2002: 10).

11. Interview with Eduardo Gonzalez, former president, Development Academy of the Philippines, Quezon City, 6 June 2006. For a different reading on the role of international donors in the Philippines' decentralisation process, see Hutchcroft (2004: 303–311).

12. Interview with Professor Somkhit Lertpaithoon, vice-rector of Thammasat University and member of the 1997 Constitution Drafting Assembly as well as Decentralisation Committee. Bangkok, 28 September 2006. He was particularly influenced, he says, by the French model of decentralisation and general French thought on public administration.

13. Interview with Dr. Orathai Kokpol, King Prajadhipok's Institute and Faculty of Political Science, Thammasat University, 28 September 2006; and with Professor Somkhit Lertpaithoon, 28 September 2006.

14. See Rodan, Hewison and Robison (2006), for an exploration of historical and economic institutionalist accounts of Southeast Asian economic growth and crisis.

15. This is so even though, in the case of sociology, new institutionalism (or new economic sociology) was at least initially a *reaction* to the incursions of economics into the discipline. The passage of time, however, has resulted in commonalities in terms of concerns, concepts and methodologies.

16. See the World Bank's 'Decentralisation Net' at: http://www1.worldbank.org/publicsector/decentralisation/Different.htm.

17. The hijacking of the institutions of governance at the local level by 'special interests' is actually a theme to be found in some neo-institutionalist and public choice theories (Bardhan and Mookherjee 2000), and is expressed as 'elite capture'. The problem with this type of theorising, however, is that it remains trapped in the worldview of rational choices being taken by individual actors whose behaviour is largely determined by such factors as different levels of political awareness and access to information, rather than by structural imperatives. This is because actors are not placed firmly within the context of broad social processes and historically entrenched structures of social interest and power—all of which clearly affect the viable options available to actors at any given time and place.

18. Interview with Joel Rocamora, executive director, Institute for Popular Democracy, Quezon City, 2 June 2006; and Professor Eduardo Gonzalez, former president of the Development Academy of the Philippines, 6 June 2006.

19. Interview with Wuthisarn Tanchai, director of the King Prajadhipok's Institute and long-standing member of the Thai Decentralisation Committee, Nonthaburi, 26 September 2006.

20. This has been sometimes similarly claimed in Thailand and the Philippines, where local politics has been understood to be the province of relatively autonomous local politicos for a longer time. For example, see the interview with Professor Somkhit Lertpaithoon, vice-rector of Thammasat University and member of the 1997 Constitution Drafting Assembly as well as Decentralisation Committee. Bangkok, 28 September 2006; and with J. Prospero De Vera, senior consultant, Office of Senator Aquilino Pimentel, Jr., Quezon City, 5 June 2006.

21. For example, see Ito (2006), who argues for the importance of civil society participation and pressure,but without much discussion of civil society's structural incoherence.

22. A third case that was more optimistic (perhaps much more contentiously so)—in the midst of notably pessimistic accounts of various localities given in the edited volume—was West Kalimantan.

23. Recently, more interesting and complex understandings of social capital have emerged. Though still writing in a Putnamian vein, Anirudh Krishna (2007) follows Berman's (1997) analysis of Nazi Germany, in the sense that he pays at least as much attention to 'social capital' that can give rise to reactionary and undemocratic social movements in India.

24. Such groups are dismissed by Diamond as not being part of civil society—though it is unclear why they should be excluded except for ideological reasons.

25. There are certain historical quirks in the evolution of Thai governance that have amounted to the seeming institutionalisation of the tensions between the legacy of the bureaucratic authoritarian state and more recent democratic aspirations. In practical terms this has meant the existence of separate administrative bodies effectively responsible for the same territorial areas, one linked and responsible to the Ministry of the Interior, and the other considered a unit of elected local governments. Thus, provincial governors are basically functionaries of Bangkok and head organisational units that are vertically integrated to those in the capital, recalling the centralising tendencies of the military-dominated bureaucratic authoritarianism of the past. Provincial Administrative Organisations (PAO), on the other hand, are elected bodies that are typically inhabited by local politicians and entrepreneurs, the dynamics of which are a clear product of democratisation. Moreover, there exist different types of municipal administrations governing urban areas as well as the rurally-based Tambon or sub-district or Administrative Organisations (TAO), which is the lowest level of local administrative structure. Given this context, decentralisation in Thailand notionally involves the reduction of powers and responsibilities, including over budgets and personnel, from the apparatus of administration vertically linked to Bangkok in favour of the various

local governments headed by elected officials (Nelson 2005; UNESCAP n.d. at: http://www.unescap.org/huset/lgstudy/country/thailand/thai.html; Weist 2001).

26. Corruption, broadly defined as 'the use of public office for private gain in ways that contravene declared rules' (Hamilton-Hart 2001: 66) or, more specifically, 'political corruption' defined as 'the abuse of entrusted power by political leaders for private gain, with the objective of increasing power or wealth' (Hodess 2004: 11; also see Harris 2003) remains a major source of worry for development planners globally. The main concerns are that 'corruption affects investment and economic growth', 'influences governments in choosing what to spend their money on', and 'discourages investment, limits economic growth, and alters the composition of government spending, often to the detriment of future economic growth' (Mauro 1997: 3–4). Moreover, it is said to undermine 'development by distorting the rule of law and weakening the institutional foundation on which economic growth depends' (see World Bank Group, n.d. 'Anticorruption').

27. For the full set of data, see Internet Center for Corruption Research at: http://www.icgg.org/corruption.cpi_2006.html.

28. The total Indonesian national budget for 2003 was Rp 231 trillion. *Republika Online* 12 August 2004.

29. Many observers have noted, however, that the World Bank was inclined for decades to 'tolerate' corruption in Indonesia prior to the Asian Economic Crisis. Dick (2002: 71) reminds us that the World Bank used to dismiss widespread Soeharto-era corruption by euphemistically, and perhaps quaintly, referring to it as 'common local practices'. Wee (2002: 6) argues that the Bank believed the growth generated by the New Order 'outweighed any leakages from graft', resulting in loans of about US$25 billion over thirty-two years, in spite of the clearly rapacious and predatory nature of the Soeharto regime. The view is perhaps repeated today in McLeod's (n.d.) assessment that in spite of rampant corruption, the Soeharto regime remained 'effective'—in the sense of doing what was needed to achieve economic growth.

30. This statement is attributed to Indria Samego, a political scientist at the Indonesian Institute of Sciences (LIPI) who was also a close adviser to the Habibie government. See 'Autonomy Benefits Officials, But Not People', *The Jakarta Post*, 21 August 2002.

31. For more details, see World Bank Group, n.d. 'Anticorruption' at: http://www1.worldbank.org/publicsector/anticorrupt/index.cfm.

32. It should be pointed out that culturalist arguments about corruption have frequently been made (e.g. Co et al. 2007: 139), but they are clearly inadequate analytically (see Dick 2002; Hadiz 2004b). Obviously, societies with very different cultures around the world also suffer from the same chronic disease. Within the confines of Southeast Asia few would seriously suggest close affinities between classical Javanese culture and pre-colonial Visayan even if certain features of these

are alleged to persist into the modern era. At the same time, corruption in the post-authoritarian Southeast Asian context is not due primarily to the failure to design institutions that would facilitate the ascendance of market rationality. Again the core problem lies in the nature of the interests that appropriate and ensconce themselves in the institutions of state power (and the market) following the fall of authoritarian regimes. Lindsay's reminder that anti-corruption campaigns are essentially ideological as well as political in nature (Lindsey 2002: 19)—and so too, logically, is successful resistance to them—accords very well with this point of view.

33. The Thaksin government represented the interests of a section of the bourgeoisie that survived the Asian Economic Crisis and then exerted its dominance over the state (see Pasuk and Baker 2004; McCargo and Ukrist 2005; Hewison 2006).

34. Interview with Nakharin Mektrairat, Dean of the Faculty of Political Science, Thamamasat University, 28 September 2006.

Chapter 2

1. For example, a workshop on 'Political Transition and Political Change in Southeast Asia' was held by the Singapore-based Institute for Defence and Strategic Studies, premised on the assumptions of the transitions literature, from 28–29 August 2006.

2. Even before the fall of Soeharto, Uhlin (1997) had invoked Samuel Huntington's (1991) Third Wave of Democratisation thesis, a work that can hardly be reconciled with his notorious 'Clash of Civilisations' (1996) thesis. Uhlin concentrated on the activities and concerns of identified networks of pro-democracy actors in Indonesia, mostly based in Jakarta, paying particular attention to the diffusion of 'Western' values, and ideas of rights and democracy. Jetschke (1999) had a similar concern for the diffusion of ideas and values and attributes democracy in the Philippines to a deep and long process of westernization.

3. See USAID (2005) at http://www.usaid.gov/policy/budget/cbj2005/ane/pdf/497-007.pdf.

4. While many of the Communist Party elements of the ancien regime also reinvented themselves both as democrats in post-communist Eastern Europe, the process is somewhat different in Indonesia. Former East European communists have had to transform themselves not just into democrats but also into pro-capitalist market actors. This they did so successfully that in one observer's (Shelley 2001: 247) summation, 'the political losers of the Soviet era were the financial winners of post-Soviet Russia', giving rise to 'a rare case in history in which the discredited elite of the old political system enhanced their financial power after the collapse of the system they had operated'. In Indonesia, capitalism has of course long been entrenched, and the issue is more about the persistence of the fundamentally preda-

tory relations of power of the Soeharto-era political economy, albeit within institutional arrangements that are more decentralised and democratic.

5. See Retnosetyowati (2006) for a discussion of New Order figures in currently powerful national positions.

6. See Thayer Watkins (n.d.).

7. In Russia too, former military men have played a key role in criminal organisations that have thrived in the context of democratisation and decentralisation, leading to a virtual integration of crime into the state (e.g. Shelley 2001: 249). One report suggests that up to half of the post–Soviet Russian economy is in some way connected to organised crime, which controls about 60 per cent of state enterprises and 50 to 85 per cent of banks (see Members of the Speaker's Advisory Group on Russia 2000, chapter 7). Armed with such resources, criminals have been able to buy election into local and national office (Shelley 2001: 252). In China, too, local politics have inspired the notion of 'gangsterisation' in rural villages, where officials regularly employ thugs to maintain order and collect taxes (*Economist* 15 October 2005: 28–30).

8. The link between the middle class, modernisation and democracy is actually a subject with a long history and is perhaps best represented in its earliest forms in the work of the political sociologist Seymour Martin Lipset (1959). More recently, an apologia for this type of modernisation theory was offered by no less than Francis Fukuyama (1995: 21), the 'prophet' of the 'End of History' that was supposed to have occurred as the Iron Curtain fell in Eastern Europe. Concerned with confirming the wisdom of mainstream 1950s and 1960s modernisation theory, he offers insights into the driving forces of democratisation in newly emerging market economies. He highlights the idea that in the 'Chinese and Thai cases, in particular, the leaders of the prodemocracy movements tended to be relatively well educated, "middle-class", and cosmopolitan citizens', in other words, 'the type of individual that began to emerge during earlier periods of rapid economic growth'.

Nevertheless, many (including Robison and Goodman 1996; Hatori, Funatsu and Torii 2003) have pointed out that the values and political dispositions of the Asian middle classes are substantially different than what was imagined by early modernisation theorists, owing to the 'late timing' of their emergence and the economic and political contexts in which they took place. Robison and Goodman, in particular, have argued that these middle classes have a far more ambiguous interest in free markets, democracy and human rights than, for example, their historical counterparts in the period in which Europe was industrialising and later, democratising.

9. Hewison (2001: 6) notes the resurgence of modernisation theory in Thai studies in the guise of social capital arguments. He cites a work that explains the Thai economic crisis of 1997 as being the result of a lack of social capital among non-Chinese Thais, as opposed to the abundance of it among their ethnic counterparts. This explanation, which recalls the most culturally determinist of old-fashioned modernisation theory, suggests that social capital is responsible for the

Chinese economic drive, and that the lack of it among Thais in general made it difficult for state bureaucratic elites and technocrats to foster social change and adopt rational pro-market policies. According to this explanation, the economic crisis in Thailand was essentially culturally rooted.

10. For example, see Sjahrir, republished in Chalmers and Hadiz (eds.) 1997, p. 156.

11. On Thai capitalism, capitalists and the state, see, for example, Hewison (2006).

12. See chapter 4 in Chalmers and Hadiz (1997).

13. A recent newspaper report discussed the longevity of the Ortega clan of La Union and their dominance there for over century, while discussing other enduring clans in Northern and Central Luzon (*Philippine Daily Inquirer*, 12 May 2007, pp. A1 and A22.

14. See the essays, for example, in Trocki (1998).

15. Some of the basis for this is found in the preceding Spanish period of colonialism in the Philippines.

16. That is, *kabupaten*.

Chapter 3

1. The immediate stimuli for Thaksin's sudden downfall were alleged irregularities in the sale of his company, Shin Corp., to the Singapore government's Temasek.

2. Notably absent were the annihilated and outlawed PKI and the Indonesian Socialist Party, which was the vehicle of social democratic and liberal urban-based intellectuals that Soekarno had forcibly closed down. Absent too was the Islamic-oriented Masyumi party, which was also banned during the Soekarno period.

3. For example, Rozy Munir, a close Wahid confidante, was installed in the powerful position of Minister of Investment and State Enterprises (*Kompas* 29 April 2000), replacing the PDI-P's Laksamana Sukardi.

4. This was stipulated under the legislation governing political parties and mass organizations passed in 1985 (Bourchier and Hadiz 2003: 14).

5. Pancasila is the Indonesian state ideology made up of the five principles of 'Belief in One God, Humanitarianism, National Unity, Social Justice, and Consultative Democracy.' Originally formulated by Soekarno, it was elevated to the realm of the near-sacred by Soeharto. From the mid-1980s, all parties and social organizations were forced to adopt Pancasila as their ideological basis. This was part of the Soeharto-era efforts to enforce strict controls over the political process. Under Soeharto's interpretation of Pancasila, opposition to the government was ideologically unacceptable as well as culturally unsuited to the Indonesian character, which

was supposed to privilege harmony and mutual co-operation. See Bourchier (1996) and Hadiz (2004c).

6. *Tempo Interaktif* 3 May 2000; *Kompas* 18 April 2000. Factory owners frequently hired local military units in the past in this role.

7. As mentioned in Chapter 2, the problem presented itself as that of sustaining the political reality of the Indonesian nation-state, which suddenly appeared fragile (Kingsbury 2003).This was the case after resource-rich provinces like East Kalimantan, Riau, and Irian Jaya demanded in 2001 that the constitution be replaced to enshrine the federal system. This reportedly prompted MPR Speaker Amien Rais to respond that federalism was 'the golden bridge between centralism and separatism', even though his own political party, PAN, had in fact placed federalism on its party platform in 1999 (Guerin 2002). But the prospects of Indonesia's break up were probably greatly exaggerated.

8. From this point of view, the Indonesian case diverges from that of the Philippines, where the decentralisation push of the late 1980s and early 1990s, while related to democratisation, had little to do directly with strong local demands outside such chronic 'problem' areas as Mindanao and Cordillera. Interview with Eduardo Gonzalez, former President of the Development Academy of the Philippines, Quezon City, 6 June 2006. In Thailand, too, decentralisation was a project designed by domestic technocrats after the discrediting of military rule in 1992, but to which established local politicos quickly latched on to.

9. This is reformulated with additional comments from the synopsis of the law as provided by Turner and Podger (2003: 23–27).

10. Interview with T. Rizal Nurdin, governor of North Sumatra, 7 July 2001.

11. In Sidoarjo, the *bupati* was derisive about the intellectual capacities of members of the legislature, many of whom, he said, did not have good educational backgrounds, interview on 13 February 2003. The same argument is put forward by numerous local heads of government, including Marin Purba, then mayor of Pematang Siantar, North Sumatra, 7 September 2001.

12. For details, see World Bank (2003b).

13. See UNESCAP, n. d., at http://www.unescap.org/huset/lgstudy/country/thailand/thai.html.

14. Interview with Wuthisarn Tanchai, King Prajadhipok's Institute and Thai Decentralisation Committee member, 26 September 2006.

15. Interview with Wuthisarn Tanchai, King Prajadhipok's Institute and Thai Decentralisation Committee member, 26 September 2006.

16. See UNESCAP, n.d., at http://www.unescap.org/huset/lgstudy/country/thailand/thai.html.

17. Interview with J. Prospero de Vera III, Senior Consultant, Republic of the Philippines Senate, Office of Senator Aquilino Pimentel Jr, Quezon City, 5 June 2006.

18. Interview with Joel Rocamora, Executive Director of Institute for Popular Democracy, Quezon City, 2 June 2006.

19. See Singh (2007) on how some issues pertaining to regional inequalities have appeared in the discussion on decentralisation in China and India.

20. Such was the timid nature of the Thai associations that there was little response when the military group that overthrew Thaksin in 2006 banned their political activities (*The Nation* 26 September 2006).

21. For example, interview with Wien Hendrarso, *bupati* of Sidoarjo, East Java, 13 February 2003. In this case, he complained about authority over land registration.

22. Interview with Mohammad Idham Samawi, *Bupati* of Bantul, 12 December 2000.

Chapter 4

1. Yogyakarta was, for a brief period, the capital city of fledgling independent Indonesia during the Republican struggle against the Dutch in the 1940s.

2. Arguably, these are the main questions that would or should accompany an examination of the salience of local politics anywhere. See, for example, Kerkvliet (2004: 2) on post-*doi moi* Vietnam.

3. Interestingly, examining parliamentary bodies following the PDI-P victory over Golkar in 1999, Shiraishi (2003) suggests that PDI-P local parliamentarians, nevertheless, were generally younger than Golkar ones. This did not seem to affect their political and organisational background.

4. See City Population, 'Indonesia', at http://www.citypopulation.de/Indonesia .html for details on these population figures.

5. Interview with Rusdiansyah, Surabaya, July 2003.

6. Compiled from official data and provided by Elfenda Ananda.

7. See the results as tabulated by the Indonesian Electoral Commission, at http://www.kpu.go.id.

8. Data from *Surya* daily, 26 October 2002.

9. See the results as tabulated by the Indonesian Electoral Commission, at http://www.kpu.go.id.

10. For example, I was intrigued to find that former members of the hard-line radical student-based organization, the PRD, were acting as field operators and advisers of several local politicos in North Sumatra during election period. Their contribution to the campaigns, waged by mostly bureaucrats and entrepreneurs, ranged from conceptualising campaign platforms and strategy, all the way to mobilising people to attend rallies.

11. Interview with Vincent Wijaya, Medan businessman, 13 June 2005.

12. Interview with Seno Prabowo, then PDI-P parliamentarian in Gresik, East Java, 18 December 2002.

13. Congressional, senatorial and local governmental polls held in May 2007 in the Philippines resulted in over 100 cases of murders officially deemed related to election issues (*The Philippine Star,* 11 May 2007, pp. 4 and 8). These political murders followed a longer period in which Leftists, critical journalists or NGO activists were also killed (or disappeared) in the hundreds (Tolentino and Raymundo 2006).

14. The Soekarno-era Indonesian Nationalist Party (PNI) and its descendents, the New Order-era PDI and now, former President Megawati Soekarnoputri's PDI-P, have been their traditional vehicles.

15. See for a comparison, Nijehhuis (2003), who in a study of the effects of decentralisation on political conflicts in a village in Mali suggests that political polarisation has resulted there, but that migrants who had settled in the village are now the main victims of the struggle.

16. Other analysts might include religious notables in this list of salient local elites, given the sometimes blatant deployment of religious sentiment and symbolism in electoral contests. Local religious leaders, often linked to nationally-organised religious associations such as the NU, or its rival, the Muhammadiyah, are frequently called upon by candidates for electoral office to bolster their legitimacy and standing in the community. Interview with T. Indra Bungsu, candidate for mayor of Binjai, North Sumatra, 15 June 2005. Others have tossed their hats into the ring and latched on more strongly to specific coalitions of power as expressed by local political party vehicles. These and similar kinds of observations often surfaced in interviews in discussions with local political actors in North Sumatra and East Java.

17. Interviews with Akhyar Nasution and O. K. Azhari, both members of the Medan parliament for the PDI-P, on 15 December and 20 December 2003, respectively.

18. Interview with Isman, then Surabaya member of parliament, 15 July 2003. He was a former leading figure in the local PDI-P, but lost out in a particularly vicious internal party squabble involving the positions of mayor of Surabaya and the party leadership in the city. The significance of this conflict will be discussed later.

19. Interview, 9 December 2000. Riyadi Gunawan, in fact, had an interestingly rich family background—his father was active in the Soekarnoist PNI, and his mother was active in its women's branch and hailed from a family of minor colonial-era bureaucrats. The grandson of a *kyai*—founder of a Muslim boarding school—he could count among his uncles and other relatives, noted activists of such organisations as the NU, PNI, Muhammadiyah and Masyumi. He also claimed that one such uncle was a founder of the Masyumi.

20. Interview, 7 September 2001.

21. Interview, 16 July 2002.

22. Although discrimination against Indonesia's ethnic Chinese minority has been reduced through legal reforms since the fall of Soeharto, its members remain vulnerable to political extortion. In Medan, for example, ethnic Chinese entrepreneurs made the rare public announcement that they were being forced to contribute to the campaign funds of major political parties that were gearing up for the 2004 national and local parliamentary elections (*Jakarta Post* 31 July 2003).

23. Interviews respectively on 8 September 2001 and 6 July 2001. Bakrie was to be appointed Coordinating Minister of the Economy under the Bambang Yudhoyono presidency in 2004, and he subsequently became Coordinating Minister of Social Welfare. His family owns the giant and diversified Bakrie conglomerate.

24. See 'Mengubah DPRD Sumut Jadi Ring Tinju', *Parliament Watch*, January 2000, pp. 4–5.

25. Interview with Rinto Andriyono, Institute of Economic and Development Analysis, based in Yogyakarta, 17 December 2002.

26. Interviews, respectively on 7 September 2001 and 7 July 2001. Following my interview with him, the *bupati* of Deli Serdang was scheduled to meet a group of potential Japanese investors.

27. PT Bosowa is owned by Aksa Mahmud, brother-in-law of Jusuf Kalla and a prominent businessman from South Sulawesi, Kalla's main base of power. Aksa Mahmud is also a national politician.

28. Both views are represented in numerous interviews with local political figures in North Sumatra and East Java.

29. Interview, 17 June 2005.

30. Interview, 13 February 2003.

31. Written interview with Rudolf Pardede, July 2002.

32. Interview, 11 February 2002.

33. Information provided by FITRA, Medan, 7 July 2005.

34. Interview, 15 June 2005.

35. Interview, 15 June 2005.

36. Interview, 14 June 2005.

37. For a detailed look on the role of the *jawara*, and their alliance with Golkar, in Serang, Banten, see Alamsyah (2007).

38. Interview with Soekirman, 14 June 2005.

39. Minister of Finance Yusuf Anwar estimates that the tax could be worth up to Rp 30 trillion nationally. See 'Negara Rugi Rp 150 Miliar Akibat Cukai Rokok Palsu', *Tempo Interaktif*, 5 March 2005.

40. Interview, 16 December 2002.

41. Interview, 12 December 2000.

42. Interview, 10 December 2000.

43. This is the case nationally as well. It is claimed that thirteen cabinet ministers in 2005 were formerly businesspeople. See Hendardi (2005).

44. Interview with Abdul Gani Sitepu, 15 June 2005, in which he concurred that local elections in 2005 were likely to cost candidates three to five times more than it did five years earlier.

45. Interview, 8 September 2001.

46. Interview with Sotar Nasution, 3 September 2001.

47. Interview on 13 July 2003 with Jalil Latuconsina, political, business and press figure in Surabaya, with long-time links to a number of 'youth' organizations. He had made a quickly aborted entry into the gubernatorial contest in East Java in 2003.

48. Interview 9 December 2000.

49. Interview 9 December 2000.

50. Interview with Marlon Purba, former PDI-P parliamentarian in North Sumatra and former head of the PDI-P militia in the province, 19 July 2002.

51. Interview with Marlon Purba, 19 July 2002; and with O. K. Azhari, Medan parliamentarian for the PDI-P, 5 July 2001.

52. Interview 5 September 2001.

53. See LSM Mail Archive 'KKN Bupati Langkat-Sumut (Kisah Nyata)', at http://www.mail-archive.com/lsm@terranet.or.id/msg00055.html.

54. Nevertheless, with relatively minor interests in the press industry, Masduki does not appear to have the personal material resources comparable to his North Sumatran counterparts and claims to be dependent on party allocation of funds to finance the operations of his *satgas*. Interview, 19 July 2003.

55. Interview with Agus Muslim, Pemuda Pancasila secretary in Surabaya, July 2003.

Chapter 5

1. Interview with Akhyar Nasution, member of Medan parliament for the PDI-P, 15 December 2003. References to a lucrative elections 'industry' were also made by local businesspeople in Labuhan Batu, North Sumatra, Haji Masulung and Haji A. Silitonga. Interview, 11 July 2005. Included in this industry are activities such as producing T-shirts, banners, pamphlets, 'souvenirs' and various other goods.

2. Interview with Ahmad Amin Lubis, businessman and brother of a candidate for deputy *bupati* of Serdang Bedagai, 14 June 2005.

3. The idea was supported by a decision made by the Constitutional Court in 2007. However, the decision did not clarify what the criteria of individual eligibility would be (See SCTV, at http://www.liputan6.com 23 July 2007).

4. Interview with Marin Purba, 7 September 2001.

5. Interview with Amran Y. S., a veteran Pemuda Pancasila leader in North Sumatra and member of the North Sumatra parliament for PAN (the National Mandate Party), 4 July 2001.

6. It should be noted, however, that the local Medan publication, *Edison*, furnished evidence that at least some of these parliamentarians were in fact paid a more substantial sum of Rp 125 million. It did so by actually reproducing the receipts the parliamentarians were supposed to have signed upon accepting the money! See *Edison*, 24–31 May 2000, pp. 3 and 11. It should also be noted that Abdillah's opposing camp was not beyond similar tactics. Ridwan Batubara's brother, the businessman Yopie Batubara and then head of the North Sumatra Chamber of Commerce and Industry, claims to have also bribed the same parliamentarians and was in possession of the receipts to prove it. Interview, 8 September 2001.

7. Interview with Akhyar Nasution, member of Medan parliament for the PDI-P, 15 December 2003; and Doni Arsal Gultom, ousted former leader of the PDI-P Medan branch, 16 December 2003.

8. See, for example, *Perjuangan*, 18 March 2000.

9. Personal communication, 19 December 2003, and interview, 6 July 2001, Martius Latuperisa. Also see the chronology of events provided in 'Kronologis Kasus Money Politics Pemilihan Walikota Medan', Sumatera Corruption Watch, n.d. Here, it is noted that fourteen of the sixteen PDI-P parliamentarians were, after Ridwan Batubara's defeat, held against their will in Parliament House by other PDI-P members who were furious with the result and demanded an explanation. On this occasion, they reportedly admitted that they had been bribed.

10. Interview with John Andreas Purba, PDI-P member of Karo sub-provincial parliament (with a background in the KNPI), 6 July 2001. On the fire, see 'Selamat Pagi Pembakar', *Otonom*, 13–21 December 2000, p. 8.

11. This was, for example, alleged in 'Momentum Show of Force Rudolf', *Otonom*, 22–29 November 2000, p. 13.

12. This is an estimate given by two members of his 'success team', Medan parliamentarian Yunus Rasyid, interview 16 June 2005; and Hendra D. S., Medan parliamentarian from the Pancasila Patriot Party and a leader of the local Pemuda Pancasila.

13. Maulana Pohan estimated that he only had about one-tenth of the financial resources available to Abdillah, though it must be noted that he had an interest in portraying himself as the underdog.

14. I attended a meeting of local PDI-P cadres and the Pohan-Sigit team (13 June 2005), in which Purba played a prominent role.

15. Interviews on 19 July 2002 and 15 December 2003. It should be noted that Purba denies involvement in the lucrative trade in illegal firearms, which is alleged to involve the military and police forces.

16. Interview with Darma Loebis and Bambang Soed, the North Sumatra Alliance of Journalists, 16 June 2005. During fieldwork, I observed that the Medan station of the Metro TV network—owned by New Order-nurtured businessman Surya Paloh—was running a half-hour programme every evening lavishing praise on the successes of the Abdillah administration and reporting on his daily activi-

ties. Major newspapers in the city, such as *Waspada* and *Medan Bisnis*, were also running news articles that were heavily tilted in favour of Abdillah and cast him in a favourable light.

17. In relation to the media, Abdillah's alleged actions do not depart from similar developments seen in many post-authoritarian or post-totalitarian situations. Outside of Southeast Asia, Oates (2001: 261–262) notes in the case of Russia, for example, that politicians often buy 'secret advertising' in the print and electronic media and regularly offer bribes to journalists during electoral contests.

18. Interviews with Nanang S., PDI-P parliamentarian for Surabaya and a supporter of the mayor within the party, 16 December 2002 and 14 July 2003.

19. Cak Narto held the rank of Lieutenant Colonel in the Indonesian army's Special Forces, the Koppasus (Nurhasim 2005: 104).

20. Interview with Nanang S., PDI-P parliamentarian for Surabaya, 16 December 2002 and 14 July 2003.

21. Interview with Bedjo, head of the Surabaya PDI-P paramilitary force, 16 July 2003.

22. Interview with Tito Widji Prijadi, East Java PDI-P *satgas*, 20 December 2002.

23. Some of the observations were raised as well in Hadiz 2004b.

24. Interview with Gatot Sutantra, a veteran local leader of a number of New Order-cultivated 'youth' organizations, 18 July 2003.

25. I observed this during fieldwork in Surabaya/East Java in July 2003. In the Medan case, FKPPI and other goons were supposed to have threatened local parliamentarians with physical violence.

26. Interview with M. Jakfar Shodig, deputy head of the local Banser, 18 July 2003.

27. Interview with Gatot Sutantra, a veteran local leader of a number of New Order-cultivated 'youth' organization, 18 July 2003. Also see 'Madu di Balik Kursi Gubernur', *Sapujagat*, 1–15 April 2003, p. 3; and *Jawa Pos* 17 July 2003, p. 26; as well as Ali Aspandi, 'Siapakah Gubernur Jatim 2003–2008', *Surya* 25 November 2002, p. 21.

28. Interview with Lutfilah Masduki, East Java provincial member of parliament for the PKB and head of the East Java PKB paramilitary force.

29. Interview with Lutfilah Masduki, member of the East Java parliament and head of the PKB *satgas*, 19 July 2003.

30. Initially, there were moves to put forward a party man as candidate, most prominently Saifullah Yusuf, the PKB secretary general who was often at odds with former President Wahid. Interview with Lutfilah Masduki, who supported Kahfi in the internal conflict, 19 July 2003.

31. The PDI-P policy of backing incumbents and generals for top regional and local positions was epitomised by its backing of General Sutiyoso as governor of

Jakarta in 2002, even though the latter, as Jakarta military commander in 1996, was partly responsible for the brutal attack on then opposition leader Megawati's supporters at the party headquarters.

32. Interview with Usaha Ginting, head of the PDI-P branch in Medan, 19 December 2003.

33. Interview with Amran Y. S., 4 July 2001. Also see Ryter (2002) for a detailed historical study.

34. Interview with Martius Latuperisa, 6 July 2001.

35. Personal communication, Martius Latuperisa, Medan member of parliament, 19 December 2003. It is rumoured that the failure was due to the objections of Abdurrahman Wahid. Latuperisa takes great pride in the fact that as the son of a mere corporal, he was able to order around the sons of officers in the FKPPI.

36. Personal communication, Martius Latuperisa, Medan member of parliament, 19 December 2003.

37. Literally, 'Elder Brother Olo'.

38. Also, interview with Topan Damanik, North Sumatran academic, 17 July 2002.

39. Interview with Usaha Ginting, 19 December 2003.

40. Interview with Doni Arsal Gultom, 16 December 2003. This claim was vehemently rejected by Ramses Simbolon, a top aide of Rudolf Pardede in an interview on 17 December 2003. Ginting himself claims that he also rejected Pardede's attempt to place cronies in the Medan party leadership; interview on 19 December 2003.

41. Purba, also the former head of the PDI-P faction in the North Sumatran parliament, had since departed from the PDI-P and joined a smaller party espousing a form of Soekarnoist ideology. Interview 15 December 2003.

42. One such mass mobilization, involving sections of the urban poor, took place on 15 December 2003. Ramses Simbolon, a key lieutenant of Rudolf Pardede, denied that his camp was behind the action, though this was the widely-held view among local politicos. Interview, 17 December 2003.

43. Interview with Haji Enteng, 10 July 2005.

44. Interview with Agus Muslim, East Java Pemuda Pancasila secretary, 16 July 2003. Also see 'Partai Patriot Pancasila Bisa Jadi Pilihan', *Sapujagat*, 1–15 July 2003, p. 12.

45. Interview with J. Anto, media activist, Medan, 17 July 2002; interview with Jalil Latuconsina, publisher, *Sapujagat*, Surabaya, 13 July 2003. He is also linked to 'youth' and business associations in the city.

46. Interview with Topan Damanik, 17 July 2002.

47. The Betawi people have long felt that they have been marginalised in 'their own city'—left behind by the process of modernisation and the wealth created for others.

48. Personal communication, Agus Muslim, East Java Pemuda Pancasila secretary, 16 July 2003.

49. Personal communication, Dede Oetomo, lecturer at the Faculty of Social and Political Sciences, Airlangga University, Yogyakarta, 17 July 2003.

50. Interview with Kusen Dimyati, Pagar Nusa chief in Tamaksari, Surabaya, 6 February 2003. The name of the organization evokes a sense of a protective fence around the islands of Indonesia, thus the *Pagar Nusa* is a protector of the Indonesian archipelago.

51. Key among these is Syukri Fadholi, a former Himpunan Mahasiswa Islam, or Islamic Students' Association (HMI), activist, and once head of the PPP faction in the Yogyakarta provincial parliament. He was later to be elected deputy mayor of the city of Yogyakarta. Interview 15 December 2000.

52. As pointed out by Tengku Erry Nuradi. Interview, 14 June 2005.

53. This observation contrasts with that put forward by Wilson (2006: 290), who quotes an unnamed political gangster as suggesting that smaller scale elections allow greater opportunities for victories won by intimidation.

54. Interview with Zainal Abidin, secretary general of the IPK in Medan, 18 June 2005.

55. Interview with Sahat Simatupang, IPK member, 18 June 2005. It should be noted that members of such organisations are traditionally recruited from Indonesia's masses of urban poor. This would be the case in spite of Zainal Abidin's claim that large numbers of intellectuals and people in middle-class professions now make up the membership of the IPK. Interview, 18 June 2005.

Chapter 6

1. Interviews and discussions with workers and labour activists in Medan/ North Sumatra, 8 July 2001 and 18, 20 and 21 July 2002.

2. The use of hoodlums to deter workers is denied by the SPSI leadership in North Sumatra. Discussion, 19 July 2002.

3. Still, there have sometimes been exceptions to this rule. In 2006, worker protests in Jakarta in particular, organised to mark International Labour Day, were successful in pressuring the government of President Susilo Bambang Yudhoyono to delay the implementation of labour law 'reforms' that would have made the position of workers in companies even more precarious because of new stipulations about dismissals and short-term contracts favourable to employers.

4. Interview with Eggi Sudjana, founder of PPMI, 20 November 1998.

5. See a critique of this idea by Batam Island-based trade unionist Thamrin Mosii (2006).

6. Interview with Budi Dewantoro, Justice Party member of Yogyakarta legislature, 13 December 2000. The party later became the Justice and Prosperity Party (PKS).

7. Interview, 9 May 1994.

8. Interview with Budi Setyagraha, Yogyakarta provincial parliamentarian from PAN, on 10 December 2000.

9. Interview with Elvi Rahmita Ginting, Medan parliamentarian and a local Pemuda Pancasila women's section leader, 6 July 2001.

10. Interview, 6 July 2001.

11. Interview, 19 July 2003.

12. Interview, 18 July 2003. The factory in question was the New Era shoe factory on the outskirts of Surabaya. It should be noted that Jakfar initially denied that this had happened until he later stated that Banser personnel allegedly involved were being investigated.

13. Interview. 18 July 2002.

14. Aware of problems such as these, there was some debate within the labour activist community for a short while in the immediate aftermath of Soeharto's fall about the need for labour parties. In a bizarre twist of events, it was the New Order-sponsored trade union, the FSPSI, or figures associated with it, that took the initiative by forming the Indonesian Workers Party (PPI) a day prior to Soeharto's resignation on 21 May 1998. Another labour party, the so-called SPSI Party, was later formed by a different group within the union, while long-time non-state labour activist Muchtar Pakpahan established his own National Labour Party (PBN). In addition, the Labour Solidarity Party (PSP) was formed with alleged financial assistance from a leading member of the Soeharto family. Muhammad Jumhur Hidayat—a former student activist turned late New Order-era political operator— at one time also expressed the aspiration of eventually forming a labour party on the basis of his fledgling GASPERMINDO. Nonetheless, all of the parties were unsuccessful in making a dent on Indonesia's electoral contests (see Ford 2005, at http://airaanz.econ.usyd.edu.au/papers/Ford.pdf). They failed to win any seats in national or local parliaments in 1999 and were even a lesser presence in the 2004 legislative elections.

Given the absence of a real labour party, and the array of labour organisations in existence, no single labour organisation today has the clout to 'bargain' on behalf of workers in relation to other social forces.

15. Interview with Indonesian political scientist Syamsuddin Haris in *Suara Karya*, 29 June 2006.

16. Various interviews, including with the *camat* of Tebing Tinggi and Pantai Cermin, and the secretary for the *camat* in Binjai, all in North Sumatra; the *lurah* of Sei Kera, in Medan; with the head of 'Kesbanglinmas' or office of public security, Serdang Bedagai, North Sumatra—all in June 2005.

17. Statements made at a seminar on the 2004 elections in Indonesia organised by NGOs in North Sumatra, 22 July 2002.

18. Ufen (2006), for example, notes how political parties in Indonesia are coming to resemble those in the Philippines in their character.

19. It is too early to definitively state what the real effect of the court ruling might be. It could be the case that some local bigwigs who have enough personal resources and networks will seek to by-pass parties and spend more money, for example, on direct vote-buying—a situation which would again dishearten the NGOs. However, political parties would have an interest in keeping the criteria for eligibility of independent candidates in the future at a fairly high level to maintain their relevance and grip on power. See *Antaranews* 17 November 2007.

20. Interview with Sahat Simatupang, IPK member, Medan, 18 June 2005; Hendra D. S., Pancasila Patriot Party and Pemuda Pancasila official, Medan, 16 June 2005.

21. Interview with Hendra D. S., Pancasila Patriot Party and Pemuda Pancasila official, Medan, 16 June 2005.

22. According to a local electoral commission member in Binjai, his office was initially pressured to delay the poll. *Kompas* 28 June 2005.

23. Interview with Professor Somkhit Lertpaithoon, vice-rector of Thammasat University and a member of the 1997 Constitution Drafting Assembly as well as Decentralisation Committee, Bangkok, 28 September 2006.

Conclusion

1. Of course, authors on market-preserving federalism (e.g. Qian and Weingast 1996) tend to emphasise the idea that these differences spur healthy competition between regions to do well economically.

2. Communications with Luky Djani, Indonesian Corruption Watch, March 2006.

3. The re-centralisation effort was helped by 'deceleration of Southeast Asia's globalisation' due to the Asian economic crisis, which had slowed 'the explosion of real estate values and government infrastructure investment that secured the conditions for the rise of local political bosses' in Thailand (Shatkin 2003: 31).

4. Interviews with J. Prospero De Vera, senior consultant, Office of Senator Aquilino Pimentel, Jr., Quezon City, 5 June 2006; and with Professor Eduardo Gonzalez, former president of the Development Academy of the Philippines, Quezon City, 6 June 2006.

5. This essentially reflected conflict between the centre and regions about the distribution of wealth. Of course, many such conflicts have been expressed in ethno-nationalist (or religious terms), as has been the case in Indonesia in the post-Soeharto years. As Wee (2005) argues, however, ethno-nationalist or religiously expressed local discontent will commonly have a strong material basis. In the case of Russia, where the issue of Chechen separatism is notable, Hughes (2001: 135) has observed that distributive issues had helped to foster regionalist and separatist

sentiment, especially where there has been long-standing resentment over modes of revenue sharing. He also notes (2001: 134) that the 'single most important common factor among the four most "secessionist" or autonomy-seeking republics . . . is that they all have significant economic resource endowments'.

6. Indeed, Indonesia ranked a lowly 135 out of 175 countries surveyed in the World Bank's 2007 Doing Business report (*Jakarta Post* 6 November 2006).

Bibliography

Abdullah, Irwan. 2005. Diversitas budaya, hak-hak budaya daerah dan politik lokal di Indonesia. In *Desentralisasi, globalisasi, dan demokrasi lokal*, ed. Jamil Gunawan, 81–93. Jakarta: LP3ES.

Abers, Rebecca Neara. 2000. *Inventing local democracy: Grassroots politics in Brazil.* Boulder, CO: Lynne Rienner Publishers, Inc.

Abinales, Patricio. 2000. *Making Mindanao: Cotabato and Davao in the formation of the Philippine nation-state.* Manila: Ateneo de Manila University Press.

Abinales, Patricio, and Donna J. Amoroso. 2005. *State and society in the Philippines.* Lanham, U.K.: Rowman and Littlefield Publishers Inc.

Abueva, Jose V. 2005. Some advantages of federalism and parliamentary government for the Philippines. Unpublished paper.

Achakorn Wongpreedee. 2007. 'Decentralization and Its Effect on Provincial Political Power in Thailand', *Asian and African Area Studies*, 6 (2): 454–470.

ADB (Asian Development Bank). 1999. Governance in Thailand: Challenges, issues and prospects. April. Manila: Author.

Affif, Suraya, Noer Fauzi, Gillian Hart, Lungisile Ntsebeza and Nancy Peluso. 2005. *Redefining agrarian power: Resurgent agrarian movements in West Java, Indonesia.* Berkeley: University of California, Center for Southeast Asian Studies.

Akatiga, TURC (Trade Unions Rights Centre) and Lab Sosio-University of Indonesia. 2006. Promoting fair labour regulations in Indonesia: A study and advocacy in improving local level investment environment in Tangerang and Pasuruan. May. Jakarta: Author.

Alamsyah, Andi Rahman. 2007. Bantenisasi demokrasi: pertarungan simbolik dan kekuasaan (Studi tentang demokratisasi Serang, Banten, Pasca-Soeharto, tahun 2004–2006). Masters thesis in Sociology. University of Indonesia,.Depok.

Almond, Gabriel A., and Sidney Verba.1963. *The civic culture: Political attitudes in five Western democracies.* Princeton, NJ: Princeton University Press.

Anderson, Benedict. 1988. Cacique democracy in the Philippines: Origins and dreams. *New Left Review* 169 May/June: 3–31.

Antlov, Hans. 1995. *Exemplary centre, administrative periphery: Rural leadership and the New Order on Java*. NIAS Monographs no. 68. Richmond, U.K.: Curzon Press.

Antlov, Hans. 2003a. Not enough politics! Power, participation and the new democratic polity in Indonesia. In *Local power and politics in Indonesia*, ed. Edward Aspinall and Greg Fealy, 72–86. Singapore: ISEAS.

Antlov, Hans. 2003b. Civic engagement in local government renewal in Indonesia. Logolink Southeast Asia. Quezon City: Institute for Popular Democracy. Retrieved on 15 September 2005 from http://www.ipd.ph/logolinksea/resources/SEA%20Regional%20Paper4.pdf.

Antlov, Hans, and Sven Cederroth, ed. 2004. *Elections in Indonesia: The New Order and beyond*. London: RoutledgeCurzon.

Appadurai, Arjun. 2000. Grassroots globalization and the research imagination. *Public Culture* 12 (1): 1–19.

Arghiros, Daniel. 2001. *Democracy, development, and decentralization in provincial Thailand*. Richmond, U.K.: Curzon.

Asia Foundation. 2004. *Indonesia: Rapid Decentralization Appraisal (IRDA) Second Report*. Jakarta: Asia Foundation.

Asia Foundation. 2006. Democracy and elections in Indonesia. Retrieved on 15 July 2007 from http://www.asiafoundation.org/pdf/Indo_Democracy-Elections.pdf.

Aspinall, Edward. 2005a. *Opposing Suharto: Compromise, resistance, and regime change in Indonesia*. Stanford, CA: Stanford University Press.

Aspinall, Edward. 2005b. Politics: Indonesia's year of elections and the end of the political transition. In *The politics and economics of Indonesia's natural resources*, ed. Budy P. Resosudarmo, 13–30. Singapore: ISEAS.

Aspinall, Edward. 2005c. Elections and the normalisation of politics in Indonesia. *Southeast Asia Research* 13 (2): 117–156.

Aspinall, Edward, and Mark T. Berger (2001) The break-up of Indonesia? Nationalisms after decolonisation and the limits of the nation-state in post-cold war Southeast Asia. *Third World Quarterly* 22 (6): 1003–1024.

Aspinall, Edward, and Greg Fealy, ed. 2003. *Local Power and Politics in Indonesia*. Singapore: ISEAS.

Bardhan, Pranab. 2002. Decentralization of governance and development. *Journal of Economic Perspectives* 16 (4): 185–205.

Bardhan, Pranab, and Dilip Mookherjee. 2000. Capture and governance at local and national levels. *American Economic Review* 90 (2): 135–139.

Bardhan, Pranab, and Dilip Mookherjee. 2006. The rise of local governments: An overview. In *Decentralization and local governance in developing countries: A comparative perspective*, ed. Pranab Bardhan and Dilip Moookherjee, 1–52. Cambridge, MA: The MIT Press.

Barron, Patrick, Melina Nathan and Bridget Welsh. 2005. Consolidating Indonesia's democracy: Conflict, institutions and the 'local' in the 2004 legislative elections. Social Development Papers, Conflict Prevention and Reconstruction, paper No. 31. December. Washington, DC: World Bank.

Barton, Greg. 2002. *Abdurrahman Wahid: Muslim democrat, Indonesian president.* Sydney: UNSW Press.

Baswir, Revrisond. 2000. Buloggate dan manejemen uang publik. *Kompas* 5 June.

Becker, Gary. 1996. *Accounting for tastes.* Cambridge, MA: Harvard University Press.

Berman, Sheri. 1997. Civil society and the collapse of the Weimar Republic. *World Politics* 49 (3): 401–429.

Bertrand, Jacques. 2003. *Nationalism and ethnic conflict in Indonesia.* Cambridge, U.K.: Cambridge University Press.

Betts, Ian L. 2003. Decentralisation in Indonesia: A review of decentralisation policy and the problems and issues that have faced businesses and investors since the implementation of regional autonomy in Indonesia. *Indonesian Business Perspective Online, Harvest International's Journal for Decision Makers* 5 (5) June–July. Retrieved on 30 August 2005 from http://www.harvest-international.com/perspec/Jun_Jul03/special.htm.

Bhargava, Vinay, and Emil Bolongaita, ed. 2004. *Challenging corruption in Asia: Case studies and a framework for action.* Washington, DC: World Bank.

Bjornlund, Eric. 2000. Supporting the democratic transition process in Indonesia. Statement by Eric Bjornlund, NDI Senior Associate and Regional Director for Asia before the United States House of Representatives Committee on International Relations Subcommittee on Asia and the Pacific, 16 February, Washington, DC.

Boileau, Julien. 1983. *Golkar: Functional group politics in Indonesia.* Jakarta: Centre for Strategic and International Studies.

Boone, Catherine. 2003. *Political topographies of the African state: Territorial authority and institutional choice.* Cambridge, U.K.: Cambridge University Press.

Boone, Catherine. n.d. The new territorial politics in Africa: Regionalism and the open economy. Unpublished paper.

Boudreau, Vincent. 2004. *Resisting dictatorship: Repression and protest in Southeast Asia.* Cambridge, U.K.: Cambridge University Press.

Bourchier, David. 1996. Lineages of organicist political thought in Indonesia. PhD diss., Monash University, Melbourne.

Bourchier, David, and Vedi R. Hadiz. 2003. *Indonesian politics and society: A reader.* London: RoutledgeCurzon.

Bourdieu, Pierre. 1986. *Distinction: A social critique of the judgment of taste.* London: Routledge and Kegan Paul.

Breslin, Shaun. 2000. Decentralisation, globalisation and China's partial re-engagement with the global economy. *New Political Economy* 5 (2): 205–225.

Brodjonegoro, Bambang. 2003. Breakthrough in regional autonomy? Retrieved 15 September 2005 from http://www.jakartapost.com, December 31.

Brown, Andrew. 2004. *Labour, politics and the state in industrializing Thailand*. London: RoutledgeCurzon.

Bubandt, Niels. 2004. Menuju politik adat yang baru? Tradisi, desentralisasi dan imajinasi politik di Indonesia. *Antropologi Indonesia, Jakarta* (28) 74: 12–31.

Budiman, Arief, Barbara Hatley and Damien Kingsbury, ed. 1999. *Reformasi: Crisis and change in Indonesia*. Melbourne: Monash Asia Institute.

Buehler, Michael, and Paige Tan. 2007. Party-candidate relationships in Indonesian local politics: A case study of the 2005 regional elections in Gowa, South Sulawesi Province. *Indonesia* 84, October: 41–69.

Buentjen, Claudia. 2000. Fiscal decentralization in Indonesia—the challenge of designing institutions. Unpublished paper, Manila, ADB.

Bunte, Marco. 2004. Indonesia's decentralization: The Big Bang revisited. In *Thai politics: Global and local perspectives*, ed. Michael H. Nelson, 379–430. Nonthaburi, Thailand: King Prajadhipok's Institute.

Carothers, Thomas. 2002. The end of the transitions paradigm. *Journal of Democracy* 13 (1): 15–21.

CGI (Consultative Group on Indonesia). 2003. Donor statement on decentralization. Twelfth Meeting of the Consultative Group on Indonesia, January 21–22, in Bali.

Chalmers, Ian, and Vedi R. Hadiz, ed. 1997. *The politics of economic development in Indonesia: Contending perspectives*. London: Routledge.

Chan Fong Yin, and Philip F. Kelly. 2004. Local politics and labour relations in the Philippines: The case of Subic Bay. In *Labour in Southeast Asia: Local processes in a globalised world*, ed. Rebecca Elmhirst and Ratna Saptari, 129–156. London: RoutledgeCurzon.

Charas Suwanmala. n.d. Devolving public service responsibilities to local government: A case study of Thailand. Unpublished paper.

Chatterjee, Partha. 1993. *The nation and its fragments: Colonial and postcolonial histories*. Princeton, NJ: Princeton University Press.

Chen, An. 2003. The new inequality. *Journal of Democracy* 14 (1): 51–59.

Choi, Nankyung. 2005. Local elections and democracy in Indonesia: The case of the Riau Archipelago. Working Paper No. 91, November. Singapore: Institute of Defence and Strategic Studies.

Choi, Nankyung. 2006. The 2006 Batam mayoral election: The weakening of local party politics and the realignment of local elites. Paper presented at a Workshop on 'Pilkada: Direct elections, democratization and localization in Indonesia', Indonesia Study Group, Asia Research Institute, May 17–18, at National University of Singapore.

City Population. Indonesia. Retrieved on 30 September 2005 from http://www.citypopulation.de/Indonesia.html.

Co, Edna E. A., Millard O. Lim, Maria Elissa Jayme-Lao and Lilibeth Jovita Juan, ed. 2007. *Philippine democracy assessment: Minimizing corruption*. Manila: Friedrich Ebert Stiftung.

Coleman, James. 1988. Social capital in the creation of human capital. *American Journal of Sociology* 94 (Supplement): S95–S120.

Connors, Michael Kelly. 2001. Ideological aspects of democratisation in Thailand: Mainstreaming localism. City University of Hong Kong SEARC Working Papers Series No. 12.

Craner, Lorne W. 2004. A comprehensive human rights strategy for China. Washington, D.C.: Carnegie Endowment for International Peace, January 29. Retrieved on 15 October 2005 from http://www.state.gov/g/drl/rls/rm/28693.htm.

Crook, Richard C., and James Manor. 1998. *Democracy and decentralisation in South Asia and West Africa: Participation, accountability and performance.* Cambridge, U.K.: Cambridge University Press.

Culla, Adi Suryadi. 2006. *Rekonstruksi civil society: Wacana dan aksi ornop di Indonesia.* Jakarta: LP3ES.

Cullinane, Michael. 2003. *Ilustrado politics: Filipino elite responses to American rule, 1898–1908.* Manila: Ateneo de Manila Press.

Danzer, Erick. 2006. Decentralization and commodity chain politics in Indonesian agriculture. Presentation given at a panel on Vertical Linkages and Multi-level Politics in Decentralized Indonesia, Association of Asian Studied Annual Conference, April 6–9, in San Francisco.

Dasgupta, Aniruddha, and Victoria A. Beard. 2007. Community driven development, collective action and elite capture in Indonesia. *Development and Change* 38 (2): 229–249.

Davidson, Jamie S., and David Henley, ed. 2007. *The revival of tradition in Indonesian politics: The deployment of adat from colonialism to indigenism.* London: Routledge.

Decentralization Thematic Team (World Bank). n.d. What is decentralization? Retrieved on 30 August 2005 from http://www.ciesin.org/decentralization/English/General/Different_forms.html.

Development Academy of the Philippines. 2005. *Decentralized capacity building.* Pasig City.

Diamond, Larry. 1994. Rethinking civil society: Toward democratic consolidation. *Journal of Democracy* 5 (3): 4–17.

Diawara, Mamadou. 2000. Globalization, development politics, and local knowledge. *International Journal of Sociology* 15 (2): 361–371.

Dick, Howard. 2002. Corruption and good governance: The new frontier in social engineering. In *Corruption in Asia: Rethinking the governance paradigm,* ed. Tim Lindsey and Howard Dick, 71–86. Sydney: The Federation Press.

Di Maggio, Paul, and Walter W. Powell. 1991. Introduction. In *The new institutionalism in organisational analysis,* ed. Paul Di Maggio and Walter W. Powell, 1–38. Chicago: University of Chicago Press.

Di Palma, Giuseppe. 1990. *To craft democracies.* Berkeley: University of California Press.

Dwipayana, Ari. 2005. Aristokrasi di dua kota. In *Desentralisasi, Globalisasi, dan Demokrasi Lokal*, ed. Jamil Gunawan, Sutoro Eko Yunanto, Anton Birowo, and Bambang Purwanto, 135–160. Jakarta: LP3ES.

The Economist. 'Protest in China: Democracy Chinese-Style', 15 October 2005, 28–30.

Eldridge, Philip J. 1995. *Non-government organisations and democratic participation in Indonesia.* Kuala Lumpur: Oxford University Press.

Emmerson, Donald K. 1976. *Indonesia's elite: Political culture and cultural politics.* Ithaca, NY, and London: Cornell University Press.

Emmerson, Donald K. 1978. The bureaucracy in political context: Weakness in strength. In *Political power and communications in Indonesia*, ed. Karl D. Jackson and Lucian W. Pye, 82–136. Berkeley: University of California Press.

Emmerson, Donald K. 1983. Understanding the New Order: Bureaucratic pluralism in Indonesia. *Asian Survey* 23 (11): 1220–1241.

Erawan, I Ketut Putra. 2007. Tracing the progress of local government since decentralization. In *Indonesia: Democracy and the promise of good governance*, ed. Ross Mcleod and Andrew MacIntyre, 55–72. Singapore: ISEAS.

Erb, Maribeth, Priyambudi Sulistiyanto and Carole Faucher, ed. 2005. *Regionalism in Post-Suharto Indonesia.* London: RoutledgeCurzon.

Erman, Erwiza. 2007. Deregulation of the tin trade and creation of a local shadow state: A Bangka case study. In *Renegotiation boundaries: Local politics in post-Suharto Indonesia*, ed. Henk Schulte-Nordhold and Gerry van Klinken, 177–202. Leiden: KITLV Press.

Escobar, Arturo. 1995. *Encountering development: The making and unmaking of the third world.* Princeton, NJ: Princeton University Press.

Faucher, Carole. 2007. Contesting boundaries in the Riau Archipelago. In *Renegotiation boundaries: Local politics in post-Suharto Indonesia*, ed. Henk Schulte-Nordhold and Gerry van Klinken, 443–457. Leiden: KITLV Press.

Fine, Ben. 2001. *Social capital versus social theory: Political economy and social science at the turn of the millennium.* London: Routledge.

Fine, Ben. 2002. The World Bank's speculation on social capital. In *Reinventing the World Bank*, ed. Jeffrey A. Winters and Jonathan R. Pincus, 203–221. Ithaca, NY: Cornell University Press.

Fisman, Raymond, and Roberta Gatti. 2002. Decentralization and corruption: Evidence across countries. *Journal of Public Economics* 83: 325–345.

Fjeldstad, Odd-Helge. 2003, 10 July. Decentralisation and corruption: A review of the literature. Retrieved on 15 September 2005 from http://unpan1.un.org/intradoc/groups/public/documents/UNTC/UNPAN018217.pdf.

Ford, Michele. 2003. NGO as outside intellectual: A history of non-governmental organisations' role in the Indonesian labour movement. PhD diss., School of History and Politics, University of Wollongong.

Ford, Michele. 2005. Economic unionism and labour: Poor performance in Indonesia's 1999 and 2004 elections. Retrieved on 30 November 2006 from http://airaanz.econ.usyd.edu.au/papers/Ford.pdf.

Ford, Michele. 2006. United we stand? Indonesia's labour movement needs to consolidate the gains of 1998. *Inside Indonesia*, April–June: 4–7.

Fukuyama, Francis. 1995. Confucianism and democracy. *Journal of Democracy* 6 (2): 20–33. Retrieved on 1 September 2005 from http://www.imf.org/external/pubs/ft/seminar/1999/reforms/fukuyama.htm#II.

Fukuyama, Francis. 1999. Social capital and civil society. Paper prepared for IMF Conference on Second Generation Reforms, November 8–9, in Washington, DC.

Gainsborough, Martin. 2003. Corruption and the politics of economic decentralisation in Vietnam. *Journal of Contemporary Asia* 33 (1): 69–84.

Geertz, Clifford. 1983. *Local knowledge: Further essays in interpretive anthropology.* New York: Basic Books.

Gelbard, Robert. 2001. United State-Indonesia relations in 2001. Council of American Ambassadors. Retrieved on 1 July 2004 from http://www.americanambassadors.org/index.cfm?fuseaction=Publications.article&articleid=42.

Gellert, Paul K. 2005. Oligarchy in the timber markets of Indonesia: From Apkindo to IBRA to the future of the forests. In *The politics and economocs of Indonesia's natural resources*, ed. Budy P. Resosudarmo, 145–161. Singapore: ISEAS.

George, Terrence R. 1998. Local governance: People power in the provinces? In *Organizing for democracy: NGOs, civil society, and the Philippine state*, ed. G. Sidney Silliman and Lela Garner Noble, 223–253. Honolulu: University of Hawai'i Press.

Gong, Ting. 2006. Corruption and local governance: The double identity of Chinese local governments in market reform. *Pacific Review* 19 (1): 85–102.

Govan, Hugh. 1997. Building on local culture for development in the Pacific: Community participation in natural resource management. In *Environment and development in the Pacific*, ed. B. Burt and C. Clerk, 185–200. Canberra and Port Moresby: National Center for Development Studies, The Australian National University, Pacific Policy Paper 25 and University of Papua New Guinea Press.

Grindle, Merilee S. 2007. *Going local: Decentralization, democratization, and the promise of good governance.* Princeton, NJ: Princeton University Press.

Gross, Jeremy. 2006. Direct local elections truly change the political culture. *Jakarta Post*, June 22.

GTZ (Deutsche Gesellschaft fuer Technische Zusammenarbeit). n.d. Decentralization in Indonesia since 1999—An overview. Retrieved on 30 September 2005 from http://www.gtzsfdm.or.id/dec_in_ind.htm.

Guerin, Bill. 2002. Power to the people: The Bupatis come to town. *Asia Times*, May 11.

Gutierrez, Eric. 1995. In the battlefields of the warlords. In *Boss: 5 cases of local politics in the Philippines*, ed. Jose F. Lacaba, 129–167. Pasig: Metro Manila.

Hadiwinata, Bob S. 2003. *The politics of NGOs in Indonesia: Developing democracy and managing a movement.* London: RoutledgeCurzon.

Hadiz, Vedi R. 1997. *Workers and the state in New Order Indonesia.* London: Routledge.

Hadiz, Vedi R. 2003. Power and politics in North Sumatra: The uncompleted *reformasi.* In *Local power and politics in Indonesia: Democratisation and decentralisation,* ed. Edward Aspinall and Greg Fealy, 119–131. Canberra: Australian National University and Institute of Southeast Asian Studies.

Hadiz, Vedi R. 2004a. Decentralisation and democracy in Indonesia: A critique of neo-institutionalist perspectives. *Development and Change* 35 (4): 697–718.

Hadiz, Vedi R. 2004b. Indonesian local party politics: A site of resistance to neo-liberal reform. *Critical Asian Studies* 36 (4) December: 615–636.

Hadiz, Vedi R. 2004c. The failure of state ideology in Indonesia: The rise and demise of Pancasila. In *Communitarian politics in Asia,* ed. Chua Beng Huat, 148–161. London: Routledge.

Hadiz, Vedi R., and Daniel Dhakidae. 2005. Introduction. In *Social science and power in Indonesia,* ed. Vedi R. Hadiz and Daniel Dhakidae, 1–29. Singapore and Jakarta: ISEAS and Equinox Publishing.

Haggard, Stephan, and Robert Kaufman. 1995. *The political economy of democratic transitions.* Princeton, NJ: Princeton University Press.

Hahn, Jeffrey, ed. 1996. *Democratization in Russia: The development of legislative institutions.* New York: M. E. Sharpe.

Hall, Peter A., and Rosemary C. R. Taylor. 1996. Political science and the three institutionalisms. *Political Studies* 44 (5): 936–957.

Hamilton-Hart, Natasha. 2001. Anti-corruption strategies in Indonesia. *Bulletin of Indonesian Economic Studies* 37 (1): 65–82.

Harris, Robert. 2003. *Political corruption in and beyond the nation state.* London: Routledge.

Harriss, John. 2002. *Depoliticizing development.* New York: Anthem Books.

Harriss, John, Kristian Stokke and Olle Tornquist. 2004. Introduction: The new local politics of democratisation. In *Politicising democracy: The new local politics of democratisation,* ed. John Harriss, Kristian Stokke, and Olle Tornquist, 1–27. London: Palgrave Macmillan.

Harvey, David. 2000. *Spaces of hope.* Berkeley: University of California Press.

Hattori, Tamio, Tsuruyo Funatsu and Takashi Torii. 2003. Introduction: The emergence of the Asian middle classes and their characteristics. *The Developing Economies* XLI–2 June: 129–139.

Hayllar, M. R. 2003. The Philippines: Paradigm lost or paradise retained? In *Governance and public sector reform in Asia: Paradigm shifts or business as usual?* ed. A. B. L. Cheung and I. Scott, 227–247. London: RoutledgeCurzon.

Hedman, Eva-Lotta E. 2006. *In the name of civil society: From free election movements to people power in the Philippines.* Honolulu: University of Hawai'i Press.

Hedman, Eva Lotta E., and John T. Sidel. 2000. *Philippine politics and society in the twentieth century.* London: Routledge.

Hefner, Robert W. 1993. Islam, state, and civil society: ICMI and the struggle for the Indonesian middle class. *Indonesia* 56 October: 1–35.

Hendardi. 2005. Pemerintah dan pengusaha. *Kompas* 22 November: 4.

Henley, David, Maria J. C. Schouten, and Alex J. Ulaen. 2007. Preserving the peace in post-new order Minahasa. In *Renegotiation boundaries: Local politics in post-Suharto Indonesia*, ed. Henk Schulte-Nordhold and Gerry van Klinken, 307–326. Leiden: KITLV Press.

Heryanto, Ariel, and Vedi R. Hadiz. 2005. Post-authoritarian Indonesia in comparative Southeast Asian perspective. *Critical Asian Studies* 37 (2) June: 251–276.

Hewison, Kevin. 2000. Resisting globalization: A study of localism in Thailand. *Pacific Review* 13 (2): 279–296.

Hewison, Kevin. 2001. Thailand: Class matters. City University of Hong Kong SEARC Working Papers Series No. 8, May.

Hewison, Kevin. 2006. Thailand: Boom, bust, and recovery. In *The political economy of Southeast Asia: Markets, power, and contestation*, ed. Garry Rodan, Kevin Hewison, and Richard Robison, 74–108. Melbourne: Oxford University Press.

Hidayat, Syarif. 2007. 'Shadow state'?: Business and politics in the province of Banten. In *Renegotiation boundaries: Local politics in post-Suharto Indonesia*, ed. Henk Schulte-Nordhold and Gerry van Klinken, 203–224. Leiden: KITLV Press.

Hill, David T. 2006. Media making choices: Local media in local elections. Paper presented at a Workshop on 'Pilkada: Direct elections, democratization and localization in Indonesia', Indonesia Study Group, Asia Research Institute, May 17–18, at National University of Singapore.

Hines, Colin. 2000. *Localization: A global manifesto.* London: Earthscan Publications.

Hodess, Robin. 2004. Introduction. In *Global corruption report 2004*, Transparency International, 11–18. London: Pluto Press.

Hofman, Bert, and Kai Kaiser. 2006. Decentralization, democratic transition, and local governance in Indonesia. In *Decentralization and local governance in developing countries: A comparative perspective*, ed. Pranab Bardhan and Dilip Moookherjee, 81–124. Cambridge, MA: The MIT Press.

Honna, Jun. 2005. The post-Soeharto local politics in West, Central and East Java: Power elites, concession hunting and political *premanism*. Paper presented at the 4th International Symposium of the journal *Antropologi Indonesia*, July 12–15, Depok.

Hughes, James. 2001. From federalisation to recentralisation. In *Developments in Russian politics 5*, ed. Stephen White, Alex Pravda, and Zvi Getelman, 128–146. London: Palgrave.

Huntington, Samuel. 1968. *Political order in changing societies.* New Haven, CT: Yale University Press.

Huntington, Samuel P. 1991. *The third wave: Democratization in the late twentieth century.* Norman: University of Oklahoma Press.

Huntington, Samuel P. 1996. *The clash of civilizations and the remaking of world order.* New York: Simon and Schuster.

Hutchcroft, Paul D. 1998a. *Booty Capitalism: The Politics of Banking in the Philippines.* Ithaca, NY: Cornell University Press.

Hutchcroft, Paul D. 1998b. Sustaining economic and political reform: The challenges ahead. In *The Philippines: New directions in domestic policy and foreign relations,* ed. David G. Timberman. New York: Asia Society. Retrieved on 15 May 2003 from http://www.asiasociety.org/publications/philippines/decentralization.html.

Hutchcroft, Paul D. 2004. Paradoxes of decentralization: The political dynamics behind the passage of the 1991 local government code of the Philippines. In *Thai politics: Global and local perspectives,* ed. Michael H. Nelson, 283–332. Nonthaburi, Thailand: King Prajadhipok's Institute.

Indonesian Electoral Commission. Retrieved on 15 December 2005 from http://www.kpu.go.id.

Internet Centre for Corruption Research. Retrieved on 30 January 2007 from http://www.icgg.org/corruption.cpi_2006.html.

IRI (International Republican Institute). n.d. China: Supporting reform in China. Retrieved on 1 September 2005 from http://www.iri.org/asia/china.asp.

Irianto, Edi Slamet. 2006. Pengantar: Islam, Barat dan politik kebangsaan: Rekonstruksi gerakan Islam lokal. In *Islam dan politik lokal,* ed. Syarifuddin Jurdi, 7–25. Yogyakarta: Pustaka Cendekia Press.

Ito, Takeshi. 2006. The dynamics of local governance reform in decentralizing Indonesia: Participatory planning and village empowerment in Bandung, West Java. *Asian and African Area Studies,* 5 (2): 137–183.

Jackson, Karl D. 1978. The bureaucracy in political context: Weakness in strength. In *Political power and communications in Indonesia,* ed. Karl D. Jackson and Lucian W. Pye, 82–136. Berkeley: University of California Press.

Jayasuriya, Kanishka. 2000. Authoritarian liberalism, governance and the emergence of the regulatory state in post-crisis East Asia. In *Politics and markets in the wake of the Asian crisis,* ed. Richard Robison, Mark Beeson, Kanishka Jayasuriya, and Hyuk Rae Kim, 315–330. London: Routledge.

Jeon, Je Seong. 2005. Kebangkitan kepemimpinan kelas buruh di Indonesia: Kasus PT Maspion Unit 1, Sidoarjo—Jawa Timur. Paper presented at the 4th International Symposium of the journal *Antropologi Indonesia,* July 12–15, Depok.

Jetschke, Anja. 1999. Linking the unlinkable? International norms and nationalism in Indonesia and the Philippines. In *The power of human rights: International norms and domestic change,* ed. Thomas Risse, Stephen C. Ropp, and Kathryn Sikkink, 134–171. Cambridge, U.K.: Cambridge University Press.

Johannen, Uwe, and James Gomez, ed. 2001. *Democratic transitions in Asia.* Singapore: Select Books.

Kahin, Audrey. 1994. Regionalism and decentralisation. In *Democracy in Indonesia: 1950s and 1990s*, ed. David Bourchier and John Legge, 204–213. Melbourne: Centre of Southeast Asian Studies, Monash University.

Kammen, Douglas. 1997. A time to strike: Industrial strikes and changing class relations in Indonesia. PhD diss., Cornell University.

Kasian Tejapira. 2006. Toppling Thaksin. *New Left Review* 39 May–June: 5–37.

Kerkvliet, Benedict J. Tria. 2004. Surveying local government and authority in contemporay Vietnam. In *Beyond Hanoi: Local government in Vietnam*, ed. Benedict J. Tria Kerkvliet and David G. Marr, 1–27. Singapore: ISEAS.

Kerkvliet, Benedit J. Tria, and Resil B. Mojares. 1991. Themes in the transition from Marcos to Aquino. In *From Marcos to Aquino: Local perspectives on political transition in the Philippines*, ed. Benedict J. Tria Kerkvliet and Resil B. Mojares, 1–12. Quezon City: Ateneo de Manila University Press.

King, Phil. 2003. Putting the (para)military back into politics. *Inside Indonesia*, January–March. Retrieved on 10 November 2005 from http://www.serve.com/inside/edit73/king%20satgas.htm.

Kingsbury, Damien. 2003. Diversity in unity. In *Autonomy and disintegration in Indonesia*, ed. Damien Kingsbury and Harry Aveling, 99–114. London: RoutledgeCurzon.

Kingsbury, Damien, and Harry Aveling, ed. 2003. *Autonomy and disintegration in Indonesia*. London: RoutledgeCurzon.

Krishna, Anirudh. (2007). Mobilising social capital: Community responses to gloablization. In *Gloabalization and change in Asia*, ed. Dennis A. Rondinelli and John M. Heffron, 191–208. Boulder, CO: Lynne Rienner Publishers.

Krongkaew, Medhi. 2000. The political economy of growth in developing East Asia: A thematic paper. Presented at the Third Global Development Network (GDN) Conference organised by the World Bank, June 9–10, Prague.

Kurniawan, Luthfi, Ahmad Charisudin, Nur Hadi, Afwan Khariri and Bisman Bachtiar. 2003. *Menyingkap korupsi di daerah*. Malang and Surabaya: In-Trans and YSPDI.

Lacaba, Jose F., ed. 1995. *Boss: 5 cases of local politics in the Philippines*. Pasig, Philippines: Metro Manila.

Laclau, Ernesto, and Chantal Mouffe.1985. *Hegemony and socialist strategy: Towards a radical democratic politics*. London: Verso.

Lay, Cornelis. 2002. Eksekutif dan legislative di daerah: Penelitian tentang potensi konflik antara dprd dan birokrasi di daerah. Research Report. Jakarta: Ministry of Research and Technology of the Republic of Indonesia and the Indonesian Institute of Sciences.

Lewis, Blane D., and Jasmin Chakeri. 2004. Decentralized local government budgets in Indonesia: What explains the large stock of reserves? Unpublished manuscript. Jakarta: World Bank.

Liddle, R. William. 1991. The relative autonomy of the third world politician: Soeharto and Indonesian economic development in comparative perspective. *International Studies Quarterly* 35: 403–427.

Liddle, R. William. 1992. The politics of development policy. *World Development* 20: 793–807.

Liddle, R. William. 2001. Indonesia's democratic transition: Playing by the rules. In *The architecture of democracy*, ed. A. Reynolds, 373–399. Oxford, U.K.: Oxford University Press.

Lin, Justin Yifu, Ran Tao and Mingxing Liu. 2006. Decentralization and local governance in China's economic transition. In *Decentralization and local governance in developing countries: A comparative perspective*, ed. Pranab Bardhan and Dilip Moookherjee, 306–327. Cambridge, MA: The MIT Press.

Lindsey, Tim. 2001. The criminal state: *Premanisme* and the New Order. In *Indonesia today: Challenges of history*, ed. Grayson Lloyd and Shannon Smith, 283–297. Singapore: Institute of Southeast Asian Studies.

Lindsey, Tim. 2002. History always repeats? Corruption, culture and 'Asian values'. In *Corruption in Asia: Rethinking the governance paradigm*, ed. Tim Lindsey and Howard Dick, 1–19. Sydney: the Federation Press.

Lingga, Vincent. 2006. Vested regional interests win in Cemex divestment. *Jakarta Post*, 22 May.

Linz, Juan J., and Alfred Stepan. 1996. *Problems of democratic transition and consolidation: Southern Europe, South America and post-Communist Europe*. Baltimore, MD: Johns Hopkins University Press.

Lipset, Seymour Martin. 1959. Some social requisites of democracy: Economic development and political legitimacy. *The American Political Science Review* 53 (1): 69–105.

Litvack, Jennie, Junaid Ahmad and Richard Bird. 1998. *Rethinking decentralization in developing countries*. Washington, DC: World Bank.

LSM Mail Archive 'KKN Bupati Langkat-Sumut (Kisah Nyata)'. Retrieved on 15 January 2007 from http://www.mail-archive.com/lsm@terranet.or.id/msg00055.html.

Lucas, Anton, and Carol Warren. 2000. Agrarian reform in the era of Reformasi. In *Indonesia in transition: Social aspects of Reformasi and crisis*, ed. Chris Manning and Peter van Dierman, 220–238. Singapore: ISEAS.

Lynch, Allen C. 2005. *How Russia is not ruled: Reflections on Russian political development*. Cambridge, U.K.: Cambridge University Press.

MacAndrews, Colin, ed. 1986. *Central government and local development in Indonesia*. Singapore: Oxford University Press.

MacDougall, John. 1975. Technocrats as modernizers: The economists of Indonesia's New Order. PhD diss., University of Michigan, Ann Arbor.

Maffi, Luisa, and Ellen Woodley. 2005. Report on the global source book on biocultural diversity. Salt Spring Island, BC: Terralingua.

Magenda, Burhan (1991) *East Kalimantan: The decline of a commercial aristocracy*, Ithaca, NY: Cornell Modern Indonesia Project Monograph Series no. 70.

Mallaby, Sebastian. 2002. The reluctant imperialist: Terrorism, failed states, and the case for American empire. *Foreign Affairs* 81 (2): 2–7.

Mallarangeng, Rizal. 2002. *Mendobrak sentralisme ekonomi*. Jakarta: Gramedia.

Malley, Michael. 1999. Regions: Centralization and resistance. In *Indonesia beyond Suharto: Polity, economy, society, transition*, ed. Donald K. Emmerson, 71–105. New York: M. E. Sharpe.

Malley, Michael. 2003. New rules, old strictures, and the limits of democratic decentralization. In *Local power and politics in Indonesia: Democratisation and decentralisation*, ed. Edward Aspinall and Greg Fealy, 102–116. Canberra and Singapore: Australian National University and Institute of Southeast Asian Studies.

Mangunwijaya, Y. B. 2003. Federalism as an antidote to separatism. In *Indonesian politics and society: A reader*, ed. David Bourchier and Vedi R. Hadiz, 269–271. London: RoutledgeCurzon.

Manor, James. 1999. *The political economy of democratic decentralization*. Washington, DC: World Bank.

Marijan, Katjung. 2006. Kerusuhan pilkada Tuban: Problem ekonomi politik. *Kompas* 6 May.

Marlay, Ross. 1991. Political parties http://countrystudies.us/philippines/85.htm. In *A country study: The Philippines*. Washington, D.C.: Federal Research Division Library of Congress. Retrieved on 20 January 2006 from http://memory.loc.gov/frd/cs/phtoc.html.

Mauro. Paolo. 1997. *Why worry about corruption?* Economic Issues 6. Washington, DC: International Monetary Fund.

McCargo, Duncan. Ed. 2007. *Rethinking Thailand's southern violence*. Singapore: NUS Press.

McCargo, Duncan, and Ukrist Pathmanand. 2005. *The Thaksinization of Thailand*. Copenhagen: NIAS.

McCarthy, John. 2007. Sold down the river: Renegotiating public power over nature in Central Kalimantan. *Renegotiation boundaries: Local politics in post-Suharto Indonesia*, ed. Henk Schulte-Nordholt and Gerry van Klinken, 151–176. Leiden: KITLV Press.

McCoy, Alfred W. 1991. The restoration of planter power in La Carlota City. In *From Marcos to Aquino: Local perspectives on political transition in the Philippines*, ed. Ben Kerkvliet and Resil Mojares, 105–142. Quezon City, Philippines: Ateneo de Manila University Press.

McFaul, Michael. 2002. The fourth wave of democracy and dictatorship: Noncooperative transitions in the postcommunist world. *World Politics* 54 (January): 212–44.

McLeod, Ross. n.d. After Soeharto: Prospects for reform and recovery in Indonesia. Canberra: Indonesia Project, Economics Division, Australian National University.

McVey, Ruth, ed. 2000. *Money and power in provincial Thailand.* Singapore: ISEAS.

Members of the Speaker's Advisory Group on Russia. 2000. Russia's road to corruption. Report by the United States House of Representatives, September, Washington, D.C. Retrieved on 15 February 2006 from http://www.fas.org/news/russia/2000/russia/par100-cover.htm.

Mietzner, Marcus. 2003. Business as usual? The Indonesian armed forces and local politics in the post-Soeharto era. In *Local power and politics in Indonesia: Democratisation and decentralisation,* ed. Edward Aspinall and Greg Fealy, 245–258. Canberra and Singapore: Australian National University and Institute of Southeast Asian Studies.

Mietzner, Marcus. 2006. Local democracy: Old elites are still in power, but direct elections now give voters a choice. *Inside Indonesia* January–March 2006: 17–18.

Migdal, Joel S. 1988. *Strong societies and weak states.* Princeton, NJ: Princeton University Press.

Moertopo, Ali. 1973. *The acceleration and modernization of 25 years development.* Jakarta: Yayasan Proklamasi and Center for Strategic and International Studies.

Montinola, Gabriella, Yingyi Qian and Barry R. Weingast. 1995. Federalism, Chinese style: The political basis for economic success. *World Politics* 48 (1): 50–81.

Munck, Gerardo L. 2001. The regime question: Theory building in democracy studies. *World Politics* 54 October: 119–144.

Nababan, Abdon. 2002. Revitalisasi hukum adat untuk menghentikan penebangan hutan secara 'illegal' di Indonesia. Jakarta: Aliansi Masyarakat Adat Nusantara.

National Reconciliation Commission. 2006. *Overcoming violence through the power of reconciliation.* Bangkok: Author.

Nelson, Michael H. 2002. Thailand: Problems with decentralization? In *Thailand's new politics: KPI yearbook 2001,* ed. Michael H. Nelson, 219–281. Nonthaburi and Bangkok: King Prajadhipok's Institute and White Lotus Press.

Nelson, Michael H. 2003. Politicizing local governments in Thailand: Direct election of executives. *King Prajadiphok's Institute Newsletter* 3 (3): 6–9.

Nelson, Michael H. 2005. Analysing provincial political structures in Thailand: Phuak, Trajun and Hua Khanaen. City University of Hong Kong SEARC Working Papers Series No. 79.

Nelson, Michael H. 2007. 'People's Sector Politics' (*Kanmueang Phak Prachachon*) in Thailand: Problems of democracy in ousting Prime Minister Thaksin Shinawatra. City University of Hong Kong SEARC Working Papers Series No. 87.

Nijenhuis, Karin. 2003. Does decentralisation serve everyone: The struggle for power in a Malian village. *European Journal of Development Research* 15 (2) December: 76–92.

Nishizaki, Yoshinori. 2002. Provincializing Thai politics. *Kyoto Review of Southeast Asia* March 1:1. Retrieved on 14 December 2005 from http://kyotoreview.cseas.kyoto-u.ac.jp/issue/issue0/article_31.html.

Nishizaki, Yoshinori. 2006. The domination of a fussy strongman in provincial Thailand: The case of Banharn Silpa-archa in Suphanburi. *Journal of Southeast Asian Studies* 37 (2): 267–291.

Noerdin, Endriana, Lisabona Rahman, Ratna Laelasari Y and Sita Aripurnami. 2005. *Representasi perempuan dalam kebijakan publik di era otonomi daerah.* Jakarta: Women Research Institute.

Nurhasim, Moch, ed. 2005. *Konflik antar elite politik lokal dalam pemilihan kepala daerah.* Yogyakarta: Pustaka Pelajar.

Oates, Sarah. 2001. Politics and the media. In *Developments in Russian politics 5*, ed. Stephen White, Alex Pravda, and Zvi Getelman, 254–268. London: Palgrave.

Obidzinski, Krystof. 2005. Illegal logging in Indonesia: Myth and reality. In *The politics and economics of Indonesia's natural resources*, ed. Budy P. Resosudarmo, 193–205. Singapore: ISEAS.

Ockey, James. 2003. Change and continuity in the Thai political party system. *Asian Survey* 43 (4): 663–680.

O'Donnell, Guillermo, and Philippe C. Schmitter. 1986. *Transitions from authoritarian rule: Tentative conclusions about uncertain democracies.* Baltimore, MD: Johns Hopkins University Press.

Orlandini, Barbara. 2003. Consuming 'good governance' in Thailand. *The European Journal of Development Research* 15 (2): 16–43.

Otonom. 2000. Momentum show of force Rudolf, 22–29 November: 13.

Otonom. 2000. Selamat pagi pembakar, 13–21 December: 8.

Oversloot, Hans (2006). Neo-liberalism in the Russian Federation. In *The Neoliberal revolution: Forging the market state*, ed. Richard Robison, 58–78. London: Palgrave Macmillan.

Pangaribuan, Robinson. 1995. *The Indonesian state secretariat 1945–1993.* Perth: Asia Research Centre, Murdoch University.

Parliament Watch. 2000. Mengubah DPRD Sumut jadi ring tinju. January: 4–5.

Pasuk Phongpaichit. 2004a. Developing social alternatives: Walking backwards into a khlong. In *Thailand beyond the crisis*, ed. Peter Warr, 161–184. London: Routledge.

Pasuk Phongpaichit. 2004b. Thailand under Thaksin: Another Malaysia? Working Paper No. 109 September. Perth: Asia Research Centre, Murdoch University.

Pasuk Phongpaichit, and Chris Baker. 2004. *Thaksin: The business of politics in Thailand.* Chiang Mai: Silkworm Books.

Patpui, Sompong. 1999. Decentralization update. October 29. Retrieved on 10 May 2003 from http://www.grassrootsthai.net/d1.htm.

Philippine Center for Investigative Journalism. 2001. *Investigating Local Governments: A Manual for Reporters.* Quezon City, Philippines: Author.

Pierson, Paul. (2000). Increasing returns, path dependence, and the study of politics. *The American Political Science Review*, 94 (2): 251–267.

Pimentel Jr., Aquilino. 2006. Multi-parties strengthen democracy. Speech delivered at the 4th International Conference of Asian Political Parties, September 8 in Seoul.

Posner, Paul W. 1999. Popular representation and political dissatisfaction in Chile's new democracy. *Journal of Interamerican Studies and World Affairs* 41 (1): 59–85.

Pratikno. 2005. Exercising freedom: Local autonomy and democracy in Indonesia. In *Regionalism in Post-Suharto Indonesia*, ed. Maribeth Erb, Priyambudi Sulistiyanto, and Carole Faucher, 21–35. London: RoutledgeCurzon.

Pratikno. 2006. Pilkadasung: Half a democratization. Paper presented at a workshop on 'Pilkada: Direct Elections, Democratization and Localization in Indonesia', Indonesia Study Group, May 17–18, at Asia Research Institute, National University of Singapore.

Przeworski, Adam. 1991. *Democracy and the market: Political and economic reforms in Eastern Europe and Latin America.* Cambridge, U.K.: Cambridge University Press.

Putnam, Robert D. 1993. *Making democracy work: Civic traditions in modern Italy.* Princeton, NJ: Princeton University Press.

Putnam, Robert D. 2000. *Bowling alone: The collapse and revival of American community.* New York: Simon and Schuster.

Qian, Yingyi, and Barry R. Weingast. 1996. China's transition to markets: Market-preserving federalism, Chinese style. *Journal of Policy Reform* (1): 149–185.

Ransom, David. 1970. The Berkeley Mafia and the Indonesian massacre. *Ramparts* 9 (4): 27–29, 40–49.

Rasyid, M. Ryaas. 2002. Otonomi Daerah: Latar Belakang dan Masa Depannya. In *Desentralisasi, demokratisasi and akuntabilitas permerintahan daerah*, ed. Syamsuddin Haris, 13–30. Jakarta: Asosiasi Ilmu Politik Indonesia.

Rasyid, Ryaas. 2005. Otonomi daerah: Latar belakang dan masa depannya. In *Desentralisasi dan otonomi daerah*, ed. Syamsuddin Haris, 3–24. Jakarta: LIPI Press.

Reeve, David. 1985. *Golkar of Indonesia: An alternative to the party system.* Singapore: Oxford University Press.

Retnosetyowati, M. G. 2006. Awan tebal orde baru menyelimuti Reformasi. *Kompas* 12 May.

Riggs, Fred W. 1966. *Thailand: The modernization of a bureaucratic polity.* Honolulu, Hawaii: East-West Center Press.

Rinakit, Sukardi. 2005. Indonesian regional elections in praxis. *IDSS Commentaries* no. 65, 27 September.

Robison, Richard. 1986. *Indonesia: The rise of capital.* Sydney: Allen and Unwin.

Robison, Richard. 1993. Indonesia: Tensions in state and regime. In *Southeast Asia in the 1990s: Authoritarianism, democracy and capitalism*, ed. Kevin Hewison, Richard Robison, and Garry Rodan, 41–74. Sydney: Allen and Unwin.

Robison, Richard, and David S. G. Goodman. 1996. The new rich in Asia: Economic development, social status, and political consciousness. In *The new rich in*

Asia: Mobile phones, McDonalds and middle class revolution, ed. Richard Robison and David S. G. Goodman, 1–16. London: Routledge.

Robison, Richard, and Vedi R. Hadiz. 2004. *Reorganising power in Indonesia: The politics of oligarchy in an age of markets*. London: RoutledgeCurzon.

Rocamora, Joel. 1995. Introduction: Classes, bosses, goons and guns. In *Boss: 5 cases of local politics in the Philippines*, ed. Jose F. Lacaba , vii–xxxi. Pasig: Metro Manila.

Rocamora, Joel. 1998. Philippines political parties, electoral system, and political reform, *Philippines International Review* 1 (1). Retrieved on 15 December 2005 from http://www.philsol.nl/pir/JR-98a.htm.

Rocamora, Joel. 2000. Formal democracy and its alternatives in the Philippines. Paper presented at a conference on 'Democracy and Civil Society in Asia: The Emerging Opportunities and Challenges', August 19–21 at Queens University, Kingston, Ontario, Canada. Retrieved on 15 December 2005 from http://www.tni.org/archives/rocamora/formal.htm.

Rocamora, Joel. 2004. Party building and local governance in the Philippines. In *Politicising democracy: The new local politics of democratisation*, ed. John Harriss, Kristian Stokke, and Olle Tornquist, 148–170. London: Palgrave Macmillan.

Rodan, Garry. 1996. Theorising political opposition in East and Southeast Asia. In *Political oppositions in industrialising Asia*, ed. Garry Rodan, 1–39. London: Routledge.

Rodan, Garry, Kevin Hewison and Richard Robison. 2006. Theorising markets in Southeast Asia: Power and contestation. In *The political economy of Southeast Asia: Markets, power, and contestation*, ed. Garry Rodan, Kevin Hewison, and Richard Robison, 1–38. Melbourne: Oxford University Press.

Rodan, Garry, and Kevin Hewison. 2006. Neoliberal globalization, conflict and security: New life for authoritarianism in Asia? In *Empire and neoliberalism in Asia*, ed. Vedi R. Hadiz, 105–122. London: Routledge.

Rohdewohld, Rainer. 2004. Building capacity to support decentralisation—The case of Indonesia (1999–2004). Paper prepared for the Tokyo International Symposium on Capacity Development, February 4–6, in Tokyo.

Rood, Steven. 1998. Decentralization, democracy, and development. In *The Philippines: New directions in domestic policy and foreign relations*, ed. David G. Timberman. New York: Asia Society. Retrieved on 10 May 2003 from http://www.asiasociety.org/publications/philippines/decentralization.html.

Rueschemeyer, Dietrich, Evelyne Huber Stephens and John D. Stephens. 1992. *Capitalist development and democracy*. Cambridge, U.K.: Polity Press.

Ryter, Loren. 2000. A tale of two cities. *Inside Indonesia* 63 (July–September). Retrieved on January 10 2002 from http://www.serve.com/inside/edit63/loren 1.htm.

Ryter, Loren. 2002. Youth, gangs, and the state in Indonesia. PhD diss., University of Washington, Seattle.

Ryter, Loren. 2005. Reformasi gangsters. *Inside Indonesia* 82 (April–June): 22–23.

S. Aminah. 2005. Relasi kelas buruh, kuasa dan kapital dalam kontestasi perpoliti-kan local. *Jurnal Perburuhan Sedane* 3 (2): 17–24.

Sangmpam, S. N. 2007. Politics rules: The false primacy of institutions in develop-ing countries. *Political Studies*, 55 (1): 201–224.

Sapujagat. 2003. Madu di balik kursi gubernur, 1–15 April: 3.

Sapujagat. 2003. Partai patriot pancasila bisa jadi pilhan, 1–15 July: 12.

Savirani, Amalinda. 2004. Local strongman in new regional politics in Indonesia. Masters diss., International School of Humanities and Social Sciences, Univer-sity of Amsterdam.

Schiller, Jim. 1996. *Developing Jepara: State and society in New Order Indonesia*. Mel-bourne: Monash University Asia Institute.

Schiller, Jim. 2007. Civil society in Jepara: Fractious but inclusive. In *Renegotiation boundaries: Local politics in post-Suharto Indonesia*, eds. Henk Schulte-Nordhold and Gerry van Klinken, 327–348. Leiden: KITLV Press.

Schneier, Edward. 2005. The role of constitution-building processes in democra-tization. Case Study Indonesia. Retrieved on 20 January 2007 from http://www .Idea.Int/Conflict/Cbp/.

Schulte-Nordholt, Henk. 2002. A genealogy of violence. In *Roots of violence in In-donesia: Contemporary violence in historical perspective*, ed. Freek Colombijn and J. Thomas Lindblad, 33–61. Leiden: KITLV.

Schulte-Nordholt, Henk. 2004. Decentralisation in Indonesia: Less state, more democracy? In *Politicising democracy: The new local politics of democratisation*, ed. John Harriss, Kristian Stokke and Olle Tornquist, 29–50. New York: Palgrave Macmillan.

Schulte-Nordholt, Henk (2007). Bali: An open fortress. In *Renegotiation boundaries: Local politics in post-Suharto Indonesia*, ed. Henk Schulte-Nordholt and Gerry van Klinken, 387–416. Leiden: KITLV Press.

Schulte-Nordholt, Henk, and Gerry van Klinken. Eds. 2007. *Renegotiation bound-aries: Local politics in post-Suharto Indonesia*. Leiden: KITLV Press.

Schulte-Nordholt, Nico. n.d. Pelembagaan civil society dalam proses desentralisasi di Indonesia. Retrieved on 15 August 2005 from http://www.knaw.nl/indonesia/ transition/workshop/work_in_progresso2.pdf.

Scott, W. Richard. 2005. Institutional theory: Contributing to a theoretical re-search programme. In *Great minds in management: The process of theory develop-ment*, ed. Ken G. Smith and Michael A. Hitt, 460–485. Oxford, U.K.: Oxford University Press.

Sen, Krishna, and David Hill. 2000. *Media, culture and politics in Indonesia*. Mel-bourne: Oxford University Press.

Shatkin, Gavin. 2003. Globalization and local leadership: Growth, power and politics in Thailand's eastern seaboard. University of Michigan, Urban and Re-gional Research Collaborative Working Paper Series No. 03–05.

Shelley, Louise. 2001. Crime and corruption. In *Developments in Russian politics 5*, ed. Stephen White, Alex Pravda, and Zvi Getelman, 239–253. London: Palgrave.

Shiraishi, Takashi. 2003. A preliminary study of local elites in Indonesia: Sociological profiles of DPRD members. Unpublished paper.

Sidel, John T. 1999. *Capital, coercion, and crime: Bossism in the Philippines*. Stanford, CA: Stanford University Press.

Sidel, John T. 2004. Bossism and democracy in the Philippines, Thailand and Indonesia: Towards an alternative framework for the study of 'local strongmen'. In *Politicising democracy: The new local politics of democratisation*, ed. John Harriss, Kristian Stokke, and Olle Tornquist, 51–74. New York: Palgrave Macmillan.

Sidel, John T. 2006. *Riots, pogroms, jihad: Religious violence in Indonesia*. Ithaca, NY: Cornell University Press.

Simonsen, Jarle. 1999. Democracy and globalization: Nineteen eighty-nine and the 'third wave'. *Journal of World History* 10: 391–411.

Singh, Nirvikar. 2007. Fiscal decentralization in China and India: Competitive, cooperative or market preserving federalism? Department of Economics, University of California at Santa Cruz, Working Paper No. 633.

Sjahrir. 1997. The struggle for deregulation in Indonesia. In *The politics of economic development in Indonesia: Contending perspectives*, ed. Ian Chalmers and Vedi R. Hadiz, 153–157. London: Routledge.

Slider, Darrell, 2001. Politics in the regions. In *Developments in Russian politics 5*, ed. Stephen White, Alex Pravda, and Zvi Getelman, 147–168. London: Palgrave.

Smith, Benjamin. n.d. The origins of regional autonomy in Indonesia: Experts and the marketing of political interests. Unpublished paper.

Smith, Claire Q. 2006. Rice and circuses: Power, patronage and political machines in 'post'-conflict Indonesia. Paper presented at a workshop on 'Pilkada: Direct Elections, Democratization and Localization in Indonesia', Indonesia Study Group, May 17–18 at Asia Research Institute, National University of Singapore.

Sombat Chantornvong. 2000. Local godfathers in Thai politics. In *Money and power in provincial Thailand*, ed. Ruth McVey, 53–73. Singapore: ISEAS.

Steinmo, Sven. 2001. The new institutionalism. In *The encyclopedia of democratic thought*, eds. Barry Clark and Joe Foweraker. London: Routledge. Retrieved on 20 July 2007 from http://stripe.colorado.edu/~steinmo/foweracker.pdf.

Suehiro, Akira. 2005. Who manages and who damages the Thai economy? The technocracy, the four core agencies system and Dr Puey's networks. In *After the crisis: Hegemony, technocracy, and governance in Southeast Asia*. ed. Shiraishi Takashi and Patricio N. Abinales, 15–68. Kyoto: Kyoto University Press.

Sukma, Rizal. 2003. Conflict management in post-authoritarian Indonesia. In *Autonomy and disintegration in Indonesia*, ed. Damien Kingsbury and Harry Aveling, 64–74. London: RoutledgeCurzon.

Sumatera Corruption Watch. n.d. 'Kronologis Kasus Money Politics Pemilihan Walikota Medan', leaflet.

Suryadinata, Leo. 2002. *Elections and politics in Indonesia*. Singapore: ISEAS.

Tadem-Incarnacion, Tessa. 2005. The Philippine technocracy and US-led capitalism. In *After the crisis: Hegemony, technocracy, and governance in Southeast Asia*, ed. Shiraishi Takashi and Patricio N. Abinales, 85–104. Kyoto: Kyoto University Press.

Tadjoeddin, Muhammad Zulfan, Widjajanti I. Suharyo and Satish Mishra. 2003. Aspiration to inequality: Regional disparity and centre-regional conflicts in Indonesia. Paper prepared for the United Nations University/World Institute for Development Economics Research Project Conference on Spatial Inequality in Asia, March 28–29, at United Nations University Centre, Tokyo.

Teune, Henry. 2004. The dynamics of local global relations. Paper presented at the International Sociological Association Conference on Conflict, Competition, and Cooperation: Contemporary Sociological Theory and Research in the XXI Century, May, in Ottawa.

Thamrin Mosii. 2006. Workers' rights in bonded zones must be guarded. *Jakarta Post* 25 August: 6.

Thelen, Kathleen. 1999. Historical institutionalism in comparative politics. *Annual Review of Political Science* (2): 369–404.

Therborn, Goran. 1977. The rule of capital and the rise of democracy. *New Left Review* 103 (May–June): 3–41.

Thompson, Mark R. 1995. *The anti-Marcos struggle: Personalistic rule and democratic transition in the Philippines*. New Haven, CT: Yale University Press.

Tolentino, Rolando and Sarah S. Raymundo. Eds. 2006. *Kontra-gahum : academics against political killings*. Quezon City, Philippines: IBON books.

Tornquist, Olle. 2000. Dynamics of Indonesian democratisation. *Third World Quarterly* 21 (3): 383–423.

Tornquist, Olle. 2002. *Popular development and democracy: Case studies with rural dimensions in the Philippines, Indonesia and Kerala*. Oslo: Centre for Development and the Environment, University of Oslo.

Trocki, Carl A., ed. 1998. *Gangsters, democracy, and the state in Southeast Asia*. Ithaca, NY: Cornell University Southeast Asia Programme.

Turner, Mark, and Own Podger. 2003. *Decentralisation in Indonesia: Redesigning the state*. Canberra: Asia Pacific Press.

Ufen, Andreas. 2006. Political parties in post-Suharto Indonesia: Between *politik aliran* and 'Philippinisation'. GIGA Working Papers no. 37. December.

Uhlin, Anders. 1997. *Indonesia and the 'third wave of democratization': Indonesian pro-democracy movement in a changing world*. Richmond: Curzon Press.

UNDP (United Nations Development Programme). 2002. A global analysis of UNDP support to decentralisation and local governance programmes 2001. Institutional Development Group, Bureau for Development Policy, United Nations Development Programme, September.

UNESCAP (United Nations Economic and Social Commission for Asia and the Pacific). n.d. Local government in Asia and the Pacific: A comparative study—Thailand: Country paper. Retrieved on 30 August 2005 from http://www .unescap.org/huset/lgstudy/country/thailand/thai.html.

Ungpakorn, Ji Giles. 2003a. Challenges to the Thai NGO movement from the dawn of a new opposition to global capital. In *Radicalising Thailand: New political perspectives*, ed. Ji Giles Ungpakorn, 289–318. Bangkok: Institute of Asian Studies, Chulalongkorn University.

Ungpakorn, Ji Giles. 2003b. A Marxist history of political change in Thailand. In *Radicalising Thailand: New political perspectives*, ed. Ji Giles Ungpakorn, 6–40. Bangkok: Institute of Asian Studies, Chulalongkorn University.

Ungpakorn, Ji Giles. 2007. *A coup for the rich*. Bangkok: Workers Democracy Publishing.

USAID (United States Agency for International Development). 2000. Transition to a prospering and democratic Indonesia. Country Strategy Paper, May 30.

USAID (United States Agency for International Development). 2005. USAID budget: Indonesia. Retrieved on 30 March 2006 from http://www.usaid.gov/ policy/budget/cbj2005/ane/id.html.

van Klinken, Gerry. 2002. Indonesia's new ethnic elites. Retrieved on 14 April 2006 from http://www.knaw.nl/indonesia/transition/workshop/chapter4vanklinken .pdf.

van Klinken, Gerry. 2004. Return of the Sultans. *Inside Indonesia*, April–June 2004. Retrieved on 10 February 2006 from http://www.serve.com/inside/edit78/ p25-26_GVK.html.

van Klinken, Gerry. 2007. *Communal violence and democratization in Indonesia: Small town wars*. London: Routledge.

Vel, Jacqueline 2005. Pilkada in East Sumba: An old rivalry in a new democratic setting. *Indonesia* 80, October: 81–107.

Watkins, Thayer. n.d. The Russian oligarchs of the 1990s. Retrieved in November 2003 from http://www2.sjsu.edu/faculty/watkins/oligarchs.htm.

Weber, Max. (1978). *Economy and society*. Berkeley: University of California Press.

Wee, Vivienne. 2002. Social fragmentation in Indonesia: A crisis from Suharto's New Order. Working Papers Series no. 31. Southeast Asia Research Centre, City University of Hong Kong, September.

Wee. Vivienne. 2005. Asia Research Centre Seminar Series, 1 December. Melbourne: Murdoch University.

Weiss, Linda. 1998. *The myth of the powerless state*. Cambridge, U.K.: Polity Press.

Weist. Dana. 2001. Thailand's decentralization: Progress and prospects. Paper prepared for the King Prajadhipok's Institute Annual Congress III on Decentralization and Local Government in Thailand, November 10–11.

White, Gordon. 1994. Civil society, democratization and development (I): Clearing the analytical ground. *Democratization* Autumn 1 (3): 375–390.

White, Roland, and Paul Smoke. 2005. East Asia decentralizes. In *East Asia decentralizes: Making local government work*, ed. World Bank, 1–23. Washington, DC: World Bank.

Willis, Eliza, Christopher Garman and Stephen Haggard. 1999. The politics of decentralization in Latin America. *Latin American Research Review* 34 (1): 7–56.

Wilson, Ian. 2006. Continuity and change: The changing contours of organized violence in post-New Order Indonesia. *Critical Asian Studies* 38 (2): 265–297.

Winters, Jeffrey A. 2000. The financial crisis in Southeast Asia. In *Politics and markets in the wake of the Asian crisis*, ed. Richard Robison, Mark Beeson, and Hyuk-Rae Kim, 34–52. London: Routledge.

World Bank. n.d. a. Decentralization Homepage. Retrieved on 10 May 2003 from http://www1.worldbank.org/wbiep/decentralization/about.html.

World Bank n.d. b. How we work with civil society. Retrieved on 10 May 2003 from http://lnweb18.worldbank.org/ECA/eca.nsf/Initiatives/A98CDE16184FEDFC85256BD6004F486F?OpenDcument.

World Bank. Decentralisation Net. Retrieved on 11 May 2003 from http://www1.worldbank.org/publicsector/decentralisation/Different.htm.

World Bank Decentralization Home Page Library. Retrieved on 12 May 2003 from http://www1.worldbank.org/wbiep/decentralization/regions.htm#europe.

World Bank. 2000. *Working together: The World Bank's partnership with civil society*. Washington, D.C.: Author.

World Bank. 2003a. Social development notes 82, March.

World Bank. 2003b. Decentralizing Indonesia. Regional Public Expenditure Review. Washington, DC: World Bank, Poverty Reduction Economic Management, East Asia and the Pacific Region.

World Bank. 2005b. Making decentralization work. Retrieved on 15 January 2006 from http://siteresources.worldbank.org/INTINDONESIA/Resources/Publication/280016-1106130305439/617331-1110769011447/810296-1110769045002/decentralization.pdf.

World Bank Group. n.d. 'Anticorruption'. Retrieved on 30 September 2004 from http://www1.worldbank.org/publicsector/anticorrupt/index.cfm.

Wunch, James. 1998. Decentralization, local governance and the democratic transition in Southern Africa: A comparative analysis. *African Studies Quarterly: The Online Journal for African Studies* 2 (1). Retrieved on 25 May 2003 from http://web.africa.ufl.edu/asq/v2/v2i1a2.htm.

YSIK (Indonesian Social Foundation for Humanity). 2004. Indonesian current political trend: 2004 general election: Will there be change? Unpublished document, Jakarta.

Zysman, John. 1994. How institutions create historically rooted trajectories of growth. *Industrial and Corporate Change*, 3 (1): 243–283.

Newsreports

Analisa. 15 June 2005.
Analisa. 17 June 2005.
Antaranews. www.antara.co.id. 17 November 2007.
Antaranews. www.antara.co.id. 11 February 2008.
Bali Post. 13 July 2005.
Detik.com www.detik.com. 25 January 2008.
Edison. 24–31 May 2000: 3, 11.
Financial Times. 13 September 2006.
Gamma. 12 October 2001.
Gatra. 18 July 2002.
Indo Pos Online. 18 June 2005.
Jakarta Post. 1 July 1998.
Jakarta Post. 17 July 2000.
Jakarta Post. 8 October 2000.
Jakarta Post. 24 October 2000.
Jakarta Post. 30 October 2000.
Jakarta Post. 13 February 2001.
Jakarta Post. 21 August 2002.
Jakarta Post. 23 September 2002.
Jakarta Post. 2 October 2002.
Jakarta Post. 22 January 2003.
Jakarta Post. 16 July 2003.
Jakarta Post. 22 July 2003.
Jakarta Post. 31 July 2003.
Jakarta Post. 27 September 2003.
Jakarta Post. 16 April 2004.
Jakarta Post. 18 June 2004.
Jakarta Post. 24 July 2004.
Jakarta Post. 16 February 2005.
Jakarta Post. 21 March 2005.
Jakarta Post. 27 June 2005.
Jakarta Post. 5 December 2005.
Jakarta Post. 11 January 2006.
Jakarta Post. 18 May 2006.
Jakarta Post. 26 May 2006.
Jakarta Post. 25 July 2006.
Jakarta Post. 24 August 2006.
Jakarta Post. 11 October 2006.
Jakarta Post. 6 November 2006.
Jawa Pos. 17 July 2003.

Jawa Pos. 28 July 2003.

Kompas. 18 April 2000.

Kompas. 21 January 2000.

Kompas. 23 March 2000.

Kompas. 29 April 2000.

Kompas. 27 November 2001.

Kompas. 31 January 2002.

Kompas. 2 April 2002.

Kompas. 13 January 2003.

Kompas. 6 March 2003.

Kompas. 7 March 2003.

Kompas. 10 March 2003.

Kompas. 19 March 2003.

Kompas. 22 April 2003.

Kompas. 5 May 2003.

Kompas. 11 June 2003.

Kompas. 15 July 2003.

Kompas. 27 May 2004.

Kompas. 11 June 2004.

Kompas. 11 August 2004.

Kompas. 28 June 2005.

Kompas. 10 July 2005.

Kompas. 16 December 2005.

Kompas. 24 January 2008.

Medan Bisnis. 17 June 2005.

Media Anak Bangsa. 7–8 September 2000.

Media Indonesia. 21 December 2003.

Media Indonesia. 2 July 2005.

Media Indonesia. 15 June 2006.

Media Indonesia. 6 January 2007.

Pelita. 26 May 2006.

Perjuangan. 18 March 2000.

Philippine Daily Inquirer. 12 May 2007.

Republika Online. http://www.republika.co.id/, 18 July 2005.

Republika Online. http://www.republika.co.id/, 12 August 2005.

Republika Online. http://www.republika.co.id/, 12 September 2005.

Republika Online. http://www.republika.co.id/, 25 January 2008.

SCTV. http://www.liputan6.com/, 16 January 2002.

SCTV. http://www.liputan6.com/, 15 July 2002.

SCTV. http://www.liputan6.com/, 10 October 2002.

SCTV. http://www.liputan6.com/, 23 July 2007.

Suara Merdeka. 13 June 2005.

Suara Merdeka. 14 July 2005.

Suara Merdeka. 17 December 2005.

Sumut Pos. 15 June 2005.

Surabaya Pos. 19 August 2005.

Surya. 23 March 2002.

Surya. 27 March 2002.

Surya. 31 May 2002.

Surya. 12 July 2002.

Surya. 24 August 2002.

Surya. 26 October 2002.

Surya. 25 November 2002.

Surya. 11 March 2003.

Surya. 27 March 2003.

Surya Karya, 29 June 2006.

Tempo. 27 February 2005: 26–35.

Tempo. 1–7 January 2007: 36–37.

Tempo Interaktif. http://www.tempointeraktif.com/, 3 May 2000.

Tempo Interaktif. http://www.tempointeraktif.com/, 14 September 2000.

Tempo Interaktif. http://www.tempointeraktif.com/, 14 October 2002.

Tempo Interaktif. http://www.tempointeraktif.com/, 5 April 2003.

Tempo Interaktif. http://www.tempointeraktif.com/, 7 May 2003.

Tempo Interaktif. http://www.tempointeraktif.com/, 4 November 2004.

Tempo Interaktif. http://www.tempointeraktif.com/, 5 March 2005.

Tempo Interaktif. http://www.tempointeraktif.com/, 2 June 2005.

Tempo Interaktif. http://www.tempointeraktif.com/, 19 May 2006.

Tempo Interaktif. http://www.tempointeraktif.com/, 23–29 May 2006.

The Nation. 26 September 2006.

The Nation. 3 October 2006.

The Philippine Star. 11 May 2007.

Waspada. 12 August 2004.

Waspada. 19 August 2004.

Waspada. 11 September 2004.

Waspada. 17 December 2005.

Waspada. 7 January 2008.

Index

Vel, Jacqueline, 173
Verba, Sidney, 50
Vietnam, 194n2; anti-corruption
campaigns in, 176
Vietnam War, 50

Wachid, A., 112
Wahid, Abdurrahman, 84, 85, 99, 192n3,
200n35; and NU, 67; and PKB, 91,
125, 132, 199n30; as president, 66–67
Warren, Carol, 157
Watkins, Thayer, 191n6
Weber, Max: on predictability of
corruption, 36; on unintended
consequences, 12
Wee, Vivienne, 36, 157–58, 189n29,
203n5
Wei Fan, 131
Weingast, Barry R., 5, 18, 26, 27, 37,
203n1
Weiss, Linda, 24
Weist, Dana, 189n25
Welsh, Bridget, 165, 167
West Java, 90, 109
West Kalimantan, 83, 165, 188n22
West Sumatra, 166, 170; corruption in,
175; and Semen Padang, 100–101
White, Gordon, 32
White, Roland, 18–19
Wijaya, Vincent, 194n11
Willis, Eliza, 18
Wilson, Ian, 74, 137, 139, 141, 149,
201n53
Winasa, Gede, 29
Winata, Tomy, 131
Winters, Jeffrey A., 36

Wiranto, General, 68, 138
women's movement, 31
Woodley, Ellen, 7
World Bank: and civil society, 30,
32–33, 37; and Consultative Group on
Indonesia (CGI), 20; and corruption,
37, 189nn26,29; and decentralisation,
5, 6, 18–19, 22, 23, 25, 30, 75, 97,
186n10; and democracy, 5; and good
governance, 6, 9, 23, 33, 97; on
Indonesia decentralisation, 75, 97;
on local spending in Indonesia, 81;
and market capitalism, 5, 97; and
neo-liberalism, 2; and NGOs, 9–10;
and privatisation, 54; on revenue
distribution in Indonesia, 82–83, 84;
and social capital, 31–32
Wunch, James, 34
Wuthisarn Tanchai, 188n19, 193nn14,15

xenophobia, 2, 8

Yapto Suyosumarno, 134, 137
Yeltsin, Boris, 177
Yogyakarta, 194n1, 201n51, 202n8;
Bantul, 85, 95, 112; elections in, 112;
vs. Jakarta, 88; labour movement in,
155; local elites in, 88, 95, 112, 155;
PAN in, 112–13; PDI-P in, 114; PKB
in, 114; political thuggery in, 114, 141;
Sleman, 114, 124
Yudhhoyono, Susilo Bambang, 52–53,
68, 179, 196n23, 201n3
Yusuf, Saifullah, 199n30

Zysman, John, 24

Opposing Suharto: Compromise, Resistance, and Regime Change in Indonesia
By Edward Aspinall
2005

Blowback: Linguistic Nationalism, Institutional Decay, and Ethnic Conflict in Sri Lanka
By Neil DeVotta
2004

Beyond Bilateralism: U.S.-Japan Relations in the New Asia-Pacific
Edited by Ellis S. Krauss and T. J. Pempel
2004

Population Change and Economic Development in East Asia: Challenges Met, Opportunities Seized
Edited by Andrew Mason
2001

Capital, Coercion, and Crime: Bossism in the Philippines
By John T. Sidel
1999

Making Majorities: Constituting the Nation in Japan, Korea, China, Malaysia, Fiji, Turkey, and the United States
Edited by Dru C. Gladney
1998

Chiefs Today: Traditional Pacific Leadership and the Postcolonial State
Edited by Geoffrey M. White and Lamont Lindstrom
1997

Political Legitimacy in Southeast Asia: The Quest for Moral Authority
Edited by Muthiah Alagappa
1995